Out

Out

ESCAPING JUDGEMENT
& FINDING LOVE

Lou Anne Smoot

2025 ANO Publishing
Copyright © 2000, 2013, 2025 by Lou Anne Smoot
All rights reserved.
Published in the United States by ANO Publishing Tyler, TX
ISBN: 979-8-9990818-2-7

Edited by Amanda Nail
Book Cover by Sara H. Noto of notobella designs

3rd edition 2025

Dedicated Posthumously To **Marilyn Hillyer**
whose Christlike example
led me safely through a very dark valley
and helped me bear sorrow I thought I couldn't bear

Dedicated Posthumously To **Alice Parrish**
who started me on my journey
through her words of love and acceptance

and to my loving wife, **Brenda McWilliams**
who supports me, encourages me,
and loves me.

TABLE OF CONTENTS

MY LIFE, MY MINISTRY: AUGUST 2000- DECEMBER 2015

PREFACE

*G*etting a book published isn't all it is cracked up to be. It's difficult, or at least it was for me. The book you're holding now is the third iteration of my story. The first time it was published was in the throes of my coming out and still attending my Southern Baptist church. At that time, the book was called *A Christian Coming Out,* and it was written with the hope of reaching evangelical Christians who didn't believe or couldn't see LGBTQ people as redeemable. After completing my personal story for the first time in *A Christian Coming Out,* I was pulled in two different directions. I felt excited at the possibility of trying to get my book published, but I was also filled with trepidation because I'd made my innermost secrets known to the world. And yet, "the world" didn't bother me nearly as much as having my secrets made public to friends and family. That's the thought that filled me with fear. However, I pressed on, convinced that my story could help others, and in truth, it did, though it never quite resonated with the audience I originally intended.

Instead of conservative Christians picking up my book to learn more about the LGBTQ community from a personal perspective and changing their minds and lives, it was other queer people and communities eager to connect, relate, and share who were encouraged and inspired. Because of this, I decided my story needed a rebranding, and the second version of the book was published in 2016, retitled as *Out- A Courageous Woman's Journey.*

Today, the version you hold in your hands is my final attempt at reaching as many people as possible, with not only a new cover and subtitle but a new focus and more details laid bare. This time, my story is written not just for others but for myself. It is the most honest of my tellings because I rewrote it from a place of love and celebration of a difficult life well-lived and not from a place of desperation, obligation, or fear.

Since that first version of the book, I have often questioned whether I really wanted to lay myself bare, admitting to embarrassing weaknesses, or publicizing feelings and actions that would probably be best kept hidden. Yet, I crave—like so many of us—to be known. I continue to believe that telling my story in writing and verbally is my reason for living and everything in my life has led to this purpose.

Much of my book was written in 2000, even though its first iteration was not published until June 2013. Prior to publication, I dreaded the thought of someone reading it on my computer so much that I used all kinds of passwords to keep it locked away, just in case I were to drop dead and someone would gain access to my computer. I wrote the book in a cocoon of fear.

That was twenty-four years ago. (What a difference two decades can make.) I now travel the country, sharing my story with any group that welcomes me.

I'm eighty-six now, and I'm thankful for every opportunity to tell my story. In 2013, Brenda and I traveled across North Carolina, where I spoke to eight PFLAG groups. In 2014, we traveled through New Mexico and Arizona, where I addressed ten more groups. In 2015, we traveled to Florida, Alabama, and Louisiana, where I told my story to six PFLAG groups, a large social justice group at the University of Central Florida in Orlando, four churches, plus a radio interview in New Orleans. By May 2024, I had shared my story with 87 groups in 11 states.

I sincerely hope that this book finds the people who need it—people like me who have felt scared, alone, or uncertain about who they are and what their purpose is.

I hope by reading my story, you can see that the process of coming out is possible, that loving and accepting yourself (and finding love in others) in the face of a culture and a society that tries again and again to silence and erase you, is possible, and it's worth it. If you take nothing else away from my coming out journey, remember this: God made you just as you are. You are lovable and worthy of happiness in this life and the next, and you deserve to live an "out loud life." No more secrets, no more hiding, no more shame. Let's live. Let's be proud. Let's be "out" together.

PROLOGUE
Awakening

*M*y life changed entirely in August 1999 when I asked Janie, a member of my Sunday School class, the question, "Is your son a homosexual?"

As a 60-year-old living in conservative East Texas, I should have had enough sense to avoid such a controversial subject inside a Southern Baptist Church. But as I listened to Janie describing her son as "an accomplished artist who was kind and thoughtful, especially toward his grandmother," an impulse arose from deep inside my being, and I simply blurted out the question.

An uncomfortable silence followed as I watched her struggle to answer. Finally, she gathered up her courage and proudly—almost defiantly—told me, "Yes, he is gay, but that's just the way God made him. God loves him just the way he is, and we should, too."

I was dumbfounded. I don't know what kind of answer I expected, but that wasn't it.

In all my 60 years of regularly attending a Southern Baptist church, I had never heard anything positive, supportive, or loving said about an LGBTQ person. I had never heard anyone indicate that God loves gays, and especially that God loves gays "just the way they are."

When our class ended, Janie and I stood up to leave for the worship service, and she hugged me in parting. I had always avoided touching other women, but Janie was a hugger, so I complied. I put my arms around her and briefly held her close. When I became aware of her long, blond hair brushing my cheek, I quickly removed my arms from around her and finished our goodbyes.

Returning home after the worship service, I prepared lunch for my husband, Jim, and me. He and I were married in 1963 when he taught junior high history, and I taught high school business subjects in Odessa, Texas. Although we seemed to share much, our marriage had always been a struggle.

Jim was five years older than I, a fine-looking man of medium build with graying reddish hair who had earned his doctorate, advanced in his profession, and presently served in Tyler ISD's central administration. Having previously taught at The University of Arkansas and later serving as a high school principal in Austin and Tyler, his career choice required him to be authoritative. When he used that tone in the home, it rankled, but I lived through an era in society that preached about wives obeying and complying with their husbands' wishes. Even though I may have seethed inside, I pushed down my anger and kept my feelings hidden. I seldom argued with him, especially when the children were present. I believed they should only see their parents being kind to each other, and Jim was a good man who loved his family and provided well for us.

After cleaning up our Sunday lunch dishes and changing into more comfortable clothes, I returned to the kitchen to bake cinnamon bread. Standing in our kitchen mixing the bread, my thoughts returned to my conversation with Janie that morning.

Life had dealt her some problematic blows. Her first child was born with disabilities so severe that she had to be placed in a special facility. Her second child had legally changed her name to a male name when she turned 18 and now, at 22, was asking her mother for assistance and support in transitioning. Because her only son was gay, Janie often lamented the thought of never having biological grandchildren. As I thought about the surprises life had thrown her, saturating sorrow filled me.

I was astonished as I had always been one of those stoic individuals who maintained emotional control. Consequently, I had gone through life alone, never confiding in anyone, never unburdening myself to anyone else—certainly not to my husband—and as a result, I seldom felt deep emotions. Yet, here I was, crying, tears streaming down my face, regarding Janie's struggles.

Amidst this unexpected sorrow, a new thought began to surface.

Could Janie and I be friends?

My heart began to soar with possibilities.

What would it be like to confess my inner thoughts—my great "sin"—to someone who might understand me and hopefully accept me anyway? Would I have the nerve to sit down and be open and honest with her?

With my mind rapidly jumping from one question to another, my emotions suddenly changed directions. Instead of feeling happy about a possible friendship with Janie, I experienced terrible pain, as if my heart were cracking open.

I had lived for so many years, keeping my past safely bottled up inside me. I reconciled that I would always be alone— that no one would ever really know who I was, sure that my loneliness would go with me to the grave. Until this afternoon, I had been unaware of what a burden I had carried all my life. Now, anguish flooded through me as if I were being swept up in crashing torrents and thrown against the rocks of my own body.

Hearing Janie's loving acceptance of her son earlier was breaking through the wall within me—the wall I had carefully constructed to protect myself from the world's attitude toward gays, toward *me*.

Standing over the cinnamon bread mixture in my kitchen that Sunday afternoon, holding a tear-soaked tissue, all my dormant feelings were suddenly coming back to life. I welcomed none of them. I didn't understand what was happening to me. I was inexperienced and unprepared to handle them.

I'd been at war with my physical desires for most of my life— significant battles— some lasting years, some just minor skirmishes, but always at war.

This ceaseless fighting began when I was a teenager. I refused to face the truth about myself and, in essence, started killing my soul and the being I was created to be. I did this by denying my existence as a unique individual and forming an untouchable, carefully guarded space within me that was kept private, even from myself. Simple existence became my goal, not happiness. I was convinced I could never be happy. Instead, I spent years of my life often yearning for an early death as a means of escape.

I blindly and successfully played the role that society, church, and my family insisted was mine: my marriage had lasted for 36 years, and all four of our children were healthy, kind, intelligent, good-looking, and college educated. Friends and family looked at what we had created and called us "successful." The truth is the mold governing my life didn't fit; it hurt. Looking at my outward life did not indicate my inward misery.

That Sunday afternoon, tears poured down my face when I began to envision the possibility of unburdening myself to someone, of being open and honest about who and what I was. Standing by the stove, grabbing tissue after tissue to staunch the tears, I was bewildered about what was happening and where all this emotion was coming from. My feelings were on a roller coaster, climbing and dropping from the heights of my empathy for Janie's family, her pain mixed with her acceptance, to memories of my own family and my deep sadness. It was a wild, dizzying ride and left me out of control for the rest of the afternoon. My entire being felt like raw flesh suddenly exposed to the air, and thoughts I never dreamed I would ever have again—thoughts pushed so far back inside of me I had forgotten their existence—broke the surface, wrapping me in a tangled briar of devastation, shame, and embarrassment. The only way to break through and set myself free was to take a long, hard look back into a past I'd worked my whole life to forget.

GROWING UP
1953-1960

1
SIGNS & WONDERS

*M*y story begins where most people's stories do, with my parents. Mine were good people, hard-working, religious, and college educated.

By 1953, when I was a fourteen-year-old sophomore, I began having strange feelings toward a particular girl in high school.

One evening, six or seven girls were all squeezed together in a car, having a great time at a drive-in movie. I sat directly behind the driver in the backseat, pressed up against the door. I felt crushed next to Jean, a senior I admired and had much in common. We played on the basketball team, were members of the National Honor Society, and served as officers in the Student Council; we even attended the same church. Our only difference was that she sat as the first-chair flute in the band, and I sat next to her as the second-chair. She was my role model and, despite our two to three-year age difference, was always kind to me. That night, we were crammed like sardines in the backseat, with her attractively tan, bare arm pressed up against the bare skin of mine, sending a shocking thought through my mind.

I want to kiss her!

My stomach began churning. I immediately dismissed such a notion as strange, wondering why in the world I was thinking about something like that.

This desire confused and troubled me, but I never mentioned it to anyone, certainly not Jean. I had never heard of two girls kissing, so I concluded it must be unnatural.

When that evening ended, I was relieved to have escaped the temptation but continued asking myself what that feeling toward Jean was about. It bothered me because I simply didn't understand it. I never worried about it happening again. Why would it? Our relationship never changed; but, much to my surprise, there was another incident a few months later.

Our high school band had performed at an out-of-town football game, and we had a long ride to return home. Once again, Jean and I found ourselves sitting close to each other, this time on the school's band bus. It was late, and we were all tired. Jean, always considerate, said, "Lou Anne, if you want to lie down and put your head in my lap, that's fine."

I did and thought nothing of it until Jean reached over and held my hand. I imagine she was trying to prevent me from falling to the floor but holding Jean's hand set my heart hammering. Ecstatic, I was immediately wide awake. At fourteen years old, her hand in mine was the most wondrous thing that had ever happened to me.

Jean graduated with the class of 1954 at the end of that school year, and I already missed her. I missed her smile, her happy laugh, and her words of encouragement.

When our family took our usual summer road trip, I asked my parents to stop by the college Jean was attending, Tarleton State University in Stephenville, Texas, so I could see her. They kindly obliged, and I was able to visit her and her roommate in their dorm room. She seemed to enjoy my visit as much as I did, but that was the last time I ever saw Jean because after my high school graduation two years later in 1956, our family moved 300 miles away.

My junior and senior years in high school were uneventful in terms of any type of unique attraction. I continued to date boys and enjoyed "parking" with a few of them, but kissing and holding was as far as it ever went. Mother always questioned me when I returned after a date. She wanted to know everything we did and where we went, always inevitably asking, "Did you two kiss?" Her questions were embarrassing. Therefore, I always headed to the bathroom as soon as I walked into the house, taking time to refresh my lipstick. Her questions made me feel guilty for just kissing a boy, so I usually denied doing so, even when I had.

One of my mother's regular admonitions was, "If you let a boy hold your hand, then he'll want to put his arm around you, making him want to kiss you. It just goes from bad to worse from there. It's better never to let a boy hold your hand."

Her words made a substantial impact on me. I recall holding my date's hand as I walked across the dance floor at my senior prom. When I looked toward where the chaperones were sitting, I spotted Mother looking my way, and I immediately dropped his hand, embarrassed she had seen me.

When I entered Baylor University in the fall of 1956, I was probably the most naïve college freshman. I was from Big Spring, a small town in West Texas but much, much larger than any other place I had lived before.

We had moved there a month earlier. Mother had made an effort for me to meet at least four other Baylor freshmen in hopes I wouldn't feel so alone, but they were only acquaintances, all planning to pledge sororities.[1] I had no desire to be in a sorority and never became good friends with any of those four from Big Spring. Luckily, one of my roommates, from Chicago, didn't know anyone else either, and we became quick friends despite our many differences.

Karen was sheltered from the mainstream and grew up in an adult world. Her father was an Old Testament and Archeology professor at a Chicago seminary, and her mother was a school counselor.

I used to refer to Karen as "being from the North." She would laughingly correct me by saying, "I am not from the North. I'm from the Midwest."

Although we were both Baptists, she attended an American Baptist church, whereas I attended a Southern Baptist church.[2]

Karen and I were different in other ways outside our family's geography and theology. For example, I had two younger brothers, whereas Karen was an only child. I'd always been one of the popular leaders in all my schools—from my first two years in Calallen (close to Corpus Christi) to my six years in Bishop (further south), then to Beeville (between Corpus Christi and San Antonio) where I graduated as one of 97 students in my high school class. Karen's friends were limited to students who attended her private school and lived in other parts of the city, making it difficult for her to interact socially.

I was used to walking down my street to friends' houses. Karen was accustomed to navigating the city using the "L," Chicago's rapid transit

---

1   Baylor did not allow Greek life on campus in 1956. The term sorority at the time referred to a local social club.
2   The Baptists split at the time of the Civil War. Many of their basic beliefs are still the same, but Southern Baptists are more mission oriented and presently have about ten times more members than American Baptists.

system. I was from a small town and had been driving our family car by myself since I was 12, when my Mother often asked me to drive a few blocks to pick up my dad at the end of his workday to bring him home. I received my adult driver's license when I was 14. Mother, carrying my one-year-old brother, took me to a judge's office and made the request. After passing the driving test, my "hardship license" was immediately granted. Karen, on the other hand, had never even tried driving in the big city. It scared her.

When she told me she lived in a brownstone, I had no idea what she meant. I learned it's a large apartment building and that her family had a roomy upstairs apartment. My family had always lived in a single-family house.

Our differences were many, but we felt alike in the face of our common need: a gaping loneliness the other filled by talking.

Karen's intelligence first drew me to her, so the subject matter of our talks was always immaterial. We discussed, we argued, we debated. We tossed our ideas and opinions back and forth. Hour after hour, we shared our thoughts, beliefs, ideals, and hopes. If we agreed about an issue, one of us deliberately pretended to disagree so we could have fun debating the subject. I had never found someone with whom I so enjoyed talking and sharing confidences. Having no sisters, I'd never really confided in anyone.

My conversations with my friends had never been profound, thoughtful, or weighty. They were typical teenage girl talk. Karen introduced me to a different type of conversation filled with depth, risks, and vulnerability, and I loved it.

We discussed our futures and our parents' expectations of us. Neither of us was explicitly told we had to marry and have children, but we knew it was expected. Our adolescence was filled with conversations that included comments like "You can place these towels in your hope chest. You'll need them when you marry," or asides like, "We look forward to showing off our grandchildren in the years to come." Both Karen and I accepted this plan for our lives, believing this was our lot in life.

My parents, in particular, always wanted me to be a teacher. As a girl coming of age in the 1950s, I felt my career choices were limited to teaching, nursing, secretarial work, or being an airline stewardess. No one ever mentioned any other possibilities to me. Nursing appealed to me because I enjoyed helping others, and becoming an airline stewardess also appealed, as it would allow me to travel worldwide. Still, I chose secretarial work because I excelled in typing and shorthand and loved to stay organized. I thought I'd enjoy running an office.

My parents continued to encourage me to get my teaching certificate at the very least. "You may never have to use it," they explained, "but it's the best insurance policy you can ever have. If something ever happens to your husband, you could always support yourself and your family by teaching."

I didn't take their admonitions seriously and enrolled in my first education course my third year at Baylor. Still, even as they recommended a career choice, they informed me that they assumed I would marry and have children.

Karen's and my love of conversing instigated our eventual physical relationship despite Baylor's strict expectations.[3]

Upon arrival, incoming female students were given a little gold-colored handbook containing gender-specific rules and regulations, which today seem antiquated. A direct quote from that handbook reads, "The fact that girls from Baylor do not smoke or drink anywhere,

---

3   Keep in mind that Baylor was established in 1845 when Texas was still a republic and by
      1956 was the largest Baptist university in the world and still highly governed and funded
      by the Baptist General Convention of Texas (BGCT).

anytime, means more than they are just abiding by a regulation. It is symbolic of the very highest standard of Christian living."

In line with the university's desire for its female students to live up to the "very highest standard," there were many rules about physical appearance. On campus, women were expected to wear dresses or skirts and blouses. Jeans or pants were allowed on picnics but only with special permission from your dorm mother. White shorts were restricted to the gym and tennis courts, and the only color allowed to be worn.

As freshmen, we were assigned to Alexander Hall, an older dorm, where six girls shared a suite with one small bathroom between two rooms. It was crowded, with three girls sharing each of the two bedrooms, which contained a bunk, a single bed, two chests of drawers, and two small closets. Along with our packed living spaces came constant supervision by hall monitors who rigorously enforced campus rules and curfew.

Everyone was expected to be in their rooms by 8:30 each evening, Monday through Thursday, with lights out by 10 o'clock sharp. After 8:30, we could visit only with our roommates. The only way we could talk with our suite mates were if we happened to be in the bathroom at the same time.

Karen and I would often be in the middle of a good discussion while our third roommate was always ready to go to sleep by ten. Cramped quarters required creative solutions, so as the lights were turned off each evening and everyone was supposed to stop visiting, Karen and I climbed into one of our beds and whispered. We lay there, not touching, enjoying the opportunity to enter each other's minds and thoughts. Our whispered conversations sometimes continued for hours, flowing like an elixir, healing our need for companionship.

After a few weeks, my longing to touch her, to simply hold her hand, dominated my thoughts as we lay side by side, talking. I ached with desire yet worried about doing something that might disgust her. A few months passed before I let my arm rest on the bed between us, next to hers, but not touching.

Do I dare hold her hand? I wondered. *Yes.*

A few minutes later, I gently clasped her hand, quietly shocked and pleased that neither of us mentioned what we were doing as we continued to whisper.

From then on, whenever we continued talking in bed after lights out, we held hands. It was understood without either of us ever saying a word about it. Nothing changed in our relationship. We never touched each other at any other time—just held hands in bed. Before long, I ached for more of Karen and began to imagine what it would be like to kiss her.

One night, when our third roommate was gone for the weekend, Karen and I still climbed into the same bed to visit. All these years later, I can still picture where we were that night.

We were on the top bunk next to the hall door when we somehow went from hand-holding to cuddling to me propping myself up on my right elbow and leaning down to lightly kiss Karen on the lips. She didn't seem displeased. She simply said, "I've never kissed a boy. Am I doing it right?"

I had dated throughout high school and had even gone steady my senior year, so Karen considered me an expert in this field. I explained, "Yes, just part your lips slightly. You'll find it very natural."

She followed my guidance, and we kissed—lovingly and tenderly, then longingly, desperately, feverishly—discovering a passion neither of us realized we possessed. After a while, Karen said, "We need to discuss what's happening to us—what we're doing."

"Yes. We should." I agreed.

My pleasure excited yet frightened me. I was feeling something with Karen I had never felt. My dates with boys had never brought out this almost delirious excitement I felt with Karen that night, and I worried about the possible consequences.

I had overheard enough conversations to know that homosexuals were looked down upon.[4] I was ignorant of the existence of gay couples firsthand, having never observed any, read about them, or heard the subject discussed freely. That fact made me realize we were outside the bounds of what was considered "normal" in our time.

We took turns climbing down from the upper bunk where our emotions had been awakened and slowly put on our robes and house shoes. Karen quietly opened the door to our room, and I followed as we walked down the deserted hallway to the stairs that led to a small prayer room in the basement.

The room was a 12' x 12' offshoot of a much larger, cold, and silent room meant for thoughtful and holy reflection. Once safely inside, we each took a straight-back chair and set them about four feet apart so we would face each other.

"What we just did was wrong." Karen began.

Though I replied, "Yes, it was," I'd never actually felt so in my heart.

What we shared was so natural and felt so good. I was trying to hide the worry of its wrongness from my conscience, but now a part of me knew she was right.

---

4   In December, 1950, A Senate report titled "Employment of Homosexuals and Other Sex Perverts in Government was distributed to members of Congress after the federal government had covertly investigated employees' sexual orientation at the beginning of the Cold War. The report states since homosexuality is a mental illness, homosexuals "constitute security risks" to the nation because "those who engage in overt acts of perversion lack the emotional stability of normal persons." Because of this report, over the previous few years, more than 4,380 gay men and women had been discharged from the military and around 500 fired from their jobs with the government. The purging became known as the "lavender scare."
https://www.pbs.org/wgbh/americanexperience/features/stonewall-milestones-american-gay-rights-movement/

I had always been a compliant child, probably because my parents never tolerated my questioning their decisions. If I did, it was considered "talking back" or "sassing" and was worthy of punishment. I'd always been the perfect daughter, doing the right things, saying the right things, being the individual others looked up to. I did as I was told and never did anything truly wrong. Sitting across from Karen in the prayer room of our dorm, faced with the possibility that what we had just experienced was so wicked we shouldn't ever do it again, terrified me because I wanted to do it again.

Karen said, "The Bible teaches against this. Many verses prohibit what we feel toward each other, especially in Leviticus."

Both she and I were familiar with the instructions and warnings of the Bible—the rules drilled into us from childhood. However, no one had ever discussed this subject openly with either of us. I didn't even know what word to use to describe what we shared, yet a part of me halfheartedly acknowledged we had potentially done a wicked thing.

Recalling Mother's concern each time I returned from a date, as she asked what we had done and whether we had kissed, suddenly had a deeper meaning for me. What Karen and I had done was beyond just kissing. The *love* I felt for Karen was forbidden.

The Bible said it was. From that perspective, we were sinning by breaking His law, but still, I questioned.

How can love be evil? I love Karen with all my being, all my soul. How can love be wrong?

As we sat in the chairs facing each other in that little prayer room, we acknowledged that what we had just shared was considered a sin by the Bible. Karen bowed her head, the first to suggest a kind of repentance, and said, "Then we need to stop what we're doing."

"Yes, we should," I agreed, then hesitated, gazed at her, and smiled. "But I don't want to."

A happy, goofy grin spread across her face. "Neither do I."

"I'm in love with you, Karen," I said.

"And I'm in love with you."

We radiated happiness. Those were our marriage vows, as no others were allowed to us. She was my other half.

2
THE LAWS OF MAN

*F*alling in love with a girl stunned me. Even though I'd dated quite a few boys, I'd never fallen in love with one. I spent much of my time wondering why I was drawn to a girl and how I had fallen in love with one.

When I'd wanted to kiss my high-school friend, Jean, at the drive-in movie, I never gave it a second thought because I'd never heard the words "gay," "lesbian," "homosexual," or "queer." The only word I'd ever heard was "sodomy," which was always spoken in such hushed tones that my child's mind simply concluded it was something nasty men did.

My family lived in South Texas for the first 17 years of my life, and many years later, my younger brother referred to that area as "repressed." I now agree with him. Sex of any kind was simply not discussed. My high school friends were also Baptist and must have come from similarly repressed families.

It wasn't until I arrived at Baylor that I heard an open discussion about sex. The conversation embedded in my mind was when my suite mates had a giggle-filled debate about the amount of ejaculation a man produces during intercourse. Some thought it was as much as a cup, while others suggested a tablespoon or two. I contributed nothing to this conversation, but I was hanging on to every word. These open discussions with the other girls in my dorm embarrassed me, but they also helped educate me. Even so, nothing was ever said about sex between two women. I simply didn't know that two women could fall in love with each other.

Despite this lack of knowledge, or perhaps because of it, Karen and I successfully deceived everyone around us by pretending to be just friends. When Thanksgiving break rolled around, I invited her home since she didn't have enough time to get to Chicago and back on the train. Going out to West Texas, where I lived, was an adventure for her. She was amazed by the red, barren landscape, the spectacular sunsets, and the occasional tumbleweed.

Dad called for us to enter their bedroom at about 10 o'clock on the second or third night we were there. He and Mom were propped up in bed. I expected to see them reading the newspaper as usual, but instead, Dad pointed to the sheet covering his chest and said, "Look!" Perched on the sheet was a scorpion.

I had seen scorpions in South Texas when we lived there, but Karen had never seen one. She found it so terrifying that she refused to go back to bed, thinking one would crawl into the sheets with her. If Dad had realized the effect seeing that scorpion would have on Karen, he would never have called us in to see it. Karen was so frightened that she sat up all night in our den reading.

After that taste of West Texas wildlife, Karen and I were happy to return to Baylor despite only having two or three weeks left of the semester before our Christmas vacation began. This break allowed Karen plenty of time to take the train to Chicago to be with her parents for the holidays. Consequently, this was our first separation, and I dreaded it. What would I do without Karen? She was like an extension of my very being. I helped her pack and rode with her in the taxi to the train station. I helped her with her luggage as she was taking home her summer things and planned to return with her winter clothes. I recall our being quieter than usual as we refrained from holding hands, afraid someone might see us. We would be apart for about three weeks, and we knew we would miss each other terribly. As she boarded the train, I waved to her with a lump in my throat, willing myself not to cry.

Our instinct to avoid public detection was painful but necessary. Though neither of us knew it at the time, same-sex couples could be jailed. Karen and my relationship was illegal. "Homosexual acts" of any degree were labeled a criminal offense across the U.S. until six years later, in 1962, when Illinois became the first state to decriminalize homosexuality. In Texas, homosexuality was considered a crime until 2003. That's why we had no role models—no one to reveal the truth of our suffering in silence or celebrate the beauty and depth of our love.

Television was relatively new at that time. My family purchased our first TV the year before I entered Baylor, and there were certainly no programs introducing us to LGBTQ individuals. I loved listening to the radio. Lux Radio Theater was a regular weekly program our whole family listened to, and I liked "The Green Hornet," "The FBI in Peace and War," and "Inner Sanctum," but none of these shows had LGBTQ characters represented in them.

Though I lacked the worldly knowledge and context to express it as I stood on the train platform, I was keenly aware that hiding our relationship from our parents would be just the "tip of the iceberg." To remain lovers, we would need to hide our relationship from everyone. *What kind of life would that be?*

Even my parents' promise of eternal job security by becoming a teacher came with warning bells. School teacher contracts had "morality clauses" whereby a teacher could be fired for being pregnant or gay. My parents experienced that type of judgement when they began dating. They met in Johnson City, Texas, Lyndon Johnson's hometown, where Dad was the school principal and Mom was a teacher. Even though they tried to keep their dating a secret, they failed and were fired at the end of their first year. Principals could not date teachers. The firing didn't bother them as they planned to return to college to finish their degrees, but morality clauses were quite real and could be brutal. Nearly all states, even today, have laws permitting a teacher's dismissal for immorality, immoral character, or moral depravity.

Years later, in 1964, while teaching in Odessa, I learned firsthand how easily a teacher can be dismissed. It was a Friday when I admitted to a school administrator that I thought I was pregnant. It was too early for me to be certain, but I felt compelled to report that possibility. Even though this administrator was good friends with my husband, he looked at me and said, "I'll expect your letter of resignation on my desk by Monday morning. You can't have your cake and eat it, too." Pregnant teachers were not allowed to teach high school students, though my husband was allowed to continue teaching even though he was the cause of my being pregnant.

Karen and I, aware of this type of attitude toward sex, even for heterosexual couples, assumed it would be difficult for us to hold a decent job if we stayed together. Society had set up too many barriers for us. We knew no one to consult and no books to read on the subject. We assumed no one else faced what we faced. We made our decision based solely on our religious upbringing, especially the admonition to honor our father and mother. Neither of us wanted to hurt or embarrass our parents, who were highly esteemed individuals.

Missing each other that first Christmas vacation, we wrote long letters every evening. Warning bells told me not to mail a letter to Karen every day, so I saved two-or-three days' worth of letters before putting them in an envelope to mail.

Even so, my parents became suspicious. Dad, a sociology major, was introduced to the possibility of same-sex love through his studies. Walking to his bedroom each night, he passed mine and glanced in. He couldn't help but notice me propped up in bed, always writing a letter.

One night, he told Mother, "I think we have a problem with Lou Anne. Those long letters she writes to Karen every night indicate she may have fallen in love with her."

Mother was aghast. "Surely not, oh surely not!"

"Yes," he replied. "I think that's what has happened. You need to go in and talk with her about this."

The next night, as I sat propped up in bed writing a letter to Karen, that's just what Mother did. She seldom came into my room just to visit, and I watched as she sat on my other twin bed a couple of feet away. I was immediately concerned and laid my writing materials down, wondering why she was there. She began the conversation by haltingly broaching the subject of same-sex love, and I froze.

Mother mentioned her younger brother, Warren, who had gone through life with a male companion. She had always made it clear she disapproved of their relationship, and her words that evening made it even more apparent that such a connection was sinful. I was devastated when she said, "You and Karen need to separate."

I felt trapped and didn't say anything. She wanted me to "confess" to a relationship with Karen. I wouldn't, but I didn't deny it either. I thought Karen and I had been so careful that no one would even suspect.

That's when I realized my writing to Karen every night had given us away.

Before I could interject, she continued, "No school district will hire you to teach in their school if you two stay together. You'll even have a challenging time just finding a place to live. No one will rent you an apartment, and few people would even sell you a house."

I continued to sit, mute and staring, listening to her accusations and judgements, and I felt my world crashing down around me. How much better this situation would have been if I'd fallen in love with a boy—someone my parents would approve of, someone I could marry, and someone with whom I could have children. But I hadn't. I had fallen deeply, everlastingly in love with a girl, someone my mother was telling me I would eventually have to part from. We'd never be able to marry, have a family, or simply share a life, all because I loved a girl.

The conversation continued to be one-sided, and the longer it lasted, the more troubled I felt, realizing my mother hadn't come into my room to be helpful. If she had, I would have unburdened myself and shared everything with her. I yearned for her to understand my predicament, to offer sympathy, a hug, a word of reassurance. After all, Karen and I hadn't planned to fall in love. I was heartsick. As Mother continued her interrogation, she asked, "Which of you is the male in your lovemaking?"

My mouth flew open. Not knowing what she was talking about, my curiosity got the better of me, and I asked, "What do you mean?"

"Normally, one of the girls plays the role of the male. Which role do you play? Are you a top or a bottom?"

I don't know where Mother got her information, but Karen and I didn't play any roles. We just loved each other.

I loved Karen with all my being and knew no way to suppress that love or make it go away.

As Mother's fears and phobias continued their march around the room, the fear I'd felt lingering at the edges of my mind that day at the train station grew, filling the space between us, its weight pressing my heart into parchment.

Our lives could be ruined. We were treading on dangerous ground. We'd always been careful, but now I became fearful. My mother was providing me with a small and brutal preview of the condemnation society would display if Karen and I failed to keep our relationship a secret. My heart split further as I watched my mother become my enemy.

I was being condemned. I was being shamed. I felt like the lowest of the low. My anguish and embarrassment overwhelmed me, yet I yearned for my mother to understand my predicament—to offer sympathy—hadn't she once been in love?

The next day, when I was alone in the house, I called Karen to tell her the shattering news. "Mother knows about us."

Karen was as shocked as I was. "Have you saved all the letters I've written you?"

"Yes. They're in a shoe box in my closet."

"You shouldn't have saved them. Burn them immediately. I bet your mother has read them. Don't save any of my letters!"

I'd never suspected that my mother might read my letters, but I did as Karen ordered. I carried them out to our burn barrel at the rear of our property and burned them. I never knew if Mother read them. I never asked, and she never mentioned them.

After Mother confronted me, I became much more secretive. I didn't speak to her for days, angry that she'd confronted me, angry that she knew, furious that she'd condemned me, and especially angry that she wanted to separate Karen and me. Most of all, I was angry at her lack of understanding of my predicament. I hated her and yearned for the holidays to end so I could return to the dorm and to Karen.

Somehow, Karen and I continued our affair all spring, with a third roommate in the room and three suite mates next door. I don't know if we were unusually discreet, if the others were just dumb, or if they had some idea of what was going on between us and didn't care to get involved. No one ever said a word. We were living in a paradise of our own making, and we dreaded the coming of summer when we would be apart for three months. Consequently, we delighted in being together as much as possible. Quite often, we would walk into the downtown area of Waco to occasionally shop or eat in a restaurant. Co-eds were not allowed to have a car on campus until they were seniors, so they did a lot of walking or occasionally took a taxi.

The summer after our freshman year was a long, long summer apart from Karen. I missed her terribly but stayed busy working at Cosden Oil Refinery, where I substituted for various secretaries when they took their two-week summer vacations.

Just a week or two before classes began at Baylor for our sophomore year, I received a devastating letter from Karen telling me she would remain at home for the fall semester. She'd decided we should end our affair, and this semester of separation would give us time to make a clean break.

I wanted her to be happy; if she felt that our being together was wrong, I was willing to go along with her plan to end our relationship. I didn't argue with her. Instead, I told myself, "If she can make the break, I can, too." We'd always felt guilty, convinced that our hidden love was sinful. We'd always known our relationship could never be permanent. I told myself that the three months of summer plus the four months of the fall semester would give me time to heal and overcome my desire to be with her.

When the fall semester came, I spent it telling myself I could live without Karen, convincing myself I never needed to touch her again.

By January 1958, when Karen returned, I felt I'd succeeded, believing that we could sincerely do it with both of us determined to end the affair. After all, we were merely separating a little sooner than we'd originally thought necessary.

Sophomores were assigned to a different dorm: Memorial Hall. I was lucky to have a very nice and friendly roommate, and we got along fine even though we had little in common. Karen stopped by my room to greet me, but we'd been apart the rest of the day.

When evening came, my roommate was soon asleep, and as I began to doze off myself, I suddenly realized Karen was kneeling by my bed. I felt her touch my hand and faintly heard her whisper, "Aren't you coming to my room?"

Suddenly awake, I was confused by her question. I whispered back, "I thought you decided we should stay apart? I've thought about it a lot, and I'm willing to give it a try. If we both work at it, we can make the break."

Her reply amazed me. "The only reason I came back was to be with you. I'm leaving on the train tomorrow if we can't be together. I love you so very much, Lou Anne. Please don't do this to me."

By then, she grasped my hand, imploring me to come to her room, her lovely face only inches from mine. As I shook off sleep, I had difficulty understanding what was happening. Was she sincerely asking me to resume our affair? I had worked so hard to convince myself I could live the rest of my life without her, and now she was begging me to be with her. My resolve simply melted. Disappeared. Confusion quickly gave way to feelings of elation. Delight. It didn't matter whether I had misread her or whether she had merely changed her mind. All I knew at that moment was that nothing would make me happier than going with her to her room.

Although our long separation had provided a perfect opportunity to end our affair, the touch of her hand that night, along with the thrill of seeing her so close to me, chased away all my resolve. I would have done anything for her, indeed, anything to make her happy. With only a moment's hesitation, I climbed out of bed and followed her.

3
PLAYING GAMES

*T*he next day, we walked downstairs to the dorm mother's office and asked if I could change rooms and become Karen's roommate. "No," the dorm mother replied. "That space is too small for two people."

She was correct in describing the room as small. It was about the size of the basement prayer room and designed to be occupied by a single hall monitor. It still contained a standard bunk bed, a chest of drawers, and only one small table and chair, but its big advantage was a small, private bathroom. No longer would we have to share a bath with four other girls. We pressed our case.

"We don't mind," I assured her, "we really would like to be together."

"Is there a problem with the girl you're with?" she asked.

"Not at all. She's very nice, and we get along just fine," I answered. "It's just that Karen and I are good friends and enjoy being together. We really do want to live together."

The dorm mother turned to Karen. "Is this something you want? Do you agree with this request?"

"Yes. I'd really like for Lou Anne to be with me."

"Well, the accommodation is too small for two, but if you want, I'll assign both of you to it."

We were elated.

Sharing one closet and one chest of drawers posed no hardship on us. We never gave it another thought. We set up a large record player across the room from the bunk beds, which played 78 rpm, 33 1/3 rpm, and 45 rpm records. Later that year, we splurged and subscribed to receiving monthly 33 1/3 rpm albums of our choosing. We found it fun to review the available albums and choose the ones to order. Our music tastes were similar, and we took turns with the expense and making the final selection. One of our albums was all Rachmaninoff music. That was a favorite for both of us, and I especially swooned over Rachmaninoff's Piano Concerto #2. I thought it was the most romantic music I had ever heard.

We worked together to keep our room neat and clean so we could pass our hall monitor's strict weekly inspections. We knew ahead of time which day of the week we would be checked and made sure our room was "spic and span." On that day, our trash can had to be completely empty. If we had an allergy or cold and needed a tissue, we took it with us instead of placing it in the trash can. We didn't mind the strict rules or the cramped space; this tiny corner of the world was our home, and we were finally together in the way we had once dreamed.

Karen walked in one afternoon complaining about her algebra class. Math was difficult for her. Her instructor spent the period writing problems on the board and then showing the class how to solve them. Karen tried to copy everything down but couldn't write fast enough.

Before she copied the final steps, the instructor erased the board and began the next problem. Karen was frustrated and on the verge of tears.

"Karen," I advised, "forget your paper and pencil at your next class and just sit back, listen, watch, and try to understand the steps he's taking in solving the problem. Give it a try."

Returning to our room following that next class period, she excitedly exclaimed, "It worked! I took no notes, but I understood how to work the problem. I'm so glad you gave that suggestion to me."

We celebrated when she passed her algebra class with flying colors.

Karen and I spent some of our happiest times in that tiny dorm room where we could say and do whatever we wished. We only had each other to please. Our lives were as close to perfect as we could ever hope for.

Because sophomores and juniors shared Memorial Hall, we requested the little room for the following year—our junior year—and our request was granted. We lived in that little room for a whole year and a half. It was our haven.

To keep the outside world out of our business, I regularly dated boys in the hope that no one would suspect Karen and me. What better way to hide our secret? I also went on dates because my parents taught me to be "nice," and accepting a date was, in my thinking, simply being nice to the fellow. I never wanted to hurt his feelings by turning him down.

During my junior year, I dated a senior named Eric McGill, whose father was a Baptist preacher in West Texas. Eric was tall and thin with curly, reddish-blonde hair. He was highly religious, which made him very proper, almost to the point of being priggish. Because he had little money and struggled to make ends meet, he worked in one of the dining halls to help pay his bills. He could afford Baylor because of the allowance available to preachers' kids. Consequently, when Eric and I dated, we just walked around campus, had a Coke, attended a free campus event or, occasionally, a movie.

One evening, as we were strolling across campus, he said, "You're one of the few girls I've ever dated who doesn't expect me to spend a lot of money on a date. You and I have fun just doing simple things, and you don't realize how much I appreciate it."

"Spending a lot of money on me isn't necessary, Eric. I enjoy going out with you," I politely lied. I never particularly enjoyed being with Eric. He was too strait-laced and proper.

Until Eric commented about inexpensive dating, I'd never thought about it one way or the other. What we did together wasn't that important. I wasn't dating to look for a husband or even to have fun because it was Karen I ultimately preferred being with. My purpose in dating was to fool my parents into thinking that Karen and I were nothing more than friends. Otherwise, they might forbid us from rooming together. The charade was exhausting but necessary, even on my visits home.

My family had moved from South Texas the summer after I graduated high school, so I remained a stranger in Big Spring, where my parents lived. Mother wanted me to feel at home there, so when I occasionally returned home on weekends or holidays, she would often arrange a blind date for me. I knew she did it for two reasons: 1. She wanted me to have something fun to do so I would look forward to coming home, and 2. She was helping me find a husband.

Today's dating is much different from how it was in my day. If a fellow asked me out, I'd be nice and accept, even if I didn't particularly like him. There was nothing unusual about dating two or three guys at the same time, maybe even within the same week. Dating wasn't a commitment to a single person the way some talk about it now; that was what we called "going steady." The goal of dating more than one person was to explore different personalities so you could discover who you might experience true happiness with, and that meant the more people you dated, the better your chances of finding it. Needless to say, Mother made sure my calendar was full any chance she got, certain that finding the right man would ensure her daughter's happiness.

While I was dating strait-laced Eric, Karen had become interested in Russell Hampton, a senior in her psychology class. I became accustomed to hearing, "I'm heading to the library to study. Russell may be there. Don't wait up for me."

Returning from the library, she was either disappointed because Russell hadn't shown up or elated because he had. Occasionally, she'd be thrilled because he'd asked her to go to the Student Union to have a Coke.

I wasn't jealous of Russell. After all, I had dated boys and had been doing so all the time that Karen and I were together, but Karen had never dated. She had no experience being with boys and no self-assurance, thanks to her mother's perpetual nagging that no boy would pay attention to Karen until she lost some weight. The more critical her mother became the more Karen ate; the battle between them and the scale was constant.

I didn't care about Karen's weight. I found Karen beautiful. I wanted others to notice her unblemished skin, flawless makeup, and precisely styled short, blonde hair. I wished she could see herself as I saw her; then, she would feel more self-confident.

Another reason I felt no jealousy toward Russell was that Karen and I both felt our lot in life was to marry and have children. Our parents and the church taught us to "Honor Your Father and Mother." Parents, society, peers, and the church had made it quite clear that marriage was expected of us. We saw no other option, so we supported each other as best we could in securing safe futures.

Russell was handsome, bright, and a member of Baylor's Air Force ROTC (Reserve Officers Training Corps) program. I understood

Karen's infatuation. At the end of her psychology class, Russell would suggest that he "might" study in the library that evening and "maybe" they could study together. These crumbs of attention were all it took for Karen to spend all evening sitting in the library, hoping he'd show. Sometimes he would, and sometimes he wouldn't. Observing Karen's disappointment on the nights when he never showed up caused me to dislike him. I could see he wasn't treating her right. I longed for her to be happy with someone who would place her on a pedestal, love her, be proud of her, and support her. If she had greater self-esteem, her eyes would have opened to the imbalance in their relationship. Although I wanted to protect her from the unhappiness Russell was bringing her, I knew that if I criticized him in any way, I would not only hurt her but also make her mad and probably not accomplish anything.

Helplessly, I watched her infatuation with him take control of her emotions. The more he took over her thoughts, the less she wanted to be with me. Several months into that first semester of our junior year, she returned from the library all excited. "Russell came to the library, and we've been studying together for the past hour—Lou Anne, I'm in love with Russell!"

This concerned me. Russell never actually asked her out on a date or took her out to eat, to a movie, or any campus gathering. In no way did he show her off as someone who could be special to him. He met her furtively at the library and occasionally bought her a Coke. I knew this wasn't a normal courtship, but Karen didn't. The little bit of attention Russell gave her was enough to cause her to fall in love with him. She was smitten.

As we started getting ready for bed one evening, she said, "The time has come for us to end our relationship." My heart stopped as she continued, "I realize this won't be easy for you, especially with us rooming together, but it's time. Let's not touch each other anymore."

I was stunned, but I didn't argue with her or plead for her to change her mind, at least not that first night. Her words broke my heart, and I felt wretched.

I was so accustomed to holding her each night in that single bunk bed that I found it impossible to fall asleep alone. I kept yearning to be with her, touch her, cuddle with her, and embrace her. When we turned out the lights each night, I'd be in the bottom bunk, and she would be just above me in the top.

One Friday night, as we were getting ready for bed, I begged Karen to simply let me cuddle up next to her, but she ignored me. The torturous situation of being close to her day after day, night after night, and not being able to hold her hand or put my arms around her eventually became more than I could bear. When she blatantly ignored me that evening, my emotions went haywire, and I threatened to kill myself.

I don't think I really meant it, but when she didn't believe me, it was like accepting a dare. I got up from my bed, walked into our little bathroom, opened the medicine cabinet above the sink, and located her bottle of sleeping pills. I shook out all the pills into my left hand, counted them, and realized there were only 13. Picking up my glass of water, I quickly swallowed all 13 pills. I wasn't thinking, not of my parents, not of my brothers, not of my schooling. I was simply distraught, wanting to escape her rejection and the pain of a life that made us have to choose. More than anything, I tried to awaken her to how cruel she was to me—to both of us.

After swallowing the pills, I lay back down in my bed as Karen chided, "That's not going to kill you. Those pills aren't strong enough."

She was right.

The next morning, my consciousness seemed to come crawling out of a deep hole to the vague sound of Karen saying, "Wake up, Lou Anne." Her voice was far, far away. She shook me and said again, "Wake up!" She continued to call me and to shake me. When I finally indicated I had heard something, she said, "Lou Anne, you must get up. You have a date to the football game, and you need to get up and dress."

I felt terrible as if I were in a stupor. I could hardly hold my head up, but it never occurred to me to cancel my date. I dressed, but not with any wisdom, as I wore a teal-blue sweater when the weather turned out to be very warm. My date brought me a corsage, and as I pinned it on, it drooped down from my loosely knit top. I realized it didn't look right, but I couldn't very well go back to my room and change clothes, leaving my date standing downstairs waiting for me. Besides, changing clothes would require me to think about what to change into, and that seemed like too big of a chore.

The game was a blur. I had a terrible time just staying awake. I was miserable, ill, hot, and uncomfortable. I recall nothing of the game and even less of my date. He never asked me out again.

After the night of the sleeping pills, Karen and I refrained from any type of physical relationship for the rest of the semester. We'd spent many happy hours in that little room last spring as sophomores and many more at the start of our junior year, but now, as winter approached and we found ourselves unable to avoid our shared space, we both felt the strain. My love for Karen quietly continued. My hatred for Russell grew.

Christmas was still about six weeks away and would give us a break from our stress. My depression began to lessen as I developed a plan to ensure a decent night's rest. After we turned out the lights, I waited until Karen was asleep, then quietly and carefully crawled up into her bed and curled up at her feet like a cat. I could doze off by just barely touching one of her feet. I craved her connection. I awakened first in the mornings and returned to my bed without her knowing I'd shared the top bunk with her. At least, I assumed she never knew. The act was desperate, I know, but it was all I could do to keep myself going. She was the only person in the world who truly knew who I was. I couldn't fathom the fierce loneliness of living an unknown, unseen, unheard life.

4
A LONG ROAD HOME

*W*hile I attempted to wait patiently for Karen to come to her senses about us once again, I distracted myself with more dates. Strait-laced Eric was roommates with a boy named Jeff Tatum, and one night, he suggested we go on a double date with Jeff and another girl to the movies. Shortly thereafter, Jeff called and asked me out. I accepted, and we dated a few times, after which Eric called, "Lou Anne, I like you a lot and would like to keep dating you. However, I will step aside if you prefer to date Jeff."

His phone call forced me to be unkind to one of these fellows, and I didn't like the feeling at all. I felt annoyed at the thought of having to "choose" since I wasn't serious about either.

I never particularly liked Eric, who seemed to be getting too serious about me, so, in the end, I found the choice to be an easy one. (I learned 48 years later that Eric wanted to marry me and was angry at Jeff for asking me out.) At the time, I didn't want to hurt Eric's feelings, so I weaseled out of telling him I preferred Jeff by saying, "You're a great guy, Eric, but I need to think about my decision."

When I accepted Jeff's next offer to go out, it became obvious to Eric that I had made my choice. Jeff and I ended up dating rather exclusively as the end of his senior year rapidly approached. He was asking me out so regularly that I had little time to date anyone else.

Eric's parents had recently moved to Big Spring, Texas, where my family lived and where I would be spending the Christmas holiday. Jeff planned to go home with Eric for the break, and just before Baylor let out for the fall semester, Eric asked if I'd like a ride home.

My usual mode of transportation from Waco to Big Spring was by bus, which involved a very long ride, sometimes stopping at each little town we passed through. I was delighted when Eric invited me to ride with them. I recall sitting in the car's front seat between them;[5] the three of us laughing, talking, and simply having fun.

The fellows had purchased a box of chocolate-covered cherries for us to share on the way home. While I appreciated their thoughtfulness, I never cared for chocolate-covered cherries. I ate one, then happily let them finish up the box.

Eventually, the topic of conversation turned to Karen's "beau," Russell. Eric commented, "I bet Russell is excited now."

"Yeah," Jeff replied, "it's been months since he's seen Donna. They have a lot of planning to do over the holidays."

"Isn't their wedding supposed to occur two weeks after he graduates?" Eric asked, the two of them talking over my head.

---

5   Back then, cars had bench seats in front and in back that basically went from door to door. These comfortable and convenient seats declined in use due to safety concerns as air bags could only protect two front seat passengers.

"Yeah. He sure is crazy about her," Jeff said. "Talks about her all the time."

"Are you talking about Russell Hampton?" I interjected, appalled.

"Yes," Jeff said.

"He's engaged to be married?"

"Yes. For years. Won't be much longer now."

"But I have a friend who likes him. She has no idea he's engaged!"

"Oh, I know," Eric replied, exasperated. "Russell's just experimenting with her as part of those psychology courses he's taking. He wanted to see if he could get a naïve girl to fall in love with him even if he never asked her out on a date. We've told him he shouldn't do her that way, but he won't listen."

For the first time, I realized these fellows—Eric, Jeff, and Russell-were rooming together in an off-campus apartment. At first, I didn't believe them, but then I reminded myself that Russell had never asked Karen out on an actual date. She was convinced Russell cared for her and was picturing wedding bells with him.

I don't recall the rest of that drive. I couldn't think about anything but Karen and the heartbreak ahead for her. My thoughts boiled.

What he is doing to her is unforgivable, that cad!

Should I tell her? I have to.

I'd want to know if the shoe were on the other foot.

I can't allow this to continue, but how can I warn her?

Will she hate me? It doesn't matter.

She has to know.

As we continued our drive, I began mentally writing her a letter, revising it as the fellows took turns driving the 300 miles from Waco to Big Spring.

Even after I arrived home and tried to warm to the holiday spirit, I kept thinking of how to break this painful news to Karen. While my mind kept swirling around the correct words to use, I nevertheless enjoyed being with my two brothers. One would finish high school in the Spring, and the other was a first-grader born when I had just turned 13. I felt like a second mother to him and always looked forward to being with him. Their presence was a salve to the ache of the difficult task ahead of me.

A day or two after my arrival, I propped myself up in bed to write another letter to Karen. Only two years earlier, I had been writing passionate letters to Karen regularly and looking forward to receiving similar letters in return. This letter would be much different. I was certain the letter I was composing would contain heartbreak for Karen and could cause her to be angry with me.

Finally, I wrote:

Dear Karen,

Being good friends usually means sharing happy times together. However, being a good friend occasionally requires being honest about a painful truth. Please know that what I'm about to tell you brings me no joy or happiness, only sorrow and anguish. I say these things with tears in my eyes, knowing how much my words are about to hurt you.

I then gently related to her what Jeff and Eric had told me about Russell.

I'm aware of how terribly hurt you must now feel, and I understand if you're angry with me and only hope you don't dislike me, but I must be truthful regardless of the consequences. I care for you very much, and it breaks my heart to give you such distressing news.

During the remainder of the holiday, I heard nothing from Karen. Today, I would have picked up the phone to check on her, but in the '50s, our family rarely made long-distance calls because of the expense.

Besides, I didn't know if she'd even talk to me. I had no idea how she was taking the news about Russell or whether she even believed me. I worried she might think I was just trying to win her back, but I rested on the fact that we trusted each other, and I thought she would understand my intentions.

When the holidays ended, I hitched a ride back to school with Jeff and Eric, who had to return a day or two early due to their work schedules. I never thought to check if the dormitories would be open; I simply assumed they would be, but I was wrong. We were all surprised. There I was, back in Waco, Texas, with nowhere to spend the night. The only alternative we could think of was going to the downtown hotel.

Eric and Jeff carried my luggage into the hotel lobby, and once I was checked in, Jeff asked me out to dinner and a movie, so I accepted. With only a little over an hour before he'd return to pick me up, I headed to my room to freshen up from our long drive. Since boys didn't go up to a girl's hotel room, I met Jeff in the lobby at six thirty.

As he and I were walking out of the hotel, Karen walked in. Surprised and shocked to see her, I blurted out, "What are you doing here?"

"My train arrived today, and the dorms aren't open. I'm staying here tonight."

"Me, too. Eric and Jeff gave me a ride back. I never dreamed the dorms would be closed. So here I am!"

"Where are you going?" she asked, looking at the two of us.

"Out to eat and to a movie."

"Come see me when you get back. I'm in Room 342."

"Okay."

I wanted to visit her right then, to go up to her room immediately and see how she was doing, and to find out how she had taken the news about Russell. I was mad at myself for having made a date with Jeff and resented the evening with him. The dinner took too long, and the movie took even longer. Jeff wasn't ready to call it a night when we finally exited the theater, so we walked for a short time until about ten thirty, when I told him I was tired. Reluctantly, he walked me back to the hotel. I headed immediately to Karen's room and knocked on her door. She opened it right away and said, half-jokingly, "You certainly weren't in any hurry to get here!"

"I'm sorry. I'd already made the date and couldn't back out at the last minute."

"I know. I've just been anxious to see you."

She wore her pajamas and robe and climbed back in bed, propping herself up with pillows against the headboard. I followed her no-touching rules and sat on the floor, leaning back against the bed beside her.

Soon, she gently placed a hand on my shoulder. "Thank you for the kindest letter I've ever received. I read and reread it and realized that despite the horrible news, you told me in the most loving way possible. I even showed your letter to Mother. She agreed it was the kindest letter she'd ever read and told me how lucky I am to have you as a friend. She's right. Thank you."

Delighted to feel her touch on my shoulder and hear her kind words, I explained, "I hope you realize I never wanted to write that letter. I never liked Russell and the way he led you on, but I felt so sad when I learned what he was doing to you. I'd do almost anything to keep you from being hurt, Karen." By then, tears were in my eyes and breaking through my voice.

"I'm all right," she said. "Yes, it hurt. Terribly. But I'm over it. I really am." Then she touched me on the cheek. "Would you stay with me tonight? I want you to spend the night with me. I'm so sorry for the way I've treated you."

What glorious words. Joy flooded my total being. My mind erupted with glee.

She wants me back! And the setting is ideal—a hotel room that gives us complete privacy.

Rising from the floor, I turned, leaned over, and kissed her, then lay down beside her. Touching, holding, and kissing her brought heaven down into my heart. After a short while, she suggested, "Go get your things from your room and move in with me."

"Are you sure?"

"Yes, I want you with me. I've treated you terribly. Please forgive me. I love you so much. Hurry. Don't take long. I want you back here soon."

"I'll hurry," I promised.

Going to my room, I gathered up my luggage, mussed up my bed to make it look like I'd slept in it, and then quickly returned to Karen's room. We stayed in each other's arms throughout the night and long into the morning. Eric and Jeff had to be at work early that morning, so we felt no rush to get up until it was time to check out. We enjoyed the luxury of the large room with a double bed, which was something we had never shared before, having only had twin-sized bunk beds.

Although we had a day before classes began, we never considered staying in the hotel for another night. Money was one factor, and the fear of being discovered sleeping together was the other. Consequently, we packed up without a fuss, called a taxi, and looked forward to returning to the privacy of our humble dorm room—our home.

5
BEING NICE

Although Russell was now out of the picture, Eric and Jeff remained interested in me.

That last semester of Karen's and my junior year and the last semester of senior year for the boys, a congregation reached out to the University's Religion department and asked for help in establishing a Baptist church in the small town of Robinson, just outside of Waco.

Eric saw the opportunity to be of service and talked Jeff into assisting. They agreed to work together to get the job done and invited me to join them.

Looking back, I have no idea why I went with them. I suppose because I had no good excuse not to. Once again, I was "being nice," as girls were expected to be.

The three of us worked together to establish this little Baptist church. Jeff and Eric took turns preaching and leading the music every Sunday morning, and I played the piano when no one else was available.

The church met in a small three-bedroom home. For the service, chairs were set up in rows in the den, facing the kitchen. The family's bedrooms became Sunday School classrooms as we divided up for Bible lessons using literature sent to us by the Southern Baptist Convention. The owners of this house, who had young children, made great sacrifices, having to rise early to eat, dress, clean up their kitchen, and straighten the bedrooms before our arrival.

Establishing that little church was no small feat, and forty years later, all three of us showed up for their 40th Anniversary celebration. Their facility was lovely, and it was a thrill to be there. A few of the older members still remembered us. Eric, Jeff, and I had a good visit that day before heading home in our separate directions that afternoon.

Back in our college days and the early days of that congregation, I'm sure the intense and exciting experience of building a church home together continued to spark Jeff's interest in building a literal home with me. As his last semester drew closer to an end, he became even more serious about me.

Jeff's interests were broader than establishing churches and dating me. He was also enrolled in Baylor's Air Force ROTC program, an elective course that offered benefits including scholarship opportunities to help with tuition. He was incredibly handsome in his uniform, but even without the uniform, he was nice-looking and a very kind and happy young man. I can see him now with his thick blonde, wavy hair and a smile on his face. He was always enjoyable to be around and had a clear vision for his life. When he graduated in 1959 with a degree in engineering, he planned to move to California and get a second degree at Stanford University. By any other girl's standards, Jeff was hands-down "a catch."

When Valentine's Day arrived in February 1959, Jeff sent me a bouquet of red and white carnations and proposed to me. I knew how ludicrous it looked to others for me to turn him down. I tried to do it gently, but perhaps more surprising was his desire to continue dating me.

Several weeks before he graduated, Jeff and I were parked in some scenic area, and he asked me to lie beside him in the car's front seat. "No," I replied. "I don't want to do that."

"I promise not to do anything funny. You can trust me. I just want to feel you lying beside me."

I already felt guilty for not accepting his proposal, so against my better judgement, I did as he requested. I felt so uncomfortable beside him that my body was rigid as I waited to see what would happen. True to his word, though, he gently held and kissed me. I continued to feel uncomfortable and could hardly wait to sit back up.

When we did, he placed an arm around me while holding my hand. Lovingly, he looked at me and said, "Lou Anne, I know you've already told me you won't marry me, but I want to show you what I've already bought for you." He reached into his pocket and handed me a little box.

The glint of the diamond in the dark made me want to cry for him. It was beautiful.

I knew he was hurting, and I was the cause of that hurt. I knew exactly what it was like to love someone and not have that love returned. My heart ached for him, and I knew the only way to remove that pain was to agree to marry him, but I just couldn't do that. I respected him too much to pretend to be in love with him. He was a true gentleman and I knew I wouldn't be able to make him happy, even though he believed I would.

Three or four years after that evening, when I was a high school teacher in the West Texas town of Odessa, Jeff called me one Saturday. He was living in California by then but visiting West Texas, where his parents lived. He asked, "May I stop by and see you tomorrow?"

"Of course. I'd love to see you." I said.

When I opened the door for him, he immediately took me in his arms and kissed me. Then we sat down and visited. After asking how I was doing, he explained, "I'm engaged to a girl I met in California. However, I wanted to come by and see you first to see if you might change your mind about marrying me. If so, I won't marry this girl."

"No, Jeff, there's no chance. I'm sorry."

"I am, too. But I need to buy a pair of shoes for my wedding. Will you go shopping with me?"

"Sure!"

So off we went to downtown Odessa, going into one store after another to find just the right shoes. As we walked down the sidewalk, he held my hand every chance he got. I thought it strange for him to be buying shoes for his wedding to someone else but holding my hand, but I figured letting him do that wouldn't hurt anything, so I didn't stop him.

He eventually found the shoes he was looking for, bought them, drove me back to my apartment, and left.

I didn't see him again for many years when he and I showed up at that little church's 40th Anniversary celebration. His marriage lasted for quite some time, but he and his wife eventually divorced and remarried.

One of the tragedies of being gay and feeling trapped in hiding is the potential of hurting others. I'm sure if I had been a stronger person and had turned down all offers to date men instead of "being nice," I would have been a genuinely kinder and much happier person.

6
SUMMER DREAMS

*M*y last semester as a Junior was bittersweet. Not only was I trying to let Jeff down gently after his proposal, but Karen's dad planned to spend the next year overseas on an archaeological dig and invited Karen to go with him. She didn't want to pass up such a wonderful opportunity, and she looked forward to living and studying overseas for a year, participating in an archaeological dig, and escaping her mother's constant nagging about her weight. I accepted her plans without any argument, knowing I would be thrilled to have had such an exciting opportunity. I pretended to be happy for her but dreaded the parting. We had always assumed we would have to part when we graduated, so her plans simply sped up and shortened the timeline. We talked of no future beyond that coming year.

As the semester ended, my parents relented and let me take a train to Chicago to spend the summer with Karen since she would be out of the country for our last year of college. It was a welcome surprise, given my mother's awful initial behavior toward my relationship with Karen.

Although I'd met Karen's dad once when he made a trip to Texas, I'd never met her mother, who, upon seeing me for the first time, exclaimed, "Oh, how beautiful you are! What a tiny waist! I've never seen such a tiny waist. It must not be more than eighteen inches!"

"Oh, it's more than that," I insisted.

"Oh, no. It couldn't be! It looks much smaller than that."

I was embarrassed, not just for myself but for Karen. The comparison made for a very uncomfortable atmosphere. After she and her mother talked that evening, Karen told me what her mother said to her, "No wonder Lou Anne chose you for a friend. She knows you'll never give her any competition with the boys."

I couldn't believe a mother would say such things to her daughter.

"Karen," I said, "you know better than that. Don't give her words a second thought."

"Yes, but it still hurts," she said, downcast.

"Of course, it does. That was cruel. It's just not true, and you know it."

I longed to reach out and put my arms around her, to let her feel how beautiful I knew she was, but I feared we might be seen, and I would have been sent home.

Karen's bedroom, which contained two twin beds, was just off the living room. One of her doors led into the kitchen and the other into the living room. When it was time for everyone to go to bed, Karen's mother brought covers and pillows into the living room and spread them out on the sofa. "You two girls leave your bedroom door open tonight," she said. "I'm going to sleep on the sofa so I can keep an eye on you."

That's when I knew Mother must have called and asked her to keep an eye on us. I was uncomfortable and embarrassed to know she was watching us. During the night, Mrs. Mundt got up several times to check on us. This was despite our door being left open while we stayed in our own beds, making no effort to touch each other. She just peered in at us, then returned to her bed on the sofa.

Karen and I were determined to do nothing to arouse suspicion and risk my being sent home. We never broke any unspoken rules. To our success, less than a week later, Mrs. Mundt quit sleeping on the couch and returned to her and her husband's bedroom, but Karen and I continued to leave her bedroom door open and stay apart. Even during the day, we sat cross-legged on our individual beds to talk. We only touched each other when both parents were out of the apartment, and even then, we stayed alert.

I suppose our exemplary behavior convinced Karen's parents that what my parents told them about us was untrue because they eventually left for a month's stay in their tiny cabin in the woods of northern Michigan. Karen was taking a summer school class at Northwestern University, and I worked temporarily in various offices to help pay my expenses, so we couldn't accompany them. I'm sure her parents needed some time alone before the upcoming year-long trip Dr. Mundt and Karen would soon be making, as Karen's mother would remain in Chicago as a public-school counselor. They were probably dreading the upcoming separation as much as we were.

When Karen's parents left for Michigan, we were ecstatic because we had the apartment all to ourselves. In less than fifteen minutes after the Mundts walked out the door, Karen and I grinned at each other and headed toward her parents' bed.

Those weeks we were alone in the apartment were like a honeymoon. We purchased flowers from stalls located in subway stations and had a great time choosing which ones to select.

I tasted strawberry cheesecake for the first time. Karen couldn't believe I had never had any and purchased several slices for us to take home.

We walked the Magnificent Mile and had fun looking in some high-end stores. Marshall Field's was Karen's favorite store, so we enjoyed walking through its various floors more than once. I still have a beautiful necklace she purchased for me from Marshall Field's.

Our days together were idyllic. This was my first experience living in a city where the only modes of transportation available to us were walking or taking the "L". I learned which "L" to take to get to the downtown area and which "L" to take back to the apartment. Sometimes, Karen would meet me downtown after my temporary job finished in the afternoon. My heart beat faster when she'd take my hand and suggest, "Let's walk down Michigan Avenue."

I recall the delightful feeling of breezes off Lake Michigan blowing against my face and through my hair as we walked, and I held Karen's hand.

Yes, we sometimes held hands, not caring who saw us. On days when I wasn't working, I accompanied Karen to Northwestern University and sat on the shore of Lake Michigan reading while she attended class.

We went to a few movies. I recall that's where I first saw South Pacific.

We ate out at a few restaurants, visited the zoo, and visited various museums. The memories we made would last us the rest of our lives. We were living in the moment, not talking about our future.

On one of these magical days, Karen met up with some of her former high school friends for lunch, eager to introduce me to them and vice versa. Three years had passed since the girls had been together in high school, and they had much catching up to do. I enjoyed watching their excitement as they greeted and hugged each other. There must have been eight to 10 girls, but I seemed to be the "star attraction" with my Texas accent as they all urged me to "Say something. *Anything.* Just talk!" I had difficulty thinking of what to say to them, but I complied with their request as best I could. The more I talked, the more they demanded. Naturally, I found their accents a little odd, too, but they sounded just like Karen, and by then, I'd become accustomed to her speech. I was happy to entertain her friends, saying whatever came to mind, and was delighted to know that Karen enjoyed "showing me off" at this happy gathering.

When Karen completed her class at Northwestern, her parents called and instructed us to take a bus and join them in their cabin on a very small lake. The cabin was rustic, with no electricity or running water, just a water pump next to the kitchen sink. Entering through the tiny kitchen, you walked directly into a living room. The Mundts had the downstairs bedroom, while Karen and I used the loft, which was open to the living room via a ladder.

She and I continued our long city walks in the Michigan woods. I had never seen a birch tree and was amazed at the way its white bark peeled off, so unlike the trees I was familiar with in Texas. A few times, I drove their family car, and Karen and I enjoyed driving down country lanes. We seldom saw anyone else or even another cabin. The area was so isolated that we occasionally took advantage of it to "park" and enjoy some cuddling and kissing.

Because the woods offered solitude and privacy, we often held hands as we walked. We also used a small rowboat to explore the tiny lake in front of the cabin.

As a hush fell in the evenings, Karen, her parents, and I would gather in the living room to read, visit, or play table games. Occasionally, I'd sit cross-legged on the floor and play my flute.

Neither Karen nor I addressed the realization that these days together in the Michigan woods were our last. Instead, we passed our days in forced ignorance, enjoying our bliss.

When we returned to the city, everyone began preparing for the upcoming trip abroad. We were all busy. I accompanied Karen on her shopping trips to Marshall Field's and other places to purchase items she would need during the coming year. I also sat with her in her doctor's office while she waited for her turn to receive the required vaccinations. I went everywhere with her, helping her shop and then helping her pack. Still, as we worked together, neither of us voiced the question buried below our conscious thoughts: *Will we ever see each other again?*

When the departure day arrived, the four of us drove to O'Hare Airport. We located the correct gate for their overseas flight, and all four of us waited together, unlike airports today with all their security concerns. Karen and I simply stood around, waiting. Nothing personal was said by either of us. I felt numb.

When the time came for Karen and her dad to board the plane, I wished her a safe trip and a happy year—the type of goodbye I'd say to anyone. She was pleased and excited, so I tried to match her happiness as best I could, watching silently as she walked through the gate with her dad. Once they were out of sight, Mrs. Mundt and I moved to a nearby corner area with floor-to-ceiling glass in front of us and to the left. We stood next to each other in silence as we watched the plane taxi down the runway, turn, and then head into the wind, quickly gaining altitude.

She was gone.

Still, without talking, Mrs. Mundt and I turned and began our walk back through the airport and then to the parking lot. I recall feeling numb and empty. At that time, I had nothing in my life to look forward to. I was already missing Karen.

Thank goodness there was no pressure to talk. I was afraid to even think about it, knowing how difficult it would be to hide my emotions from Mrs. Mundt, who I'm certain had her sad thoughts.

Even though she would have her counseling job to keep her occupied, she would come home to an empty apartment every night, completely alone. I remained stoic, as did she.

Mrs. Mundt took me to a restaurant that evening and then to a movie. We saw a new release, *Gunfight at the O.K. Corral*, starring Kirk Douglas, and I've never wanted to see that movie again. The following day, Mrs. Mundt drove me to the train station, and I headed home, turning my last months with Karen into a dream I was just waking up from.

photo provided by the author

MARRIAGE & FAMILY MATTERS
1963 – 1999

7
NEW LIFE

*W*hen I graduated from Baylor in 1960, I was awarded a teaching assistantship at the University of Texas at Austin. I taught typewriting and shorthand while working on my master's degree in management. I took additional required education courses while working on my master's and was able to graduate by the end of the following summer with both a teaching certificate and an MBA.

As I began seeking a job as a teacher, I thought it would be nice to live within visiting distance of my parents but not in the same town. They were still in Big Spring, almost 300 miles west of Dallas, so I accepted a position teaching in Odessa, sixty miles west of Big Spring—close but not too close.

Several weeks after I signed my teaching contract, my parents informed me they were moving to Little Rock, 670 miles from Odessa. I was shocked. I knew absolutely no one in Odessa, but Mother helped me locate an apartment, and that fall, I began teaching business classes at Odessa High School.

I was twenty-two, and most of my high school classmates were already married, leaving my mother concerned that I didn't have a steady boyfriend. I was certain her compulsion to set me up on blind dates, as she did throughout college, would continue to haunt me, even now, as a graduate with a steady job and a place of my own.

My parents had two goals for me: to earn my teaching certificate and get married, and no one could accuse my mother of not doing her part to help me find a husband. I never questioned this common societal standard, but that didn't change my frustration. By the time I was twenty-three, I told myself to just pick out a nice fellow, marry him, and get it over with. Not long after I conceded to the idea of marrying without love, a friend arranged a blind date for me. There was no escaping it.

Jim was a nice-looking man of medium height with dark, sandy-colored hair, blue eyes, and five years older than I. He was a Texan who had served in the military and had lived in California for a while. While there, he worked various jobs, including cutting up the concrete used in the Red Sea scene from the movie The Ten Commandments. He had also worked as a police dispatcher in Snyder, out in West Texas. He was an interesting conversationalist who taught history in an Odessa junior high school. He had set his sights on eventually becoming a school administrator, meaning he would need to return to school to earn advanced degrees. His goals appealed to me, as my dad was a school administrator. Jim's dad was a Southern Baptist minister, so we held similar religious beliefs. Jim loved children and wanted to have a family. I, too, wanted to have children, so I asked myself, "What more am I looking for? He fits the bill."

We were married in March 1963.

It took me less than three years after we'd married to realize I'd made a terrible mistake.

I wanted out of the marriage almost as soon as it started, but I never shared this with anyone. I was miserable and unhappy, but my parents and my church had taught me that marriage is an unbreakable commitment—"till death do us part."

Through the years, Jim and I struggled with our marriage. A primary area of conflict was in the bedroom. I didn't enjoy intimacy and quickly realized Jim was a very sexual being. Even though I wanted to please my husband, I dreaded going to bed. My mother's words often came back to me: "If you don't give your husband what he wants, he'll find it somewhere else."

I, therefore, acquiesced to his desires as I genuinely wanted to be a good wife. I often "escaped" by letting my mind wander elsewhere. One of my mental fantasies was pretending to be a prostitute and telling myself I was earning a lot of money for what I was doing. Other times, I would "fly away" to somewhere else. There were nights when I yearned just to be held and cuddled, but that was impossible. At one point, Jim told me it just took a touch to "stir him." After hearing that, I avoided any touch for fear of instigating sex.

By the time I began to consider divorce seriously, Jim and I were already parents. When we initially discussed having children, we both agreed to wait two years after our wedding to start trying to get pregnant. However, after we were married for a little over a year, I changed my mind. I was unhappy in the marriage and wanted something in my life to look forward to.

I was ready to have a baby.

Jim went along with me, and it didn't take long for me to get pregnant. Our first son, Jimmy, named after his dad, was born in July 1965.

Jim was the proudest dad I've ever seen, showing off his son every chance he got. He became so involved in his son's care that stinky diapers never phased him. He enjoyed bathing Jimmy, dressing him, and holding him. He loved attending various gatherings and proudly showing off "his son." They played together on the floor, and little Jimmy enjoyed crawling up and over his dad just as much as Jim wanted it. Watching them play together, I told myself it would be cruel to ask for a divorce and separate Jim from his young namesake, of whom he was so proud.

Then I thought of my parents. Dad and Mom would be hurt and embarrassed to have their only daughter a divorcee. I couldn't do that to them. I vividly recall my parents discussing the Presidential candidates in 1952: Adlai Stevenson vs Dwight Eisenhower. My parents typically voted Democratic, but that year, their votes canceled each other out. The simple reason this happened was that Stevenson was a divorced man, and Mother refused to vote for a divorced man. That strong stigma against divorce was just as active in the '60s as it had been throughout the '50s.

Having genuinely accepted me as their daughter, Jim's parents were so loving and proud of me. Divorcing their eldest son would be a terrible blow. Siblings on both sides of the family would be hurt.

Each time I contemplated asking for a divorce, I thought, *I will be the only one benefiting from a divorce. I've been taught my whole life not to be selfish—to be nice.* I couldn't break that ingrained pattern. Ultimately, I honored my wedding vows, "Till death do us part."

Jim and I eventually had four children. They brought light and joy into my life and still do. When Jimmy was born, we had been married for a little over two years. I was 26, and Jim was 31. We were both delighted to have a son. My second pregnancy ended in a miscarriage after four and a half months, but I became pregnant again rather quickly.

When occasional bleeding made me think I might be having another miscarriage, my doctor told me my chances were 50-50 of bringing the baby to term. He admitted that some doctors might tell me to stay in bed, but he encouraged me to go on with my life, suggesting that whatever might happen would happen regardless of whether I stayed in bed or not.

In 1968, Jim completed work on his Ph.D at the University of Texas in Austin and was subsequently hired as an instructor at the University of Arkansas, so we moved our family out of Texas and into Fayetteville.

Despite the packing and unpacking I did during this pregnancy, the bleeding finally stopped a few months after our move. That's when I begged God, again, to give me another boy despite Jim's constant reminders of how much he wanted a daughter.

I didn't want a girl because I didn't trust myself with a daughter. I know now my fears were irrational, but at that time, they felt very real and were connected to the "unnatural" feelings I felt toward girls. I didn't understand why I had those desires or how they might transfer to or affect any female children I might have. I still didn't know there was a name for people like me. Nothing in popular media or literature related to me. I was an island unto myself. I didn't seem to fit anywhere.

Luckily, my anxieties were soothed, and my prayer for a second son was answered when Michael was born in April 1969.

A little over a year later, I became pregnant again, and our third son, Josh, was born in February 1971. Three boys. I was ecstatic, but Jim was terribly disappointed. He wanted a daughter so badly. Consequently, guilt poured over me for begging God for the boys because I was convinced then and am convinced now that our three boys resulted from my desperate pleas.

Since I believed God answered my pleas for boys, I also felt God had something to do with my inability to love a man. My entreaties to God to fill my heart with love for Jim were never answered, and I couldn't fathom why. Wasn't it His word that said I should? Consequently, I've always regarded my inability to love a man, especially a decent man like Jim, as a dirty trick God played on me.

At the same time, I'd tell myself God has tried to make up for the dirty trick He played on me by giving me a good life! He granted my request for sons, and I married a fine man. By all outward appearances, I had an ideal, secure life. My mind was a constant swirl of cognitive dissonance.

Despite my inner turmoil, we had a good home life.

Throughout the 60s, 70s, and 80s, our household operated the same way as many homes did then. Jim went to work in the mornings, and I stayed home with the children. I prepared three meals daily, mostly from scratch, and we all ate together at the table.

Cooking and baking brought me pleasure, and we celebrated each family member's birthday with a homemade cake or other dessert of their choice. I also encouraged Jim and the children to choose the main dish for our evening meal on their birthdays.

Jim's favorite cake was German chocolate until I made an Italian cream cake, which became his favorite. Josh wanted a big berry cobbler with ice cream instead of a cake, so I made that for him. Michael's favorite meal was chicken tetrazzini, and Jimmy's favorite was meat pie. We had good meals, but few, if any, snacks between them. We didn't keep sweet snacks or chips on hand. The children ate all their meals at the table.

I planned out a week's worth of meals before shopping for groceries, and I was very careful with how the money was used. We lived comfortably, adhering to the detailed budget I developed.

Each day, the evening meal was a time for family when Jim could be with the children, and we could share the happenings of our day and any upcoming plans with each other. I sought to maintain a pleasant atmosphere at the table, so the television was turned off, and nothing was brought to the table, such as books or toys.

It sounds ideal and typically was, but there were times when Jim's temper took control when one of the boys misbehaved. He once jerked one of the younger ones up from the table and marched him outside for a good talking to and punishment. My heart would seize up when this took place, as I wanted everyone to be happy and enjoy their food. No one dared say a word after incidents like that.

On weekends, Jim stayed busy around the house, mowing and edging the yard, washing and tinkering with the cars, changing their oil, and doing minor repairs. He was good at pitching in when I needed help with the children, but he had a short temper, and his discipline was swift and harsh. For that reason, I disciplined the children most of the time.

Michael and Josh, who were only a little less than two years apart, had the most trouble getting along. A punishment I regularly doled out was to require the boys to sit in straight-back chairs, facing each other, about 6 feet apart. I then required them to take turns saying 10 nice things about each other. They hated having to do that when they were mad at each other, but eventually, I'd hear laughter coming from that room.

We attended church regularly on Sunday mornings, Sunday evenings, and Wednesday evenings. I took the children to the Sunday evening and Wednesday evening services so they could participate in choir programs and children's mission programs. Jim, a preacher's son, always told me he received all the church he needed by attending on Sunday mornings. He participated in no other services.

Jim also helped with cleaning the house when I was unable to get it all done, even cleaning the toilets. He pitched in and occasionally made breakfast tacos for the family's breakfast. On the weekends, he sometimes treated us to Dunkin' Donuts, which was a big treat for all of us. Our "eating out" at a restaurant was limited to once a month, usually a Sunday lunch at Luby's Cafeteria.

As the years passed and the three boys got older, I considered having a fourth child. My threshold for starting that process was when the boys could all bathe themselves. Our house had a sunken bathtub, which was beautiful and unique, but hard on the back when I had to lean over and scrub the boys. I knew I couldn't handle that job when I was pregnant.

By the time Josh turned 5 years old in 1976, I had turned his bathing over to him. At that time, Michael had recently turned 8, and Jimmy would soon be turning 12. I realized the time was approaching when Jim and I would be alone in our home, just the two of us. I wasn't ready for that.

The boys had always served as a buffer—as an excuse— to avoid being alone with Jim. I wanted another child to prolong that buffer a while longer.

I suggested to Jim the possibility of adopting a child. I knew there were children who needed a home, and I told myself we could afford to bring one of those children into ours. I wasn't against physically having another child as I rather enjoyed pregnancy. Still, in a way, I hated to keep populating the world when children were already available in foster care. Jim wouldn't even discuss adoption and asserted, "I want my children to come from me." His inflexible reply left no room for discussion.

I was reaching an age when few women continued to have children, and I still yearned for another child to serve as a buffer with Jim. When I was 37, I asked Jim, "Would you like to have another child?"

"Yes," he excitedly replied. "I'd love to have a daughter!"

Realizing we would probably have another boy, I warned him, "We can't go into this wanting a girl. The doctor told me our chances of having a daughter are one in eight. We either go into this wanting another child, regardless of what gender it is, or we don't do it at all."

Jim immediately replied. "I want another child, regardless." So we began trying to conceive a baby.

I didn't get pregnant immediately. It took almost a year. When our fourth child was born, I was 39, and Jim was 44. My pregnancy was difficult this time. Despite following my doctor's orders to watch my weight, the baby was big, and I was carrying it out in front of me like an over-inflated beach ball.

When I was seven months along, a clerk in a store exclaimed, "You must be ready to deliver any minute now!" I laughed and said, "I've got another two months to go!"

During that summer of 1978, my second son, Michael, was 9 years old and in Little League. I attended all his games along with Josh and Jimmy, who were 7 and 13 years old. I recall overhearing a woman talking to her friend as I slowly climbed up the stadium steps. "She's here AGAIN!" I knew they were expecting me to have had the baby before that game, but at that time, I still had over a month to go.

My back ached, so I borrowed a unique corset from a young mother with twins. She was delighted to lend it to me, and that contraption helped quite a bit.

Before the baby arrived, I developed a relentless cough. I ended up coughing so hard that I cracked a rib. Nighttime in bed became a painful experience. I couldn't lie on my stomach because of the baby, and I couldn't lie on my back because the baby's weight made it difficult to breathe, and the cracked rib made getting up, lying down, or turning over excruciating. I learned to hold all laughing, coughing, or sneezing actions in check to avoid the pain in my rib.

One of my last doctor visits brought tears when the doctor jokingly brought out a yardstick to measure me. He began to have second thoughts that maybe there was more than one baby and sent me to have a sonogram.

During this pregnancy, I started praying for a girl.

Because I continued to live in terror of someone realizing I was gay, I never read any books on the subject. My education about same-sex attractions came solely from the Ann Landers and Dear Abby columns. Their positive answers to letters sent to them helped me understand myself. I found further comfort in the 19 years that had passed since Karen and I were together. Since Karen, I'd had no other feelings of attraction to women. I was finally able to consider myself "all right," and it allowed me to start imagining having a daughter with me in the kitchen—a genuine helper and companion. The more I thought about having a daughter, the more I wanted one. I began to petition God for a girl, promising to always protect her. Luckily, my "whopper" arrived just before my next doctor's visit.

Laura weighed 10 pounds 6.5 ounces. All my boys had been eight pounds and above, but this baby girl was something else. Because she was so large, she quickly began sleeping all night due to her ability to consume large quantities of milk. She was my easiest baby—a gift that eliminated all but a few sleepless nights.

I was delighted with her, and Jim was ecstatic to finally have a daughter.

8
A HOUSE DIVIDED

Through the years, Jim and I struggled with our marriage despite the joy each of our children brought us. Eventually, after Laura was born, Jim realized I didn't enjoy having sex, and we finally decided to have sex only on Friday nights. I woke up every Friday morning with dread and kept dreading all day, but I was thankful that the decision had been made. It finally dawned upon me that the more I participated and generated excitement, the quicker the activity was successfully ended. I'd start looking at my bedside clock and make a mental game of it, trying to best my previous speed. He never knew I was doing this, but he appreciated my participation.

Amidst babies being born and raised and compromises being managed, we moved from Fayetteville, Arkansas, to Austin, Texas, in 1973. Once there, we spent years joining and leaving three Baptist churches, hoping to find one we could call "home." No matter where we settled, something about each church eventually angered Jim, and the family was uprooted from one community to the next.

As soon as we arrived in Austin, we joined Hyde Park Baptist Church, the largest Baptist church in the city. The church provided my primary social outlet because I no longer worked outside the home. I actively participated in its programs, directed a fourth-grade Sunday School department, worked in its Mother's Morning Out program, played in its handbell choir, and enrolled our children in its choirs and mission programs.

Seven years after joining this ultra-conservative church, it decided to establish its own private school. I knew as soon as they announced it that Jim would be immensely upset.

In 1980, Austin, Texas, was involved in a court-ordered busing plan.[6] Jim and I supported integration and even chose to purchase our home in a racially integrated neighborhood. Despite knowing it would affect the sales value of that house, we put our money where our mouth was and ignored the realtor's warnings. In addition to Jim's strong feelings about integration, he believed that if the new church school were successful, he could conceivably lose his job.

He was Austin's newest high school principal, having recently chosen to step down from a position in central administration. He felt that if the church's high school were successful, Austin would need one less public high school, and, as the newest principal, he would be the one to lose his job.

Laura was less than two years of age when, one night around the dinner table, Jim announced his desire never to set foot inside Hyde

---

6   Busing plans were government instituted efforts aimed at integrating schools by transporting students of all races to different schools throughout the city. It was done in an attempt to satisfy the Brown vs. Board of Education ruling, but was fought against for over a decade within the city, as many wondered if the solution was enough to meet integration requirements.

Park Baptist Church again. "We'll locate another church to join. None of my church contributions will ever be used to support a private church school. This school is being established to enable prejudiced people with money to keep their children segregated from minority students. That's what it's all about, despite our Director of Education's assurances that they just want to take advantage of this opportunity to 'spread the word.' That's not what it's all about, and I'll have no part of it."

When Jim announced that we would not return to Hyde Park, silence prevailed around the table. The children and I were clearly upset, but none of us disagreed with his decision. We dared not stand up to Jim, to argue with him, or to plead. Jim was the "head of the family," and we abided by his wishes. I understood his fear and anger, but quietly found fault in his desire to leave a community we could influence. Nevertheless, he concluded that his church was personally threatening his job, his standing in the community, and his livelihood, so we all had to leave.

The following week, we began visiting new churches.

In a short time, we joined a neighborhood church, Windsor Park Baptist. I again became quite active, playing in their handbell choir and agreeing to direct their fourth-grade Vacation Bible School.

We had been members for less than a year, when Jim was asked to serve on the church's education committee. The first meeting he attended was a disaster. Upon returning home from that meeting, he said, "Would you believe I sat in that meeting tonight listening to everyone knock down public education and discuss the possibility of establishing a private school?" Anger was in his voice as he continued, "They did nothing but run down the public school system. We aren't going back to this church ever again."

This time, I spoke up and said, "I've already agreed to direct the fourth-grade department's Vacation Bible School. It starts in less than a month, and there isn't enough time to get someone else. Besides, I'm not going back on my word. They're depending upon me. Wait until Vacation Bible School is over; then I'll be willing to quit this church and hunt for another one."

Jim abided by my request, and in the summer of 1981, as soon as Vacation Bible School was over, we began visiting other churches—all of us, except Michael, who was twelve at that time. He dearly loved Windsor Park because many of his school buddies attended, and he was involved in their active youth group. He didn't want to leave and became quite adamant about it. Jim told him, "We are a family, and we'll attend church as a family. We are not going to be divided on Sunday mornings."

I disagreed with Jim's decision, and when he and I were alone, I gently suggested he let Michael continue to go to Windsor Park Baptist. "We ought to be happy he wants to go to church. Most boys his age must be dragged into a church, but he enjoys going. If we force him to go with us, he may end up hating the church altogether. I think forcing him to come with us will be a terrible mistake."

Jim immediately disagreed. "It's wrong for our family not to worship together on Sunday mornings. That's what family is all about. Besides, how do you propose we get him to and from his church while we go elsewhere?"

"We'll drop him off on the way to whatever church we attend." I offered. "Yes, he will arrive earlier and stay later than usual while he waits for us to get him, but we can explain this to him; if he still wants to go to Windsor Park, let's let him go."

Jim conceded, and we spoke with Michael, who was more than willing to arrive early and leave late. Many a time, when we finally came to pick him up, he was standing all by himself in the parking lot. Still, he never complained, probably because Michael could avoid Jim's grumbling every Sunday morning after dropping him off, unlike the rest of us. "This is not right," Jim would say every week, "all of us not staying together on a Sunday. I don't know why I let you talk me into this; this isn't right. We shouldn't have a son attending a church that is different from the one we attend. This is just not right, and I'm sorry I ever gave in and let you talk me into this."

Every Sunday, without fail, we listened to the same spiel from when we dropped off Michael until we arrived at whatever church we attended that day. The atmosphere in the car was unpleasant every Sunday.

By the spring of 1982, we had settled upon University Baptist Church on Guadalupe, close to the University of Texas.

After we had been members for a while, an incident occurred one Wednesday evening that instigated another church move.

Our youngest son, Josh, who must have been around eleven or twelve years old at the time, was given a lead role in a children's choir performance based on the life of David, the shepherd boy who killed the giant Goliath. Josh was extremely intelligent and socially immature, which always caused him problems. His peers assumed that whenever he used big words, he was showing off. He had no idea he was setting himself apart from his peers by the intelligent questions he asked, the correct answers he gave, and the words he used. Josh was good-natured without a mean bone in his body and was elated to finally be given this chance to "shine" and prove he belonged with his peers.

When Josh proudly announced his part in the musical, he handed me a paper listing the rehearsal dates (every Wednesday) and the rules, which clearly stated that a missed rehearsal meant being dropped from the performance. I was careful to take Josh and Laura to church every Wednesday evening, and he attended all the scheduled rehearsals.

One day, a card arrived in the mail announcing an extra rehearsal scheduled for Monday afternoon just before the Wednesday performance. As I showed the card to Josh and told him we needed to plan to attend rehearsal, he quickly stated, "Mom, I don't have to go."

"Why not?" I asked, surprised at his statement.

"That rehearsal is for those who don't yet know their parts. I know my part. So, I don't have to go," he explained, full of self-assurance.

"But Josh, they'll need everyone to be there."

"Not me. They don't need me. I know my part."

I should not have listened to him, but I did. I had other children needing my attention that Monday afternoon and felt relieved that I wouldn't need to spend hours driving Josh across town in heavy traffic for this surprise rehearsal.

Wednesday night arrived, and Jim joined us at the church for dinner and the choir program. Everyone looked forward to Josh's performance. As we sat together in the Fellowship Hall, finishing our meal, the children were summoned to dress in their costumes. A few minutes later, Josh returned to our table in tears, obviously heartbroken. Confused, I asked, "What is it, Josh?"

"I'm not in the play anymore."

Shocked, I asked, "What do you mean?"

"They took my part away because I didn't go to the rehearsal on Monday. I don't have the part anymore. I'm not in the play."

Others in the room became aware of the scene playing out at our table, and Jim was appalled that anyone would treat a child this way. His anger overflowed, and he started making a scene. I got up and ushered the children out of the room, with Jim following. Several church members came over to help us smooth out the problem, and one even went to talk with the choir director on our behalf. However, the director was resolved to hold fast to the rules. Josh had missed a rehearsal, so he could not be in the play. However, as a peace offering, the director offered Josh a minor role in the performance. Josh didn't want the minor role and was in no condition to perform by then.

While Josh continued to cry, our family sat on some indoor steps near the Fellowship Hall and watched the costumed children file into that room to perform. After they passed, we got up and walked out of the church, and Jim informed us that we would never set foot in University Baptist Church again.

Throughout parts of 1984 and 1985, we visited more churches but couldn't find a congregation we wanted to join. I became fed up with our rootlessness, especially the absence of children's participation in children's and youth activities. So, contrary to my normal acquiescence to Jim's leadership, I decided during the summer of 1985 to return to our original church, Hyde Park, and to take seven-year-old Laura with me.

One afternoon, as Michael, Josh, Laura, and I were sitting on the grass in our front yard, visiting, I shared my decision with them. I explained to the two younger boys that they could choose which church they wanted to attend. (Jimmy was in college by then and living in Waco.) Michael, who had continued to participate in Windsor Park Baptist, quickly indicated that's where he wanted to go. Josh hesitated a little, then said, "Mom, since you're taking Laura with you, I'll go with Dad so he won't be alone."

"That would be great, Josh," I replied.

The next step was to disclose to Jim my decision. So seldom did I "rock the boat," I found it difficult to broach the subject with him, but I finally gathered the courage. "I'm tired, Jim, of visiting churches and moving from one to another. I'm going to return to Hyde Park, where so many of my friends are, and I'm going to take Laura with me."

Jim stared at me in disbelief. "You know I will never go back there. What you are proposing is to break up the family! This is the same as asking me for a divorce! Is that what you want?"

"No, all I'm proposing is to return to Hyde Park. But if you want to talk divorce, we can talk divorce." Our discussions went downhill from that moment.

When he questioned whether I loved him, I finally admitted I didn't. I didn't want to say it, but I needed to be honest. My high esteem for honesty back then struck me as strange when I consider that my whole life had been a fabrication, yet I always felt I was doing what was expected of me, what was "the right thing to do." I interpreted my misery all those years as a punishment, a cross I had to bear for the sin of being "unnatural"—and I bore it alone, silently.

Soon after that discussion, Jim called our younger sons, Michael and Josh, into our bedroom one evening and said, "Boys, your mother and I are planning to divorce because your mother doesn't love me anymore."

I was shocked when he made that statement, placing all the blame upon me. He wanted to hurt me, and there was no better way than to harm our children. He knew how crazy I was about them and how I detested seeing them hurt. Jimmy was not in on this conversation as he was in college, and neither was Laura, who was only seven years old at the time and also away, spending two weeks with my parents in Little Rock, Arkansas. As I recall that evening, I remember feeling a deep anger toward Jim. His laying all the blame on me infuriated me, but I refused to argue with him in front of our children and make matters worse.

Several days later, my parents called to tell me that Laura was homesick and was begging to come home. The drive from Austin to Little Rock is over 500 miles, so we agreed to split the difference and meet outside a cafeteria in Mount Pleasant, Texas. Michael had other plans on the day of that drive, so only Josh rode with us.

Before we arrived in Mt. Pleasant, we told Josh, "Give us a few minutes to visit with your grandmother, granddad, and Laura. Then we'd like you to take Laura a little ways off and play with her so your daddy and I can talk privately with your grandparents. We don't want Laura to hear of the divorce right now. We'll sit down and talk with her about it later."

"Sure, Mom," Josh replied. I knew he would do as we asked.

74

All of us were quieter than usual that day. We didn't play our usual car games, which helped make time pass quickly and kept the atmosphere light and happy. None of us seemed to have much to say.

We made good time to Mt. Pleasant. Laura was delighted to see us and kept clinging to me, but she was also pleased to see Josh, who was just as happy to see her. All the boys adored her, and she felt the same about her three big brothers. I eventually suggested that Josh and Laura could walk to another area and play for a few minutes. He took her hand and led her away, and we watched as they played chase.

Turning to Mother and Dad, I said, "Jim and I are planning to get a divorce."

They stared at us. "What?"

"Yes. We've already talked with Michael and Josh."

"But I don't understand!" Mother said, "Why?"

"We think it's best" was all I could come up with.

My parents just stood there, silent. Finally, Dad looked at me. "Lou Anne, does this decision make you happy?"

"No," I admitted. Although I wanted a divorce, I hated to break up the family. I dreaded telling everyone our marriage was over. I wasn't sure how I'd be able to support myself and the children. All I felt was misery and guilt— lots of guilt. I sincerely thought I was doing the right thing by marrying a man, but after 25 years, I realized I had been very unfair to Jim because my heart still yearned for Karen.

I thought of her daily and convinced myself that only by dying could I escape from my yearnings to be with her. That's when the thoughts of suicide would come to my mind. My whole marriage, I seemed always to be thinking of various scenarios whereby I could kill myself. I realized, even as I dreamed up these multiple possibilities, that my desire to die was selfish and conflicted with the deep love I felt for my four children. I would never want to leave them. They were my very life.

When Jim and I mentioned divorce, we didn't go into any details. We hadn't even discussed who would take the children when we got divorced. I assumed I would, but Jim may have had other plans. All these conflicting thoughts kept swirling through my mind, making "no" the only possible answer to my dad's question about my happiness over the decision.

Dad took my admission to mean that I wasn't in favor of the divorce, which was the furthest possible thing from the truth. He looked at both of us and said, "You need to work this out. Find some way. Get counseling but try to make a go of it. You two don't need to be doing this."

I didn't know what to say. I was forty-six at the time and still felt like a child. I'd spent my entire life obeying either my father or my husband, so when my dad told me not to divorce and to try to make a go of it, it was all I thought I could do. "All right," I said.

Jim and I didn't talk much as we drove home to Austin with the children. We didn't want to discuss the subject in front of them.

Jim suggested I get a lawyer and start proceedings because it would be better if I instigated the divorce. I didn't understand why I had to be the one to make that move, so I didn't. He didn't either. We ended up not divorcing by way of a stalemate, but we were both miserable. We lived in silence for months until we finally agreed to see a marriage counselor Jim chose for us.

The counselor visited with us separately, then brought us together for a final meeting. He knew I wasn't telling him the whole story, but there was no way I was going to admit to anyone that I was gay.

I was aware of Jim's prejudice against gays. I recall standing by the kitchen table one afternoon with the newspaper opened to the Ann Landers column. The word "homosexual" was in a headline, and as he glanced at it, he said, "I'll never hire a homosexual to teach in any of my schools. Everyone knows they are all pedophiles."

I felt sure if the counselor knew about me, he would tell Jim, and I would lose the children in a divorce. I had always guarded that secret and continued to do so.

9
MOVING ON

*T*hree years after we first talked about divorce, Jim was offered a high school principal position in Tyler, located in East Texas, about halfway between Dallas and Shreveport, Louisiana. Living in a much smaller place appealed to both of us. I had spent my childhood in small towns and regretted that my children didn't have the same advantage of having their friends within walking distance. We'd spent fifteen years in Austin but looked forward to a slower pace of living and a less complicated existence, given the complexities we were still battling within our home.

For one thing, navigating the heavy traffic in Austin was becoming unbearable, and Jim disliked the politics he sometimes had to deal with in the school system. At this time, I was 49 and Jim was 54. Our eldest son, Jimmy, had just received his bachelor's degree. Michael was taking some time off from college to work. Josh had one more year of high school left, and Laura had just turned ten.

When we moved to Tyler in 1988, we were amazed at all the Baptist churches. They seemed to abound on every corner, and the two largest ones began vying for our membership. We joined the smaller of the two, First Baptist, and were all back in the same church again. As usual, I became active in various programs and especially enjoyed playing in their handbell choir.

The year after we came to Tyler, I began teaching part-time at Tyler Junior College, where I taught for four years. In 1994, I returned to teaching full-time at the local high school. After a semester, I transferred to the district's alternative high school. I retired early in 1998, soon after my 88-year-old mother moved to Tyler from Little Rock. She was in excellent health but required a good bit of my time as she adjusted to living in her new retirement home. When I first thought about retiring, I wasn't sure my pension check from 11 years of teaching would cover my healthcare expenses; luckily, it did, and as soon as that was confirmed, I happily retired in 1998 at the age of 59.

It was one year later that I accepted a position at First Baptist teaching a ladies' Sunday School class and found myself asking Janie about her homosexual son—the year my life truly changed.

After all my efforts to avoid feelings of love and desire for a woman, Janie's words of acceptance for gays were all it took to turn my world upside down and seize control of my emotions. Janie's compassion and understanding, the day she spoke so boldly in acceptance and support of her son, stirred the dead spot in my heart where my feelings for Karen had once abided, and I began to feel myself falling in love with her because of it. I was devastated. I never told anyone I was gay. I avoided forming close female friendships for fear that I might fall in love with someone, yet it had happened anyway, with a woman I was just getting to know.

From that day on, I thought about Janie constantly, wanting her, desiring her, imagining scenarios where we were together. It was a type of insanity derived, I'm sure, from years of repressed desire.

After almost five months of living with these newly ignited feelings, I gathered my courage to talk to Jim. It was another Friday night after dinner in a new year— in a new millennium, January 2000— when I finally said, "Jim, I'm very unhappy. You've probably sensed this."

"Yes," he said, "something's going on with you."

Something *was* going on with me, and her name was Janie. Ever since that Sunday conversation, I was having trouble sleeping, had lost my appetite, and felt constantly on edge. The only way I could think to regain my sanity was to get out of my marriage, so I pressed on.

"I don't know any other way to say it, but I need to take a sabbatical, a leave from the marriage for a while."

Jim appeared to droop all over. "I'm very, very sorry to hear this."

"I plan to sleep in the other bedroom, and I'm going to Lubbock after church Sunday to stay in Laura's apartment for a week or two and think through some things."

Laura, our youngest at twenty-one years old and the only one still "at home," was a beautiful, intelligent, tender-hearted senior at Texas Tech University. Five days earlier, I broke down and confided in her that I was gay. "Mom," she said immediately, "you've got to get a divorce."

Every day since then, she'd said, "Mom, you've got to do it. Don't keep putting it off. You've got to talk with Dad." At the time, Laura was the only person in my life who knew I was gay, though I suspected Janie might also be catching on, given the many talks we'd had about her son's coming out journey and identity. Regardless, both encouraged me to do what was best for me and leave Jim; my anguish was palpable to them, regardless of why they thought it was there.

81

"Do you think that's the only solution?" Jim asked me. "To separate?"

"Yes. You know how many years we've tried to make this work. You'd be much better off having somebody you could love."

"I don't want anybody else," Jim said.

"You'd be happier."

"No, I'd be happier with someone who's—"

"A different person than I am." I interrupted.

Jim stared at me with tired eyes, "No, Lou Anne, just let me behind that wall. I've never been able to go there." Continuing to stare directly at me as we sat at the table, Jim said, "This hurts. It cuts to the inner part of my soul because we've always said that no matter what, we'd make it work, that we're survivors."

He was right, but I didn't want to just survive anymore.

" If you can't have some kind of happiness, it's just not worth it," I said.

" I disagree. You *have* worked hard and made me happy, but I evidently haven't put forth enough effort to do the same." He stared at the table before asking, "Do you really think our marriage is irreparable?'

My answer was simple, "Yes."

"If you feel that way, you're talking about divorcing!" he exclaimed unbelievingly.

His use of the word "divorce" brought me a sense of relief—almost joy. I didn't want to ask for a divorce, thinking the conversation would be too difficult if I did, which is why I decided to ask for a temporary separation. Now that the word divorce was part of the conversation, I took my chance. "Yes, that's probably what will happen."

Jim looked like I'd hit him with an iron skillet. "I've always said that if we ever got a divorce, it would be because you left. I tolerated the unhappy parts of the marriage to keep the family together. Do you have anything else to say besides that you're unhappy?"

"No. I don't think I can." I admitted.

Part of me wanted to be truthful about my being gay, but it was a very, very small part of me. I thought that would be like putting salt in an open wound, making my request for a divorce more painful than it already was. I never wanted to hurt Jim; I only wanted to get away from the marriage, at least for a while.

Dejected, Jim remained slumped in his chair before finally conceding, "If you've already made up your mind and we can't try to reconcile, let's just go ahead and get a divorce."

I watched unblinking, hardly believing what I'd heard.

Jim continued, "Once upon a time, I hoped and prayed that you would have an affair. Does that make any sense? I wanted to know there was somebody in this world who could make you happy because I have tried so hard. Maybe if you had an affair, at least I could say there was *somebody* capable of reaching in and touching those innermost strings I could never grasp."

I sat unflinching in my resolve despite the pain of his words. "Well, I didn't. And you didn't."

"I asked your dad once if there had been any kind of tragic experience with a man in your life because there just seems to be a wall around you that I can't get inside of, but he said, 'No, not a thing.'"

The conversation continued, sometimes touching on hurtful incidents of the past, such as his conceding to let Michael attend a different church from the rest of the family. It never stopped troubling Jim that he had given in on that request or the time I refused to have sex with him during a memorable family vacation we'd taken to Colorado. We were in a beautiful mountain cabin, and since it was his vacation, he wanted us to forget the "Friday night only" rule and enjoy sex more often. I rebuffed him, which made him mad and ultimately hurt his feelings in a way I knew felt cruel or unusual to him, given I was his wife. I'm aware that the failings of our marriage were not all Jim's fault and that our lack of intimacy contributed significantly to both of our unhappiness, but my orientation made sex with a man unbearable for me; it was a feeling I could never overcome no matter what games or tricks of the mind I concocted for myself.

I had finally reached a breaking point, and there was no turning back. I understood Jim needed to vent, and as I listened, I couldn't help but mentally pat myself on the back for initiating this difficult conversation; I had put it off many times. Jim had no way of knowing at that moment that these were the necessary steps to set us both free.

Later, as I continued to reflect on the marriage, I realized how Jim and I harmed our four children by rearing them in a home where their parents didn't display love for each other. We were polite and considerate to each other, but unaffectionate. The blame falls on both of us, but more on me. I found it impossible to show affection when I didn't feel it. Because of this perceived coldness, Jim believed I would never need anyone else as I could live happily alone. He then ventured closer to the truth than he imagined when he stated, "I just can't get inside that private shield of yours, Lou Anne. It just rips me apart." After he expressed his love for me again, we decided there was nothing else to say. I asked Jim for a divorce, and he agreed.

My heart was heavy as I stood up and walked out of the kitchen and into the guest bedroom.

I should have felt happy to have finally broken free of a relationship that had transformed me into a disconnected person, detached from who I knew myself to be, from intimacy and genuine connection, and from joy.

Denying who and what I was—accepting the role of a submissive wife— I'd learned to hate myself. For years, I'd felt like I was walking around as a shadow of the real me. Sitting down on the bed now, I was numb, almost in shock. I no longer recognized myself.

A short while later, Laura entered the bedroom that evening to see how I was doing. As we sat on the bed together and held hands, she said, "Mom, you need to talk to a professional counselor."

Her suggestion hit me at the right time. I'd been telling myself for over four months, ever since falling in love with Janie, that I needed to talk with someone. My life was a mess. My sorrow and pain for the past several months had made me feel as if I had only three choices: suicide, a mental institution, or divorce. These three choices had been going through my head constantly. The divorce was just a stop-gap solution. I knew I needed help.

"I don't know anyone I can talk with," I replied.

"I do, Mom. A psychologist who's a professional counselor taught one of my classes at Texas Tech. He's great. I'll call him right now and schedule a time for you to see him. You can stay in my Lubbock apartment for a while, okay?"

"Yes," I said. "I'll talk with him if he can see me."

Laura located the professor's number and called him at home that evening. His schedule was full, but he agreed to work me in for an hour's appointment. This would be a first for me—admitting to someone the pain I was experiencing due to my feelings for Janie. But I was ready. I had to do it for my own sake.

I slept only a little that night, still disbelieving that I'd asked Jim for a divorce just hours ago and was now spending the night in another room. I felt relief and guilt, along with the continuing deep pain I'd felt since my life-changing conversation with Janie five months earlier.

The next day, I talked with our second-born, Michael, who was now a single, thirty-year-old entrepreneur, and told him I'd asked his father for a divorce.

"Have you been planning this all along?" he asked, "Were you just waiting until Laura finished college?"

"No," I truthfully answered. "I haven't. And it has nothing to do with Laura."

His following words spoke a truth I had lived with for a long time but never realized anyone else had noticed. "Mom," he said, "you and Dad are just on different planes—completely unable to communicate. I can say something to Dad, and it doesn't bother him at all, but if you say the same thing, it pushes his buttons."

I had always felt this was true, but it was a gift to have Michael substantiate it. I had so often cast myself as the secret villain in our relationship because of my sexuality, but the truth was, Jim had his faults, too, namely his short temper.

"You're right, Michael. That's one of the things I tried to tell your dad last night."

So often, when Jim and I disagreed about something, and it became apparent that I was correct in what I had stated, instead of graciously admitting that I was right, he would angrily retort, "Oh, you know it all! You're always right about everything!" I'd always been worried about upsetting him, but over the years, that worry often turned into intimidation, enforcing my silence on many different things.

As Michael hugged me, he said, "Mom, I just want you to be happy."

His love and support were welcome words, as I knew he was very close to his dad.

Later in the day, I visited with our eldest, Jimmy, now a thirty-four-year-old bilingual pre-kindergarten teacher here in Tyler. His young students and their parents loved him because they sensed his kind, loving, and supportive attitude toward them. When I shared the news of the upcoming divorce, I was relieved to hear him say the same thing as Michael. "Mother, we love you and want you to be happy."

The following day, I taught my Sunday School class as usual, with seven members present—a big group for us. As simply as possible, I let these women know I would be out of town the following Sunday and had already asked one of their favorite substitutes to step in. I gave no hint of the trauma I was experiencing.

When I left the church, I drove to Mother's apartment in her classy retirement home. Mother, eighty-nine and in excellent health, was a beloved resident, respected, and a humdinger of a bridge player. Tall and thin, impeccably dressed, she regularly received compliments on her beautiful white hair. Mother never had any problems speaking her mind or speaking out. I managed to grow up in her shadow, like a sapling fighting for light in the shade of an oak, and now, ironically, I see myself being a lot like her: determined, focused, staunch.

When I arrived at her apartment, Mother had just returned home from church and was about to walk down to the dining hall for lunch. She was shocked to see me when she opened her door. As soon as I walked in, I greeted her by saying, "Mother, I'm not staying but a minute," and I meant it. I had no desire to have any type of extended conversation with my mother about my marriage. I had dreaded having this conversation because I expected Mother to shame me into staying married, just as she had shamed me into feeling guilty about my relationship with Karen at 17. After that condemning conversation, we never discussed anything personal again, except for the time I became engaged to Jim.

He and I had driven from Odessa to Little Rock for Thanksgiving in 1962 so that I could show off my engagement ring and introduce Jim to my parents, and vice versa.

Since their first meeting, I've always believed Mother could probably tell I wasn't in love with Jim. She once asked me if I loved him. I lied and assured her that I did.

Now that I was admitting to her my plans to divorce Jim, I was filled with the same trepidation I had felt that Thanksgiving in 1962 and was determined not to let her interfere in my plans. Now that I had finally found the courage to ask Jim for a divorce, and Jim had acquiesced to it, I was in no mood to hear any suggestion from her that I stay married. The two of us faced off in the middle of her small but always elegant-looking living room, and I got right to the point: "Mother, my car is packed, and I'm driving to Lubbock to spend a couple of weeks in Laura's apartment."

Stunned, she asked, "What?"

"I'm driving to Lubbock as soon as I leave here."

"I don't understand," she replied.

Gathering courage, I wasn't sure I had, I finally stated what I had come there to say, "I've asked Jim for a divorce, Mother, and that's why I'm going to Lubbock for several weeks."

"You're getting a divorce?"

She was confused, but I yearned to conclude this visit quickly.

"Yes, I am."

Just as she was stunned by my news, I was amazed at her response: "I know you've been unhappy for a long time, Lou Anne. This doesn't surprise me. I just want you to be happy. When did you say you were going to Lubbock?"

She supported my decision, and I had trouble believing it at first.

"Right now, Mother, just as soon as I leave here. The car is already packed. I'll stay in Laura's apartment, so you have her phone number. I'll call home tonight to let everyone know I've arrived safely."

We said a few more words, hugged, and she admonished me to drive carefully, as any caring mother would. I left with my heart much lighter than before, but also much fuller. I'd braced myself for condemnation that never came, and I wondered if any still would.

10
TEARS & TEACHINGS

I arrived in Lubbock around 7:00 p.m., feeling exhausted. After all, I'd awakened at 3:15 am, taught a Sunday School class later that morning, and then driven 400 miles.

Climbing into bed, I wanted to read for a few minutes. I'd brought library books on the legal aspects of divorce and the financial decisions that needed to be made, as well as some books I thought would help me better understand homosexuality and my deep emotional pain.

When I had gone to the library and looked up "homosexual" in the card catalog, I was nervous someone would somehow see what I was searching for, so I made certain no one was nearby when I pulled up our library's slim assortment. I chose a memoir by Mel White, a former evangelical pastor and ghostwriter for Pat Robertson, Billy Graham, and Jerry Falwell. The title was *Stranger at the Gate*, and I was delighted that the title didn't indicate the book was about homosexuality. When I checked it out, I placed it between the books on divorce, hoping no one at the library would see my selection.

After putting on my pajamas and propping myself up in bed, I picked up *Stranger at the Gate* and spent the evening reading and crying over its pages.

I was sixty-one years old, and this was the first book I'd ever read about homosexuality. I placed a box of tissues beside me on the bed, and every few minutes, I stopped to blow my nose and wipe away tears. Mel expressed my feelings exactly when he stated, "Feeling abandoned by God, by the church, and by society, I longed to end my life."

For the first time in my life, I discovered that other people like me exist, have similar feelings, and have suffered in much the same way. Just as I fought my homosexual urges, so did Mel, who spent more than 30 years of his life in counseling and anti-gay "therapy" that involved praying, fasting, exorcisms, and electric shock treatments in attempts to "make the gay go away;" until he was able to reconcile his Christian theology with his sexual orientation.

I didn't realize the book would explain all of this when I chose it, but how fortunate that, in my ignorance, I nevertheless decided to read such a popular book among gay Christians. I'd always believed I was an atypical, maladjusted, isolated case, but now I was no longer alone. There were others like me. I cried for the lost years, for all the loneliness, silence, and fear. I cried for years of repression and the unwarranted guilt I carried all my life for something I couldn't help, and when I thought my tears were finished, I would read another page that applied directly to me, and the tears would start again. I'd never cried like this.

A purging was taking place, an emptying, a release of repressed emotions as I learned I wasn't the terrible sinner I always thought I was. White's statements excited me. "Misusing the Bible to support old prejudice is not a new phenomenon," he said and pointed to issues besides homosexuality, including the injustices of slavery, anti-integration efforts, and its use (to this day) of keeping women out of pulpits and other forms of leadership in the church.

Eventually, when my body couldn't cry any longer, I cut off the light and slept a little.

As soon as I awakened, I picked up White's book and continued to read. This time, I took the time to note page numbers, enabling me to summarize the points I considered most important later.

He wrote, "Doing justice begins by walking away from the churches and the synagogues, the preachers, priests, and rabbis, who use God's word to condemn homosexuality and into churches and fellowships where we are loved and respected as God's children who happen to be gay."

Everything he said hit home. All my life, I'd avoided reading about this subject. I thought it would just go away if I ignored it. The only information I gleaned came from the Ann Landers or Dear Abby columns, written by two sisters well known for their sound, compassionate advice, which is offered in a straightforward style. The letters they received and answered covered a wide range of topics. A few dealt with questions about gays and lesbians. No wonder their columns were the first I looked for in the daily newspaper, as their comments supported gays and condemned prejudice against them.

As I took a break from reading that Monday morning, I thought back to the previous day when Janie had lingered for a few minutes after I completed the Sunday School lesson. She was the only group member who knew I'd asked Jim for a divorce. I'd called her on Saturday to tell her of the events of the night before when I'd asked him.

I could still hear her saying in the preceding weeks, "Lou Anne, this is something you must do. You've got to get a divorce." Over and over, she encouraged me to leave the marriage. I knew she was right each time she said it, but doing what was right can sometimes be very difficult. After the other class members left yesterday morning, Janie asked, "Are you all right, Precious?"

"Yes, I'm fine," I replied, though I was probably still shocked. She handed me a little bag containing a book wrapped in gift paper and tied with a bow. "I want you to read this," she explained. "I didn't think the other class members needed to see it, so I wrapped it up like a gift, but I had it at the house and thought it would be good for you."

After thanking her for lending me Bruce Bawer's *A Place at the Table*, I visited with her for a few minutes and explained how my request for a divorce from Jim had unfolded.

"One of the things Jim said to me as we discussed the divorce was that there had always been a wall between us," I told her. "He didn't realize how right he was."

"Lou Anne," she replied, "he knows what it is. He just doesn't want to admit it, but he knows."

I didn't believe it had ever occurred to Jim that I was gay, yet a part of me wished he did know, so I'd never have to explain it to him. Then, a wave of fear passed through me. What if he found out before our divorce was final? Would he make the divorce difficult? This fear instilled in me the pressure to continue protecting my secret.

After reading some more in *Stranger at the Gate* that morning, I made a trip to the grocery store and then climbed back into bed. I propped myself up as I snuggled under the covers and continued to read. I also called Josh, the only son with whom I hadn't talked.

Josh is our third son and will soon be twenty-nine. He lived in the Houston area with his sweet, supportive, and pregnant wife, Sandy. As an engineer, he worked for a company that subcontracted with NASA and was involved in preparing experiments launched into space. His comments mirrored what my other children said: "Mom, I just want you to be happy." However, he did add, "I can't help but selfishly wish our baby could have the same family togetherness that I had as a child."

I thought this a strange statement, knowing the family togetherness he'd experienced as a child was a pretend closeness between his parents. I managed to feel relief instead of grief that the charade had ended.

After two days of solitude, reading, and phone conversations, I met with Dr. Kerns, the psychologist Laura recommended. After arriving at his office, I was asked to complete a lengthy questionnaire. When I read, "Tell me in what way you think I will be able to help you," I wrote, "Frankly, I don't think you can."

When Dr. Kerns read my statement, he laughed. "You really don't think I can help you?"

"That's right." I said, "No one can do anything for me."

In my mind, my problems were insurmountable and unsolvable. I kept the appointment as a place to bare my soul.

I confided precisely why I married Jim and how miserable that decision had made me for so many years. Although I despised the person I'd become, I was very proud of my children and showed Dr. Kerns an 8" x 10" color picture of the six of us. I told him everything—my pain and misery, the reason for it, and the hopelessness of my situation.

I mentioned Jim's extreme prejudice against homosexuals, believing they were all child molesters. "He had no idea a homosexual was mothering his four children. His attitude made it impossible for me to be open with him." I told Dr. Kern.

"Do you think he might have a good attitude if you explained to him 'the wall' between the two of you?" Dr. Kerns asked.

"No. No way in the world."

I cried continually as I poured out my heart to him that afternoon. A dam, well fortified for the past forty years, was finally cracking open, and my anguish poured out. He placed a box of tissues next to me as I sobbed for most of the hour. Several times, he became so concerned about me that he left his chair to sit beside me, patting me on the back.

Several times, he asked, "Do you believe God loves you despite your homosexuality?"

"Yes," I sobbed. "I know He loves me, but I don't know why He made me this way."

"If Jesus walked into this room right now, do you believe He would put His arms around you and tell you how much He loves you?"

"Yes," I admitted. "But I don't understand this heartbreak. I don't understand why I'm hurting so many people or why I will have to endure the disapproval of others; none of it makes any sense unless God has always planned for me to use my life experiences to help someone else. That thought is all that keeps me going."

"You do have difficult times ahead of you," he said, "But you don't have to place an ad about your situation in the paper," he added as he looked at me with a slight grin on his face.

I appreciated his comment and realized he was right. I don't have to put myself out there. I could slow down and protect myself more than I had been.

As he moved back to his chair, he advised, "You need to make some definite plans prior to returning to Tyler and be specific. Decide before you leave here where you'll spend the night, where you'll eat your meals, whom you will see, and whether you will attend church. Make these decisions ahead of time."

These suggestions gave me direction and a sense of control amid a life that felt increasingly chaotic, and I was grateful to him for helping me form a plan to return home.

When our session was over, and I stood up to go, Dr. Kerns said, "I don't normally do this, but would you mind if I prayed?"

"No, of course not," I answered.

Dr. Kerns held my hands as we stood facing each other, asking God to watch over and comfort me. As I left his office, I realized he had never questioned my divorce from Jim.

Having been so tied to a Baptist church all my life, I have always assumed all Christians saw divorce as a sinful act. I expected this overtly Christian counselor to suggest I stay in the marriage, but he didn't. There was no hint of condemnation, and I found peace in that relief.

Although I didn't turn out my light until eleven that night, I was awake by five the following day and decided to splurge on breakfast at IHOP. My weight had dropped, and I didn't need to lose any more pounds.

The food was good, but I had little appetite. I ate half a small omelet and a biscuit and drank half a glass of orange juice. When I couldn't push any more down, I paid my bill, got in my car, and drove the loop around Lubbock.

I set the speed control, listened to Beethoven's Piano Concerto #1 in C Major, and drove a practically empty highway lit by streetlights and a sprinkling of stars in a dark sky. It took twenty-four minutes to circle the whole city.

When I returned to Laura's apartment, I climbed back into bed, feeling a headache, and finally slept for a little while.

After supper that evening, I called Mother. I'd been feeling guilty about not communicating with her and attempted to keep the conversation upbeat to hide how depressed I was. At one point, she said, "I woke up before five this morning thinking about Jeff Tatum."

"What in the world made you think of him?" I asked.

Mother's answer surprised me. "I figure he's probably the one you have on your mind— why you've decided to leave Jim."

My mouth dropped open, "Oh, Mother! I can't believe you said that."

"Isn't he the one who drove out to Big Spring to give you a big diamond ring?"

"He offered me a diamond ring while we were at Baylor. You must be thinking of Allen Adair. He drove up from South Texas to Big Spring to see me."

"Yes, I remember him. He gave you that pretty sweater from Germany. I remember all those fellows. I figure it's one of them you're thinking about."

"Mother, you're wasting your time. Quit thinking. And that's all I'm going to say on the subject. You're worrying about something that's not happening."

My insides writhed with frustration and anger. *Mother still refuses to remember what she accused me of in 1956. If she felt that I was gay back then, why doesn't she realize that I am still gay now? She is convinced I have my eye on another man— It's insane!*

I awoke Friday at three thirty-five in the morning, recalling the questionnaire I'd completed at Dr. Kerns' office two days earlier. Listed at the bottom of the questionnaire, in relatively small print, were perhaps up to a hundred problems I might be experiencing. I circled quite a few, including sadness, marriage, suicide, depression, sexual issues, and sleep disorders. I then marked the two I believed to be the most critical: depression and marriage.

At some point during the interview, after I'd expressed my long-standing desire to die and the many, many times I considered killing myself, Dr. Kerns asked, "Why didn't you ever commit suicide?"

"Because of the children," I replied. "I knew they needed me. Suicide would be so unfair to them and to my parents."

At that point, we discussed my homosexuality and the fact that, because Dr. Kerns works for a Christian counseling service, he's had little contact with gay patients. We spent a few minutes discussing it in very general terms, and then I said, "That's where the hate comes from, you know. From Christians."

"Yes, you're right," he said.

His affirmation validated my belief that organized religion and churches are the root of prejudice against gays.

Mother called again that night to say, "I think I've figured out who you're interested in." I rolled my eyes, waiting for her estimation. "When you asked for that good-smelling hand lotion for a birthday gift, I decided I knew then who it was."

My heart began to pound because the hand lotion connected me to Janie. The scent was her scent. Fear set in. I didn't say a thing, and she continued. "It's Frank Smitherman, isn't it?"

I laughed with relief, along with the ridiculousness of her conclusion. Frank and I had taught together in the alternative high school and shared a classroom for several years. We supported each other in that environment and were undoubtedly friends, but our relationship never went beyond that. Besides, he was at least fifteen years younger than I, maybe twenty.

"Mother," I said, "your imagination's working overtime. I can't believe what you're doing. I'm not interested in Frank Smitherman, for goodness' sake!"

"It dawned on me that you were up to something when you asked for that expensive hand lotion. If it's not Frank, it must be someone at the church."

"Why would you think that?" I asked.

"Because you're always going to the church for meetings."

Once again, I set to dissuade her, "You're wasting your time, Mother. I told you that last night, and I'm telling you again now. Quit thinking! It's not going to get you anywhere. I'm not interested in anyone."

"Well, I figured you want to be free to be with someone else."

"I don't have someone waiting for me. There's no one." I reassured her once again, feeling very put out.

We talked for a while longer about the children and her new hairdresser, and then I closed the conversation by saying, "I can hardly wait for your next phone call to see who in the world you've thought of next."

Several hours passed, and the more I thought about Mother's meddling questions, the angrier I became. Memories flooded back from my teenage years and how she put me through the third degree after every date. "Where did you go? Who was with you? What did you do? Did you kiss?" Oh, how I hated her questions. I dreaded walking into the house after a date, knowing I'd have to endure her inquisition.

It's sad to think about it now, in my old age, that we were never close enough for me to share my thoughts and feelings with her. She was a good person and a good parent, but I think of our relationship as oil and water - always divided. I don't recall ever feeling close to her after she condemned me for loving Karen, yet I cared for her for the last few years of her life. At that time, one brother lived in California, and the other was in North Carolina. They both visited her and supported me in all my decisions, but I was there with her at the end.

11
NAVIGATING DIVORCE

*J*im called while I was still in Lubbock and couldn't have been more pleasant. I appreciated him not pleading for me to change my mind. Instead, he said, "I'd like us to keep everything friendly, and you're welcome to stay at the house until you find a place to live. I want us to go over the financial details of the divorce. We don't need to get involved with lawyers. The two of us can work everything out in a friendly way."

"I agree with you," I replied. "I'm working on proposed budgets to enable each of us to maintain the standard of living we've been used to."

"I certainly hope you are right," he replied. "I'll gladly maintain your car in exchange for a few home-cooked meals. And when Josh, Sandy, and their baby come to Tyler to visit, I'd like you to come over so we can all be together."

I thought this was a rather odd scenario, but I was delighted to hear Jim being so nice and friendly, and I quickly agreed. "I'd be glad to come over and cook for all of us."

His desire for us to be together for visits made me realize that the divorce would be easier than I had expected. I also felt his plans for family gatherings would be short-lived because once he became interested in someone, he certainly wouldn't invite me over, but I told myself we'd cross that bridge when we came to it.

After two weeks, I returned home from Lubbock with some type of respiratory virus and stayed in bed for almost a week. As soon as I was able to get up, I started looking at apartment possibilities and found a small apartment in a gated senior community for only $470 a month. I was delighted to have found a place so quickly and easily, as my strength was gone.

I regularly wondered, during this time, if I was crazy for getting a divorce and making a mess of my life at the age of sixty-one. I was giving up everything I'd ever known and stepping out into an unknown world as a single person—a divorcée—and I often asked myself if this was what I really wanted.

The answer: *What's the alternative?* I knew being married to a man for the rest of my life was impossible, just as I knew it wouldn't solve my problem of being in love with Janie. I knew my misery would continue, but that divorce would help lessen it significantly.

By January 31, 2000, Jim and I agreed on how to divide the money. I was satisfied that I could live on the smaller portion I had asked for, determined to show Jim that he would have enough to continue making the house payments and maintain his standard of living. We'd always lived on a strict budget, which was my responsibility because I genuinely enjoyed it. Finances were my forte, and I even completed our yearly tax returns. Now, at sixty-six, Jim would be forced into new financial areas, and I hated to leave him unprepared. I promised to balance his checkbook at the end of February and showed him some basic steps before heading to the bank to open a checking account in my name.

Jim called a lawyer to check on the cost of handling the divorce: $400 plus a $150 filing fee. We agreed to split the cost, knowing that if we filed right away, it would still be April before the divorce was final.

I moved out of our home into the one-bedroom apartment the following day. Having been ill for almost two weeks, I decided to take only a few essentials to get partially settled in and to pick up additional items from the house in the next few days. Jim was helpful in the move, and we both worked hard all day.

As he assembled the bed for me in my apartment, I silently thanked God for Jim's willingness to help and his generous attitude. We completed the last load after dark, and when I made no move to get back in the car with him, he said, "You are coming back to the house to sleep, aren't you?"

"No, I plan to stay here."

"But you don't have anything set up."

"The bed's put together. That's all I need. I can find some sheets to put on it. I'll be all right. Really. I want to stay here tonight."

Reluctantly, Jim left me alone in the apartment. Later that night, I drove to Walmart to purchase shelf paper and a few food items in an attempt to start nesting.

The following day, Jim and our son, Michael, both called to check on me. I appreciated their concern and assured them I was doing fine, which was true to a certain extent. I hadn't slept well during my first night in the apartment as I kept hearing noises I wasn't used to. Nevertheless, I stayed busy on my first full day in the apartment, organizing the few items I had brought into my new home, plus my Walmart purchases from the night before. I organized the clothes in my closet, the towels in my bathroom, and began putting down shelf paper in the kitchen.

Before long, my strength played out as I was still weak from my long illness. When I took a break, I relaxed in my only chair, a comfortable, blue, cushioned swivel rocker that I had placed next to the front window. The light in that location was excellent for reading, and I could look out at a large dogwood tree in my tiny front yard. When it bloomed a month or two later, I was amazed to see both pink and white blossoms as two trees had obviously grown together. It made me think of Jim and I, separate as those blossoms but working hard to grow together, even now as our branches are no longer intertwined.

The books I chose to read during this period were religiously oriented non-fiction books because I found them comforting and inspiring. This morning, I chose to read a book of meditations by Ted Loder. When I read, "The most powerful yearning is for a past one never had," I was stunned. Those words described my exact feelings.

During my long marriage, I had consistently yearned for a life I denied myself when I was twenty. I was always wishing for something I could never have.

Someone gave me a beautiful mini journal, and I started recording passages that held special meaning for me. I titled my little journal "Struck Chords" because reading a particular passage struck a chord with me. One of the first passages I wrote down was a quote from Albert Einstein, "I must be willing to give up what I am in order to become what I will be," and a quote from Carl Jung that read, "Thinking is difficult. That's why most people judge."

I spent ten blissful days making my apartment livable. I purchased a large desk from Office Max consisting of over 300 pieces, which was a challenge. It was a type of hutch with shelves and cubby holes attached to the back. I worked and worked on that desk, carefully reading the instructions prior to each step. It never dawned upon me to purchase a power drill, which would have saved the palms of my hands from blisters.

When the desk was complete, with the door opening and shutting, and the drawer sliding in and out, I felt very proud of my accomplishment. That desk would be my Ebenezer—a monument to my strength and capability that I still use over twenty-four years later.

One of my next purchases was a comfortable office chair. Then Michael offered me his extra sofa, which I gladly accepted. Heading to a thrift store, I purchased two matching upholstered dining chairs and a small dining table. I eventually had my piano brought over from the house and set it up on an inside wall in the living room. My little apartment was comfortable, and I enjoyed it very much, especially the freedom to do what I wanted when I wanted. More than that, I could relax, knowing I no longer needed to weigh my words before I spoke.

When the building, purchasing, and decorating were done, loneliness crept in. I'd always felt lonely, even around people, but now my mind had plenty of time just to think. To fill the void, I continued to live in a fantasy world, thinking about Janie, a person I had no right to yearn for.

Even as I took pleasure in the visualizations of Janie and me being together, I felt I was sinning in doing so. I kept asking myself why I was so crazy about her. Even though I continued to remind myself it was just an infatuation, the pain, nevertheless, persisted. I felt too old to be experiencing this type of emotion. I was like a teenager with my first crush. The pain was indescribable, pure agony. It developed into a terrible feeling of hopelessness flooding me with despair because there was no chance of my fantasy coming true. Janie was off-limits.

I had no doubt she loved her husband, and I knew from the way he looked at her that he worshiped her. To do anything that might cause dissension between them would be unpardonable.

I awoke at three-thirty the following day and couldn't go back to sleep, so I finally got up at six. My emotional state was still affecting my physical condition. I'd lost my appetite completely, with my weight now down to 110 lbs., an 18 lb. drop in four months. Divorce was proving to be equal parts salvation and suffering. I was happy to be free from the lie of my marriage to a man, but I wondered if a woman like me could ever access, ever deserve, genuine happiness ever again.

photo provided by the author

COMING OUT
December 1999 – July 2000

12
NO MORE HIDING

I shall never forget February 28, 2000, because of an e-mail Jim sent to me late the night before and my decision when answering it. I had heard little from him since I requested the divorce almost two months earlier. Consequently, when I began reading his long letter, my heart began to pound as I realized what he was asking.

Lou Anne,

I feel certain you were aware I could not walk over and speak to you this morning before Sunday School…To the best of my ability, I want you to know and try to understand the feelings that have built up during the last several weeks.

During January and early February, I experienced feelings of sadness, grief, and hurt, asking why the request for divorce happened. I was determined to help you move and get established in your new apartment, even though it took great effort to sublimate my feelings. I was determined to keep communications open for the sake of our children. That approach seemed to work for the first 5-6 weeks.

But about two to three weeks ago, a real anger began to permeate my very being. I thought for a while that, indeed, it would have been easier to cope with your death than it would with this awful thing called divorce.

I felt anger because you have turned my world upside down, and I do not know why….I've lost my helpmate of thirty-seven years, and I do not know why. It was a wave of anger growing from the reality that I had worked so hard for thirty-seven years to raise a family with you (and I've told you many times that you deserve most of the credit for the way they have turned out.) I was looking forward to the next twenty years when we would have an extra $1500 each month to do some of the things we had denied ourselves through the thirty-five years of raising four fine children.

Now, I am forced against my will to divide our retirement income and maintain two households, leaving us with less. And the most pervasive source of anger is that I still deeply love you, and now that love has been rejected. You have left a gigantic hole in my heart that simply hasn't had time to heal.

You, of all people, know that I have never been as good as you are at hiding my emotions. I wish I could tell you 'Thank you' for doing what I did not have the courage to do, but that is not the case right now. When I saw you at church this morning, my whole body flushed with anger and resentment on the one hand and, on the other, a wish that I would suddenly awaken and realize the days since January 7th have been just a bad dream. I have considered leaving the church to see if 'out-of-sight, out-of-mind' would hasten the pain, but I enjoy the men in my class, and it is getting easier to face the group each week.

The closest answer to 'why' goes back to our conversation on Friday night, January 7th, when I returned from an emotionally draining day with my brother Mark. If I recall correctly, you said you were "miserably unhappy."

As I've lain in bed at night during the last several weeks thinking about that statement, I've allowed myself to think selfishly about the many times over the previous thirty-seven years when I was unhappy with your behavior or lack thereof. And I ask myself why I didn't ask for a divorce. You know the answer to that... divorce wasn't and isn't my path to solving problems. Your asking for a divorce was a selfish act on your part, which did not make sense because you were always the most unselfish person with your time, talent, and resources. That was particularly true of your behavior toward my family members. In addition, you could always share so unselfishly with people who were mere acquaintances.

Finally, the real source of anger is why I didn't see this coming and why I didn't know you were so miserably unhappy. To help me reach mental and emotional closure in this phase of my life, I need to know precisely why this is happening.

Would you do me the courtesy of sitting down at your computer and sharing the specific things over the last several years (or the last 37 years) that have caused you to ask for a divorce? And, if your answer still comes up as 'unhappy,' please identify the ten or so things that contributed to your unhappiness. This request is not aimed at providing me with a list of behaviors that I can seek to correct and attempt to reconcile. The Rubicon has been crossed, and there is no turning back now. I simply need to know why, so I can understand specifically and accept those reasons as closure to the anger eating at my soul.

In the meantime, I hope you will find the peace of mind you seek with something, somebody, or even the fact that you are away from the primary source of your unhappiness. I mean this from the bottom of my heart.

Jim

When I finished reading, I resolved to tell him the truth. It wasn't fair to keep him in the dark, and despite our different reasons, he was hurting as badly as I was.

Even as I had these thoughts, other thoughts began to take over: fears that he wouldn't want to hear what I needed to tell him, or worse, that once he heard the truth, he would retaliate by delaying the divorce or causing problems with the division of money. These fears made me wonder if I should wait until the divorce was final to be truthful with him. Our divorce would not be final for almost six weeks, and I realized it would be cruel to withhold the truth from him longer than I already had.

I sat at my computer and wrote Jim a letter explaining to him the years of dark depression I suffered and the way I begged God to fill my heart with a deep love for him the entire time we were married. I shared with him the many times I had thought it would be easier for God to simply let me die once the children were older and out of the house. Then, I explained how Janie Robbins perceived my unhappiness and how I eventually admitted to her that I was gay.

I know how the knowledge of my being gay will hurt you, and I have a pretty good idea of how you are hurting right now. I've tried for many years to soften your views on homosexuals but have been unsuccessful. The only difference between heterosexuals and homosexuals is their sexual orientation, which is mysteriously imprinted upon each of us by God. Other than that, we are just like everyone else.

I started off to make this a very long letter, wanting to explain what it is like to be gay in a bigoted world and to constantly long for something you can never have. I also thought about spending time refuting the six biblical passages used to condemn homosexuality, but this is not the time for all that because you are hurting and confused. I don't fit the stereotype of what you have always perceived to be "homosexual." That's because the only ones you hear about are the oddballs. The rest of us are so afraid to "come out of the closet" that no one knows who we are. We're the teachers, lawyers, doctors, and businesspeople that you interact with day after day and never dream that we are gay. We are rich and poor, young and old, parents and grandparents, children and grandchildren. We come from every possible race, religion, and ethnic background.

I realize you will need to talk with friends about this letter, and that's fine with me. You might even want to speak with our pastor, Bob Watson. I'm so tired of living a lie that I'm almost anxious for it to all come out. It wouldn't surprise me to be asked to give up my Sunday School class and even leave the church. So, hang in there with your church buddies. I probably won't be around much longer.

You can talk with our daughter, Laura, about all this. She knows. Janie urged me to tell her. Janie thinks Laura "hung the moon." She saw her sweet spirit and instinctively knew she would react lovingly and understandingly. It was as Janie predicted.

I'm so sorry to have hurt you like I have. I never intended for it to end this way. We are both victims of the homophobia present today that tells gays, "Just get married, and the problem will go away." But it won't go away. I can't decide to be straight any more than you can choose to be gay! We have both suffered needlessly because of society's bigotry and prejudice, but I continue to cling to the promise in Romans 8:28 that "all things work together for the good to them that love the Lord."

Despite the years of suffering, we have produced four wonderful children. We have lovingly served not only our families but also public-school systems, churches, and various facets of society. We have been productive members of society and will continue to be.

If it eases the hurt at all, just know that I accept all the blame for the failed marriage. I always knew you loved me. I always knew you were faithful to me (and I was always faithful to you). We both did our best.

Lou Anne

The die was cast. The secret I had protected all my life was no longer a secret. My life was changing, and I was unsure about what would happen. All I knew was that my heart felt lighter and was no longer bound by that all-encompassing vise-grip of fear.

A second email from Jim arrived in the morning.

Lou Anne,

I do not want to discuss this matter over the Internet. It may surprise you, but I have known deep down in my heart that this might have been the problem. As soon as I can eat and go get my exercise, I would like to come by and visit with you. Please know that the deep love I expressed last night in my email is still present for the person I thought was the most beautiful girl I had ever met.

Jim

When Jim arrived about 9 a.m., he took me in his arms, pulled me up tight to him, put his cheek next to mine, and began sobbing. I put my arms around him and cried. Our emotions overflowed. When we eventually sat on the sofa, I placed a box of tissues between us and gave him the opportunity to vent about all the years of frustration when he had tried to be close to me but just couldn't. I listened as he talked about the feeling of futility and the heartache he had experienced, and I answered all his questions.

Jim called the next day, asking if he could come over again.

"Sure," I told him.

As we sat together on the sofa, Jim told me about his conversation the night before with our son Michael. "He had a tough time accepting your news," Jim said. "He knows you're a good mother and still loves you very much, but he just doesn't understand."

"Please get Mel White's book, *Stranger at the Gate*," I urged. "I want both of you to read it. I really think it'll help you understand what's happening."

"Michael is concerned about all of this being known. He asked me some very pointed questions last night that made me stop and think. He asked, 'Why do you want everyone to know about this, Dad? This is a family matter.'"

Fearing Jim felt a duty to tell everyone, I quickly interjected, "Jim, don't think you are doing me a favor by telling others. I'm quite capable of telling those I want to know. I just want you to feel free to tell your close friends *if* you want them to know. I'll handle telling my own friends."

Jim said he'd probably unburden himself to a few close friends, and I told him I wanted to be the one to tell my mother. I indicated anger toward her, saying, "I think that deep down, she's known the truth for a long time."

"She never hurt you on purpose," Jim said.

"I know that. Mother just did what her society and her religion demanded. But I want to tell her. I owe her that."

Jim then said he planned to inform our son, Josh, in Houston. It bothered me somewhat that he was the one telling the children, but I kept quiet.

Then he surprised me by asking, "Did you think about your sexual orientation every year during our marriage?" Jim asked earnestly.

"Every year? It was more like every day!" I said.

"It must have been a miserable life."

How true, I thought, but I didn't say a word.

After my interaction with Jim, my emotions were raw. I was sleep-deprived for days and constantly full of turmoil. I kept telling myself, *Keep your head on straight, girl. Don't lose it.*

Laura called one afternoon. "Hi, Mom. I just called to see how you're doing. Now, be truthful."

After explaining that I'd told her dad, I said, "It's been rough, sweetie. Others are finding out that I'm different, and I don't know from one day to the next who's heard and who hasn't. I'm afraid my emotions aren't holding up very well."

Laura began crying, and I assumed she was feeling sadness for herself and the upheaval in her life—her mother moving out of the house, her parents divorcing, and now others finding out her mother is gay. I imagined that would upset anyone, so I asked, "Are you going to be all right? I'm so sorry you have to go through this."

"Mother," she replied, "I'm crying because of you! I'm so worried about you. Are *you* going to be all right?"

"I'll be fine, dear. It's a little rough right now, but I'll make it," I said, trying my best to put forth a brave face.

"I had thought about talking with my friend, Kristy, but was afraid she might tell someone else, so I didn't say a word. I haven't talked with anyone about it."

I let her know she could share any of this with her friends if she needed to talk to someone. "I'm through trying to keep this a secret."

13
TELLING MY SONS

*J*im wanted to tell our three boys about my sexual orientation, but knowing how prejudiced he had always been against homosexuals, I inwardly balked at his suggestion. I felt it was my right and my duty to tell the boys, who were now adults and responsible for their own lives and households. That old feeling of "walking on eggshells" returned when Jim was around, and despite these misgivings about him taking charge, my primary desire was for the divorce to go smoothly, so I said nothing.

When Jim explained his plan to sit down and personally visit with each son, I knew I didn't want to use that method. I was convinced the best way to reveal my sexual orientation was through writing, specifically by sharing Jim's letter to me and my response to him. I felt the letters revealed the pain both of us had been in for so long and afforded the reader time and privacy to absorb what would probably be shocking news—shocking because my sons were raised in Southern

Baptist churches that condemned homosexuality. Their first reaction could be instantaneous denunciation, even anger, and I didn't want to see that reaction. I wanted to give them time to think and absorb the information. I knew they were intelligent and loving sons and hoped for supportive responses.

Jim told me he planned to drive to Houston to tell Josh, our youngest son. Our other two boys, Michael and Jimmy, lived locally. For some reason, I didn't want Jim to tell Josh. I reasoned that I should tell Josh since I had already spoken to Laura, meaning I would have told two of the children, and Jim would tell two. That sounded fair to me. Without hesitation, Jim began calling our eldest sons, Jimmy and Michael, while I gave myself time to think about how best to contact Josh.

Josh

I sent my letter to Josh and his wife, Sandy, via email. Later that day, Sandy called and visited with me by phone for almost an hour. Even though she was extremely kind, loving, and non-condemning, I kept crying off and on throughout the conversation. Coming out to my family and close friends kept my emotions at a high pitch. I cried at the slightest little thing and constantly fought depression and loss of appetite.

"Mom," she said, "I want you to talk Josh out of riding his motorcycle to Tyler tomorrow. Your news has hit him rather hard, and he feels he needs to talk with you personally. He's in such an emotional state that I don't want him to drive that long."

"Put him on the phone," I replied, then squashed his plans by promising to drive to their house the following afternoon.

Although Josh is my youngest son, he was the first to marry. When he first talked to me about his marriage plans, he was still in college. He thought I'd be surprised, but I always knew he'd be first. Josh always needed more hugs, physical contact, and reassurance than my other boys; he preferred being with others rather than alone, and Sandy was, and remains, a perfect match for him. They are always affectionate to one another, and Sandy has always been a loving and supportive wife.

Her intelligence and sense of responsibility have placed her in a managerial position in a large, extensive hospital system. Tall and statuesque, she towers over Josh, who proudly shows her off to anyone and everyone. It was always a joy to see them, and the four-hour drive to their home in Houston typically passed quickly, but this drive was longer than usual and filled with fear and worry.

Just before leaving, I had an extremely emotional two-and-a-half-hour visit with my friend Barbara before my four-hour drive to Houston. I tried to keep my emotions in check, but I couldn't help replaying our conversation repeatedly in my head. I also couldn't stop thinking about Janie and the unrelenting hopelessness of my feelings toward her.

I arrived safely at Josh and Sandy's house, tired on every level. My life was changing rapidly from 60 years of secrecy and pretense to a life of openness and honesty. I never thought I would come out, and consequently, I seemed to stay upset and depressed most of the time. I only hoped these talks with Josh and Sandy would go smoothly.

Josh was still at work when I came in, allowing Sandy and me to have long conversations. Sandy listened, asked a few questions, and made me feel loved and accepted. I felt relaxed talking with her, and our closeness grew.

Sandy thought Josh and I needed some time together. She admitted he was finding it difficult to come to grips with having a homosexual mother, so that evening, Josh and I went out to dinner.

Our conversation that evening drained me.

When Josh is convinced of something, arguing with him is impossible. He possesses a logical, well-ordered mind, and his college degree is in biomedical engineering. He has more than a smattering of knowledge about the body, including genes, and was convinced, in 2000, that people couldn't possibly be born with a different sexual orientation. Today's research still hasn't identified a particular gene that determines a person's sexual orientation. Still, scientific research is getting closer to understanding the biological factors that contribute to a person's sexual orientation, beginning before birth. We just don't know with certainty what those biological factors are.

"All behavior is learned," Josh confidently stated.

"Josh, we aren't talking about behavior because there's been no 'behavior' on my part since I was in college. This is the way I am, the way I feel. *Me*. I've tried all my life to change, but I just can't."

"But Mom, something has caused you to be this way—environment, perhaps—you can't convince me a person is born this way."

I tried to keep my composure as I explained, "Josh, all I know is who I am and what I've experienced. I'm positive this isn't something I chose. No fool would choose to be homosexual in the world we live in. That's the most ridiculous supposition I can imagine. Just think about that for a minute."

"Are you trying to tell me the baby we're expecting in July could be gay?"

"Yes, and so what?" I could hear the irritation rising in my voice. I was feeling frustrated because, at the time, I had no science-based facts to support my position. All I had was the truth of my existence and my lived experiences, and it was defeating to know that couldn't be enough.

Looking back, even if I had known of the current discussions and data being collected among scientists, I couldn't have held my own against Josh. His brilliance has always amazed me. Angry at myself for being so impotent in our argument and angry at Josh for his persistent logic and lack of compassion, I finally said, "If your baby turns out to be gay, you'll treat it just like you would if they weren't. Just love and accept them the way they are without making them feel guilty."

By then, Josh was becoming upset. "Well, I can't accept that. I can't believe our child could be gay."

Hearing my precious son echoing the voices of prejudiced individuals who declared, "Being gay is a choice," without ever actually talking with or listening to a gay person, flooded me with disappointment. "I hope they're not, Josh. But if they are, just love them. That's all. Just love them."

When I made this declaration to my son, my heart ached with the wish that someone had given my parents that advice long ago.

The following day, despite the raw emotions from our difficult talk, Josh took me to see his office and laboratory.

Ever since Josh was a young child, I pictured him in a lab, and I was thrilled to see what I always assumed would be his destiny: workstations and tables filled with his experiments.

He worked for a company that did product research for NASA and proudly explained the various projects he was working on. He talked about microgravity and showed me the wiring and parts of a box he was building for a space experiment with a liquid that had to be kept moving, but not too fast or too slow, because otherwise, the particles would separate. He explained that the astronauts had to be given pure oxygen for five to six hours before walking into space; otherwise, bubbles formed in their blood. He then walked over to another experiment involving microphones implanted in the astronauts' suits, next to their hearts. He was working on allowing NASA to hear other sounds in the space capsule without interference from the astronauts' heartbeats. I stood, staring around the lab, bright-eyed and immensely proud of all Josh was accomplishing, but my heart still ached. I wished he could design a microphone to hear the truth inside his mother's heart— to approach me with the same curiosity, questions, and determination to seek understanding as he did all the experiments he toiled over. Some discoveries take time. I committed to being patient and loving Josh as I always had, and I hoped he would find it within himself to continue doing the same.

The future was not easy for Josh and Sandy. Their only child, born about four months after the conversation I just described, is transgender. They love and support her and have helped provide her with medical and psychological assistance. They are truly wonderful parents. I like to think, despite Josh's attitude and perspectives that night of our conversation, that maybe my advice to "just love them" helped pave the way towards them supporting their trans daughter.

Several years later, despite all logic, when Mother's Day rolled around, Josh and Sandy sent me a beautiful gift and duplicated the same gift for my partner. I was amazed and so thankful they included her on Mother's Day! That gesture assured me of their acceptance and love for us as a couple. And every year thereafter, their Mother's Day gift(s) have been to both of us. We have never felt anything but love and respect from those two.

Jimmy

When Jim told me he would be informing our sons that they had a gay mother, he began his "job" the very afternoon I sent my email to Josh and Sandy. The next day, I received an email from our eldest, Jimmy, who was currently working as an elementary school teacher and supplementing his salary by driving a school bus every morning and afternoon.

Hey, Mom,
Yesterday, as I was arriving at the bus barn, Dad called my cellular

and said that he needed to come over to the house later and talk with me. When I got to the house (and saw what a mess it was in!), I called him back to suggest that I drive over there, but he was insistent.

"You'll understand when I get there," he said. Boy, that put my mind to wondering. First, I decided he was having a giant garage sale and selling the house and everything in it and was preparing to move somewhere far away. The other scenario I imagined was that he'd already found someone, and she was already living at the house.

I'm glad that you had the courage to be so honest with him and with all of us. Now, I'll admit the idea that my mother is gay may take a while to get used to. But it really doesn't change anything about how I feel about you. You're still the same mother I've loved for thirty-four years. To me, the divorce brings more changes to my life (no more family dinners at the house) than the news of your sexual orientation does.

I hope and pray that people will be loving and accept you as you are.

I love you, and that's never going to change.

Your Son,

Jimmy

I immediately replied, expressing my deep-felt thanks. Jimmy was my "missionary son," and God had used him in so many precious ways. From missionary trips to Russia, where he worked in orphanages, to mentoring young boys throughout the local community in Waco through his church while attending Baylor, he had made a significant impact. Even his teaching position was a service, as he spent years perfecting his Spanish to be certified as a bilingual pre-kindergarten teacher.

After I gave him permission to share this information with his friends, he wrote to me three days later, updating me on the people he had told. "Mother," he said, "I have yet to receive a negative reaction." One of his friends told him, "Your mother really has a lot of courage."

Michael

Despite receiving "the news" at the same time as his brothers, a month passed before Michael contacted me.

Michael is my entrepreneur son who graduated summa cum laude with a degree in finance but never desired to be under a supervisor. He wanted to work for himself and taught himself to be a finish carpenter. He's skilled and widely appreciated for his expertise, dependability, hard work, and honesty.

His father also enjoyed working with his hands, doing yard work, car repair, and woodworking, so Michael naturally inherited his interest and skill. He and his dad were like two peas in a pod. They both enjoyed hunting and fishing, they were both hard workers, and they were both prejudiced against homosexuals.

Of all my children, he would have the most significant struggle with accepting and understanding the fact that his mother is gay. I knew the news would distress him most because he was prejudiced against gays.

A lesbian had recently hurt him both emotionally and financially, and I had heard him make multiple ugly comments about gays. Growing up, making small talk with his dad, Michael would sometimes ask of characters on TV, "Hey, Dad, that fellow is a little 'light on his feet,' isn't he?

"Yes," his dad replied. "He's a fairy for sure!"

My heart would always skip a beat as they shared a laugh, hoping neither of them would notice the distress or disappointment on my face.

I decided to let Michael think about the news of my orientation without pressing or intruding.

That month of waiting seemed to take forever.

When the mail finally brought a letter from Michael, I anxiously opened the envelope.

Dear Mother,

I am writing you this note not because I can't or don't want to visit with you personally, but because I need the forum to make my point without the distraction of a give-and-take discussion. I love you because you're the reason I'm on this earth and because I'm reasonably happy with the way I've turned out.

If you told me you needed me to stand on my head and sing nursery rhymes in a prison visiting room, I'd do it for you. Put simply, any decision or action you take regarding your coming out is okay with me. I support you. Your happiness is more important to me than my own.

You are who you are based on what you have said and how you have acted over the course of your life. You are defined by the actions of your children, whose greatest role model is the person reading this note. I agree that sexuality is a major part of the human experience, but that it is a paltry standard by which to evaluate others.

Frankly, I don't understand the positive benefits of sharing this with others. If that is what you want, I support you. If that is not what you want, then I need to talk with Dad because he is under the opposite impression.

In closing, I hope the next time you feel depressed, you will think about me and how much I love you.

I love Dad, too, but he may not be totally objective when it comes to sharing his wife's secret. After all, you've just provided him an opportunity to completely abdicate any role he may have played in his failed marriage.

Michael

I breathed a sigh of relief. Michael still loved me. All four of my children had declared their love for me, and even though they may not have fully understood all the implications of having a gay mother, they were willing to walk with me on my journey. As I had done before, I braced myself for total rejection, primarily because I hadn't heard a word from this son in a month. However, when I read his letter, my heart leaped for joy and immense gratitude. His words meant the world to me.

My entire family officially knew the truth about who I was, and that part of my world hadn't come crashing down as I'd feared. Instead, I felt more bolstered to face the world outside and continue fighting the battles still waged within.

14
BARBARA

*W*hen I told Jim he was free to share with others that I am gay, I envisioned the news rapidly spreading throughout the church. He wasted no time calling our eldest sons, and the minute I agreed to his telling others, I knew our friends would be close behind.

Coming out all at once—to my children and my closest friends within the same week— had me in an odd state of relief and severe depression. The constant worry about what others might think weighed heavily on me, and the tears were ready to fall at the slightest provocation. To bolster my spirits after my talk with Jim about how to break the news to others, I went through a box of old letters and notes, many written to thank me or praise me for something or another. Many were from Barbara Lawrence, who is about two years older than I am.

Barbara's intelligence amazed me, and I admired how she always seemed to know what was happening in the church. Her deceased father had been the pastor of a large Baptist church in a neighboring town, and she was well-grounded in scripture. Everyone regarded her as an excellent Sunday School teacher.

She made tremendous efforts to be my friend by contacting me frequently, yet I did so little for her in return. Guilt crept over me. Since first meeting her, I'd treated her shabbily, and I knew why. I was abiding by that old promise: to never again have a close female friend.

I looked at the evidence of Barbara's generosity and perseverance: notes, gifts of books, help with Sunday School lessons, invitations to lunch, and written encouragement. She was always there for me, willing to be my friend, and an overpowering urge came over me to unburden myself to her and share my story. How strange that I should even consider such a thing, yet I felt a need to explain my aloofness, my pulling away from her offers of friendship. I imagined her reaction when she heard of my sexual orientation and pictured her as totally amazed, perhaps repulsed, or maybe just smiling as she said something like, "I kind of figured that," but who knew how she would react?

I felt an uncomfortable churning deep inside, not just in my stomach but in my spirit. My whole being was sad. Barbara had been too friendly to me to let her be blindsided by this news. She was bound to hear about it from someone in the church, so I decided to warn her by sending her the letters between Jim and me that outed me. Along with that letter, I included the following explanation:

Barbara,

I've spent my life trying not to have a close friend, always fearful I'd feel something toward her I shouldn't. I've done little to encourage our friendship, and that's why.

If you have questions or want to talk, that's fine. If not, I certainly understand. It's no problem.

Lou Anne

Late that afternoon, I received Barbara's response, which I had anxiously awaited all day. I trembled with fear and excitement as I read it. She assured me she loved me and that she'd suspected I was gay but didn't want to risk our friendship by asking. I was relieved to hear she was willing to set up a morning and time to meet, despite it landing on the same day I was to travel to speak with Josh and Sandy about my coming out letter to them. Even with the toll it was taking on me, I thought it best to go ahead and get all the difficult conversations over at once.

When Barbara opened the door for me the following day, my tears began falling. For two and a half hours, I explained who and what I was, confessing to feelings and relationships I'd previously kept to myself. Barbara brought out my innermost feelings because she was gutsy enough to lead with her curiosity and intelligent enough to know what questions to ask and which would cross a line.

I confessed it all: my first crush on a girl in high school, my falling in love with Karen while attending Baylor, and our two-and-a-half-year affair in our dorm room.

After I finished my story about Karen, Barbara asked, "Did you ever see her again?"

"Yes, several years later, but we were surrounded by others and restricted to a public conversation. We never had an opportunity to really talk."

"Where is she now?" she asked.

"I have no idea. The man she married, Louis Van Meter, is of British ancestry and settled in South Africa before moving to Israel. I don't even know what country she's living in now or if she is still alive. I don't know how many children she has, though I know her firstborn was a boy, born a year and a half after my first, and I know his name. She and I broke off contact a long time ago."

"Why?"

"For about twelve years, we corresponded regularly. Then, in 1971, when I was especially unhappy in my marriage, I wrote some things I shouldn't have. Our letters were always generic, so we could show them to anyone. I usually shared her letters with Jim, and she did the same with her husband, Louis. Yet, in that particular letter, I bemoaned how unhappy I was in my marriage and concluded by expressing my thankfulness that I was at least fortunate to have had the opportunity to know what love really was all about. After I mailed the letter, I realized I shouldn't have said that. How would she explain that statement to Louis?"

Barbara stared intently, not missing a word.

"I never received a reply and decided not to write again. Karen evidently had a happy marriage. I was pleased for her and glad she was happy. My letter could have caused problems in her marriage, and I regretted making things tough for her." I continued, pausing to fight the tears as I relived that final contact with Karen.

"But I miss her, Barbara. I've always missed her. When I'm in a crowd of people, I often look around, thinking I might just see her. I sometimes dream of being with her. Just the other night, I dreamed we were meeting on a public street, yet we greeted each other with hugs, kisses, and held each other close, oblivious to the passersby. When I awoke, I thought, 'We never showed any affection toward each other when others were around.' We didn't even do what female friends normally do—hug or kiss each other on the cheek," I said, pausing to see how Barbara was taking my truth-telling. I expected condemnation to be heaped upon my head at any moment, but I felt nothing other than concern coming from Barbara, so I continued.

"To have a dream in which we were publicly affectionate seemed strange. We were careful never to touch in public, but it revealed how much I continue to miss her, even after forty years."

"Is there someone else in your life now?" Barbara asked, catching me by surprise.

Tears started again, and I didn't answer.

"You don't want to talk about it, do you?" she asked.

"No," I mumbled as I shook my head.

We went to another subject for a few minutes, and then Barbara again surprised me by clarifying, "It's Janie, isn't it? You're in love with Janie, aren't you?"

I'd never intended to tell anyone this secret I feared was so horrible, but Barbara had guessed it, and I sobbed anew at the realization that my affections were so obvious.

Barbara said in a sympathetic, gentle voice, "If I were you, I'd be in love with Janie, too."

Barbara's words were the kindest, coming from the heart of this woman who had been born and bred a Baptist and whose father was a minister. Of all the things I expected from her mouth, loving friendship and concern for me were not on the list. I expected what I'd always had from most Baptists: condemnation, so how truly fortunate I felt—how blessed— to have a friend like her.

"I know I shouldn't be in love with Janie," I said. "I don't want to be. It's wrong. I know it's wrong. She's happily married. She's heterosexual. I've promised myself never to touch her, ever."

"Does she know you're in love with her?" Barbara asked.

"Oh, no! I don't want her to ever know. It would kill me if she found out. She loves her husband so very much. I don't want to be in love with her. It's embarrassing to have such feelings about her. I've never been so miserable."

I started to sob again. "All my life, I have done everything right to prevent something like this. After Karen, I never allowed myself to have a close female friend again, fearing I might fall in love with her. I avoided physical contact with women. Even with Janie, I did nothing wrong—not a thing—so I don't know why these feelings are there. It's so unfair. If I did something wrong, I'd be getting what I deserved, but I didn't. It just happened. It was as if someone were standing behind me with a 2 × 4 and slamming it into my head with all their might. That's how it hit me: completely out of the blue. I was standing in the kitchen on a Sunday afternoon, and 'wham!' I started having romantic thoughts about Janie. I didn't do anything wrong. It just happened!" I wailed.

Barbara moved close to help comfort me. I was in agony, admitting what I'd always been told was a deplorable weakness and feeling ashamed for having fallen in love with Janie.

After a few minutes, Barbara suggested, "You need to give up teaching your Sunday School class, at least for a few months."

"I can't do that."

"Why not?" she asked incredulously.

"I need to see Janie occasionally. I couldn't stand it if I didn't."

"Lou Anne, you've got to quit teaching that class. It doesn't have to be a permanent change. I'm teaching a class on that same floor with some younger ladies; I think you'd enjoy being with them. Come visit our class."

"No, I can't," I insisted, but her suggestion made me think about it. I decided to teach my class that coming Sunday, after visiting with Josh and Sandy, to see how things went.

15
PASTOR BOB

*B*arbara had urged me to tell our pastor, Bob Watson, the reason for the divorce. After initially rejecting her suggestion, I considered her advice and realized I'd much prefer he hear the news from me rather than Jim or someone else.

I emailed Pastor Bob copies of the letters Jim and I exchanged when I finally gave Jim an honest answer as to why we needed a divorce. It felt like the most honest way to relay the whole story and show the mixed pain and freedom of both sides. As I clicked "send," I felt that same sense of trepidation every time I came out to someone new, not knowing what kind of response I would receive. I didn't wait long and received a response from Pastor Bob that same afternoon.

He told me that my message had moved him to tears and wrote that he was relieved to have received my letter. He appreciated my entrusting such heartfelt matters to him, and the rest of his letter, depicted below, are words I still cherish.

Lou Anne,

Your response to Jim showed so much courage and care. It grieved me to know of your long struggle in coming to grips with your sexuality. Furthermore, I know it wasn't (and won't be) easy to continue sharing such a delicate understanding of who you are. I am grateful that Janie was there for you. It doesn't surprise me. I consider her a person of perception, sensitivity, and intelligence.

I want you to know that you matter to me. If you need to talk or vent, please don't hesitate to do so. I realize that the issue of sexual preference is an emotional, misunderstood, and volatile subject. I do hope and pray that we can be the church for you in this time, in the best sense of the word. To that end, pray diligently and lean on brothers and sisters in Christ, like Janie and Barbara, not to mention others, including me. Please know that my thoughts and prayers are with you.

Your brother in Christ,

Bob Watson

I rejoiced that my pastor seemed to understand the long, long road I had traveled trying to be the wife I was expected to be and that he was rejoicing with me in the newfound feeling of freedom brought about by being open and honest about myself. Few Baptist pastors, at that time, would have passed up the opportunity to condemn me for what they perceived as a perversion. Bob hadn't condemned me, and I felt truly blessed to have him as my pastor.

About a month later, on March 29, I made an appointment to sit down and visit with Bob again. Even though I had been a member of First Baptist for 12 years, this was the first time I recall ever being in the pastor's office. I was immediately impressed by its roominess and the numerous bookcases. When I entered, Bob was sitting behind an enormous mahogany desk, working, but he immediately stood and greeted me with a smile and a hug. He indicated a chair for me to sit in and took the one close by, so we could look at each other.

I found it challenging to know what to say, but his kindness led me to share a lot about my life and what it had been like to pretend to be heterosexual. One of my purposes for visiting with him was to ask whether I should let my Sunday School class know that I'm gay.

He advised me not to speak to them about it as a group but to talk with one or two at a time. "If you talk to them as a group," he said, "you'll experience the very lowest opinions in that group." I've thought of his advice many times since that afternoon and realized the wisdom of his answer. Those individuals prejudiced against gays would have been the first to speak up and condemn, while others would quietly hold back to mull over how they really felt about the subject. I avoided suffering shame thanks to his advice.

Then he said, "Various church members have asked me if I'm aware of your sexual orientation." *So, the news was spreading through the church*, I thought. "They weren't upset or condemning but inquisitive. You will be pleasantly surprised by all the support you will find among church members who think very highly of you."

"Can you tell me who's come to speak with you about me?"

Looking rather uncomfortable, he said, "No, I can't. And be prepared for others who will say some unkind things to you. Decide ahead of time what you will say to them." Several times during our conversation, he urged me to be prepared for unkind words. I was less sure what he meant each time he made that statement. How volatile did he anticipate people to be, and how does someone prepare themselves for cruelty?

"It might be a good idea for you to give up teaching your Sunday School class, at least for a while," he suggested.

The statement shocked me out of my contemplation. I didn't expect him to say that, but I should have. *Was this the start of the cruelty he was warning me of?*

Most churches have difficulty filling the volunteer position of teaching Sunday school. Usually, churches beg members to accept a teaching assignment. A good teacher spends many hours each week preparing a lesson simply for the satisfaction of serving their church and their God. Classes that lose their teachers typically do so because of health problems, lack of preparation time, or because the teacher moves from the church for one reason or another. I'd never heard of a teacher who was asked to step down.

He must have discerned my discomfort with his suggestion of resigning, as he quickly changed the subject. "How is your mother taking this news?" he asked.

When Mother moved to Tyler two years earlier, she joined this church to be with me and my family. At the time of my conversation with Pastor Bob, she was 90 years old and hard of hearing but otherwise quite energetic and alert for her age.

"I haven't told her yet," I replied, "and I'm not certain I will."

"You need to."

"I feel angry toward her." I confessed. "She knew when I was in college that I'd fallen in love with a girl, but she did nothing but condemn me. She also pressured me to get married—the same kind of pressure I felt from society at large. That's why I married Jim and lived a very unhappy life. I don't know if I'll ever discuss this with her."

"How is Jim taking this?" He asked.

"He seemed sad at first, but I think he's now becoming angry, which doesn't surprise me."

"Telling him the truth about yourself was an act of grace, Lou Anne. You did a wonderful thing. How are your children taking the news?"

(This meeting with Pastor Bob was amidst my letter writing and visits with my children when Michael was still unresponsive.)

"Laura and Jimmy are all right with it. Josh is having trouble, and I haven't heard from Michael yet. I know it's not easy for him. He's like his dad in that they are both very prejudiced against gays."

"You need to give them time."

"Yes, I know. I'm trying to."

I shifted the conversation to mention two couples in the church who were friends to Jim and me, and close in age. "I'm certain they know about me, but no one has said a word to me personally."

Bob looked uncomfortable and embarrassed (probably because they were the ones who had come to make certain he was aware of the reasons behind the divorce).

Concernedly, he reminded me, "You need to give people a chance. This is all new to them. You're probably the only homosexual they've ever known. They don't know what to say. Just don't begin a crusade. Whatever you do, share this information on a one-on-one basis."

I trust the pastor's purpose in warning me was twofold: 1) to avoid creating divisive controversies in the church, which could cause a "split" by one faction breaking off from the other, and 2) to protect me personally.

Both Pastor Bob and I had lived in Tyler long enough to know the city had a poor reputation when it came to its treatment of homosexuals. For people of our age and experience, the atrocities weren't memories from a distant past but nightmares we witnessed unfold.

I'm sure he remembered, as I did, the 1993 abduction of Nicholas West, a 23-year-old medical records clerk, taken from a central park in our city.

Five men had transported him to a clay pit 10 miles away, where they stripped him of his clothes, brutally beat him, and sadistically murdered him simply because he was gay. The most unsettling part of the crime was the boldness of the five men, as they proudly boasted to authorities that they looked for homosexuals to rob and assault; they clearly thought they would receive no punishment because the man they killed was gay. Luckily, they did, but you must wonder what kind of culture nurtures such a mindset. Their admission frightened gays and lesbians in East Texas, who stopped venturing far from home for years after.[7]

East Texas culture is an extension of the values of the Old South, brought here by Southerners who migrated to our area after the Civil War. The Ku Klux Klan flourished in East Texas, and I've heard it is still present, though not as visible as it used to be.

During the Civil War, Tyler was the site of the largest Confederate ordnance (artillery) plant in Texas, and in 1863, a large Confederate prison camp known as Camp Ford was built four miles to the northeast. The camp held as many as 6,000 prisoners.

The city still has a street named Confederate Avenue, which contains a large "hanging tree"[8] used at one time to lynch six Black Union soldiers during the period of Reconstruction.

The Old South mindset, the Confederacy, and the Ku Klux Klan have kept this area of Texas immersed in old traditional values, making change hard to come by.

Pulling my mind back to the present, Pastor Bob asked, "Are you taking care of yourself? Exercising? You've lost a lot of weight, haven't you?"

---

7   Tyler Morning Telegraph, Feb. 8, 2024, "Board denies parole for Flint man serving life sentence for 1993 hate crime" by Vanessa E. Curry.

8   https://www.weremembertyler.org/lynchingstories/1868-black-union-soldiers-lynched-tyler-tx

"Yes, but I'm watching it. I do exercise, and I walk a little." I sighed. "I keep asking myself why I've had to suffer so much internal anguish, and I'm beginning to believe that God wants me to do something. That's why I've had to come out of hiding. You can't imagine how wonderful it would have been to have had someone to talk with when I was a teenager and was confused about my feelings. There are bound to be other people in this church just like me, each hiding in their own little cubbyhole of fear and secrecy. I want to do something for them, especially the children who'll grow up feeling the same guilt and condemnation I always felt."

"There probably is a reason all of this has happened to you," he said. "Just be patient, and those needing help will eventually find you."

Eventually, after serving First Baptist for nine years, Pastor Bob left Tyler and moved to another city. At that time, I told him he was too intelligent for East Texas. I wished him the best and kept up with where he and his wife were living and what church he was pastoring. I noticed his new pastorates tended to be in more liberal churches than the one here in Tyler.

Years later, during my first book tour in New Orleans, I had the opportunity to visit with Pastor Bob. We had dinner with him and his wife, and as we stood up to say our goodbyes, he hugged me and whispered in my ear, "Thank you for your ministry." His words thrilled me. I was fortunate to have had such a kind pastor when I first "came out."

After I visited with my pastor, I wrote to Barbara, sharing our conversation with her. She replied:

Lou Anne,

As I told my Sunday School class recently, my favorite poster shows a pool of light (as if from a flashlight) surrounded by darkness and the words, "Faith is going to the edge of all the light you have and taking one more step." I suspect that may be where you are. But if you're walking in the Light, you'll be able to see when you take that step.

I hoped she was right because I certainly felt like I was walking in darkness, not knowing what would happen next or how others would react. The possibility that each step of my coming-out journey would have light at that last minute to guide me was a comforting assurance that, so far, proved to be true.

16
DOUBTS

The Sunday School lesson that week went well, and the group was much larger than usual. Many went out of their way to compliment me on the lesson I taught, which made me question the results of my conversation with Pastor Bob a few days prior.

Afterward, Janie walked with me to the parking lot, saying. "Your lessons are so good, Precious. You really ought to tape them. You do save them, don't you?" (My heart always beat a little faster when she used that pet name for me.)

As we talked, Janie ignored where she was going among the cars in the church parking lot and ran into a rearview mirror. She received quite a jolt and probably a nasty bruise. I exclaimed, "Oh, honey! Are you hurt?"

She didn't seem to react abnormally to my words, but I knew I'd goofed and hoped she didn't later give my endearment more thought. I knew I had to get over my feelings for her, yet I couldn't imagine living my life without ever seeing or talking to her. I continued to imagine scenarios such as driving somewhere with Janie beside me. It would be a dream come true.

On March 8th, Jim found an excuse to call me and, with pain in his voice, wished me a Happy 37th Anniversary. My heart went out to him.

The following night, Mother hosted a family dinner at a Mexican restaurant because my brother, Tom, had come from California for a short visit. Michael was living with Jim, so when I called days earlier to invite Michael to join us, I assumed Jim would prefer not to come. Michael quickly informed me I was wrong. Both Jim and Michael joined us, along with our eldest son, Jimmy.

I felt uncomfortable having Jim sit at the table with all of us, and it was clear that everyone else felt awkward too. Afterward, as we headed to our cars, Jim handed me a small, gift-wrapped package. I thanked him and waited until I got home to open it. It was a CD of "I Will Survive."

The enclosed card read, "Lou Anne, I ordered one of Gaynor's 'I Will Survive' for myself and thought you would enjoy listening to the full track. Your favorite song has become my personal anthem… regardless of what has been dropped on me…I will survive! I play the CD morning and night, just to remind myself, 'You're OK. Jim'"

Jim knew the song was a favorite of mine thanks to a video short on the internet of a green, one-eyed space alien singing the first refrain while prancing around until unexpectedly getting crushed by a fallen disco ball. I loved the video because it captured the irony of my situation: Surviving? Continually crushed by the weight of my own "performance" as a heterosexual? Absolutely.

I emailed him a thank-you for the CD and received the following reply:

Lou Anne,
Glad you enjoyed the Alien CD. Even though it is sung by a woman

about a man who has done her wrong, it still speaks to my current feelings...As you have suggested, I have talked with several people in the church. Interestingly, they seemed to sympathize more with the burden you've had through the years. They are very accepting of alternative lifestyles, more so than yours truly.

...I can't seem to shake the anger I feel over all the years of happiness that I could have had with someone who really loved me. I think of the hundreds of nights that I lay beside you, trying to ask the Lord why we could not be close...and I never got an answer. I wish I had been enough of an SOB to tell you how miserable I was and file for divorce. But you, of all people, know I stayed with you for one reason: the children. The children are a great source of pride for me, but if I had it all to do over again, I would do it differently.

You bet, I will survive, and I hope you do also. I cannot understand how two people could play this game of charades for thirty-seven years. I only need time to forget what has happened and try to find someone who will let me know how special I am to them. That will make me climb mountains for that kind of person.

Jim

His letter made me feel uncomfortable, angry, and guilty all at once. I somehow felt I deserved this "slap in the face" and was only thankful I no longer had to live with him.

When I shared his letter with Barbara, one of the things she said was, "I am a touch surprised that Jim continues to use the term 'alternative lifestyle' (always sounds to me like moving into a commune) instead of 'sexual orientation' or something similar. Evidently, he's still buying into the theory that homosexuality is something a person chooses."

I appreciated Barbara more and more. She voiced many things I thought and felt but didn't exactly know how to put into words at the time.

Soon after that painful "gift" from Jim, I received a letter from my brother, Tom, whom I'd seen just a few days earlier when he came to visit. He wrote:

Sis,

Congrats to you. I'm glad to see you being independent. Your new place looks like it is really yours.

It's difficult not to be affected by the actions of your "ex," but it is worth the effort. The therapists I went to (Tom's twice divorced) *taught us that people with a hidden agenda always adopt one of three strategies— being a victim, a persecutor, or a rescuer. Often, they combine two in one move, such as persecuting someone by claiming to be their victim.*

The therapists suggested one way to step out of the circle is to resist the feeling that the other person is trying to induce. E.g., don't feel guilty when they claim to be a victim; don't feel injured or helpless when they try to persecute, and don't feel gratitude or a sense of debt when they offer help at a time no help was asked for. All in all, it's exciting and rewarding. My love and best wishes go with you.

Tom

My life seemed to be moving at breakneck speed. I asked for a divorce at the start of the new millennium in January, moved into my little apartment on February 1, admitted to Jim I was gay on February 28, and immediately began coming out to children and friends. The upheaval in my life triggered sleep problems.

One morning, I awoke exceptionally early and eventually got up around five-thirty, experiencing an overwhelming sadness for the fourth straight day. Though I'd finally decided to free both Jim and me to find true happiness, this decision to divorce and then to admit that I was gay had introduced me to the most tremendous misery I'd ever faced. And to make matters worse, I'd fallen in love with a happily married woman. How could that happen?

I was ready for an upward swing in my mood. Feelings of depression weren't uncommon for me, but I'd been down in the dumps longer than usual this time. I just wanted to crawl into bed, stay there, and count the hours until I saw Janie. Simple phone conversations with her always raised my spirits.

One morning, we talked for over an hour. "I hope Jim finds someone special," she said, then added, "Lou Anne, you need someone in your life, someone to love. I hope you find such a person soon."

Thoughts of her raced through my mind as I mumbled, "Yes, that would be nice." She was right, of course. If someone else came into my life, that would help subdue my feelings toward her. I needed to get over her.

Perhaps I needed to make a conscious move toward finding a partner, but I had absolutely no idea how to go about finding someone. Sometimes, I desperately yearned to put my arms around a woman— any woman— and just hold her.

Several days later, Janie called to tell me about a conversation at one of the weddings she'd attended. Jim's close friend, Milton, had made a point of walking over to her and saying, "Thank you for being such a good friend to Lou Anne. I know how difficult and painful it is for her now, and I appreciate your helping her out."

As Janie shared Milton's words, my mind seemed to shut down from amazement. Their conversation must have been extended, but I recall little of what else she said. Janie told Milton, "I'm sure this is also difficult for Jim." Milton agreed yet returned to the subject of me and the "brave step" I'd taken. Milton was probably Jim's best friend. Since neither Milton nor his wife had spoken to me, his sympathy and understanding came as a welcome surprise.

It was hard for me to explain, even to myself, why the loving, kind reactions from Barbara, Janie, Laura, Jimmy, Milton, and our pastor Bob Watson amazed me. It might have been related to living with a feeling of guilt all my life, a feeling that was such a part of me I didn't understand why everyone wasn't heaping additional feelings of guilt and sin on me. Part of me wished someone would haul off and beat me to a pulp and get it all over with. The physical pain appealed to me, like a cleansing or something I deserved.

One day, I read a very interesting verse in the New Testament book of Romans.

"But who are you, O man, to talk back to God? Shall what is formed say to him who formed it, 'Why did you make me like this?'" (Romans 9:20)

This verse became an affirmation to me that God deliberately formed me as a gay person and that I had no right to question His decision. From then on, it helped me feel better about myself and who I am.

After sharing with Janie the conversation Pastor Bob and I had, I received an email from her the following morning:

Dear Lou Anne,

I really find it hard to believe that Dr. Watson would think it best for you to quit teaching, even for a little while. Hasn't he noticed that our attendance is up, and we are an active class once again, thanks to YOU! Also, I still hold to the belief that your situation is far more common than we can imagine, and to think that this is so foreign to "church members" is just not, in my opinion, accurate. If this is so, then these church folks live with their heads buried and their eyes closed. We send missionaries all over the world, healing the wounded, helping the lost, embracing the sick at heart, and WE cannot even help one of our own flock through a really tough time? I stand behind you and rejoice in your creation.

How are you going to answer the questions from others? God will tell you how. Just listen to what He says. He is the only one you must answer to. If you quit teaching, I will take my own stand and will not return to the class. I love you,

Janie.

I then wrote the following to my pastor:

Dear Dr. Watson,

First, thanks for taking the time to visit with me. I welcome your advice. However, I need some clarification on your suggestion of giving up my Sunday School class, at least for a while.

I should have asked you yesterday, but it wasn't until later that I began to wonder what prompted that statement. Since everything else you said seemed to be well thought out, I feel this suggestion falls in that same category. Are there members of my class who are coming to you? Or are there church members thinking it inappropriate that I be teaching? Or do you foresee the latter occurring and want to head it off before the complaints start coming in? For me to make the best decision regarding this suggestion, I need some clarification.

Also, I'm having great difficulty even thinking of what people might say to me or what questions they might ask me. Consequently, I keep hitting a brick wall trying to plan my answers. Do you think they are just going to walk up to me and ask me if I am gay? Or do you have other comments in your mind?

Thanks again for your loving support. You have no idea how much this means to me. I realize that in most churches, I would not receive such kindness from my pastor.

Lou Anne

I sent Janie a copy of my letter to Dr. Watson and added the following paragraphs:

Dear Janie,

Thanks for your support. Please be patient. Don't quit the class, regardless of what happens. You are their "salt." They need you, and I need you to be with them. Quitting the class just plays into the hands of those we don't want to "win this game."

At the present time, I have no desire and no plan to quit teaching. I enjoy teaching, and I really enjoy this group of women. After being in this church for 12 years, this is really the first group that I feel completely comfortable with, so I'm not going to give it up without having a very good reason. And whatever that reason turns out to be, I need you to support it. Sometimes, "teams" need to "divide" to better accomplish their assignment. That may be what you and I are called upon to do. Keep your chin up.

Lou Anne

When I awoke the following morning, I seemed to be doing much better, probably because Janie called me twice yesterday, early in the morning and again close to suppertime. We chatted for over an hour each time—just friendly talk. I finally felt I was being as good a friend to her in these conversations as she had been to me. Overall, I was sleeping a little better and had gained a pound. And I was making some progress in shutting down some of my fantasies about Janie. What a relief!

My pastor emailed me an even longer explanation of why he thought I should reveal myself to church members one at a time and resign from teaching Sunday School.

Dear Lou Anne,

Thanks for your conversation on Wednesday evening and then the follow-up e-mail. ...I know this is a difficult time for you. Furthermore, I know that you are trying to do the right thing.

As to your question about Sunday School leadership, my recommendation that you step aside for a while is based on my heartfelt concern for you and the church. Because you have struggled with this issue for so long, it may be hard for you to realize that most people have not struggled with this issue, do not care to struggle with this issue, and simply respond in an emotional manner, particularly when it intersects an area of their lives which is sacred to them (i.e. the church). I have seen this tinderbox ignited many times in the past few years (from women in ministry to the Southern Baptist Convention controversy to local church matters), and when the issue becomes a public issue without proper prayer and preparation, then it becomes a "lose-lose" situation, permanently dividing people.

I am very much afraid that in a public discussion, you would be attacked and vilified, and I don't wish to see that happen. For instance, in situations like church business meetings, when a volatile issue is brought up on the floor of the church, more often than not, emotions win out over logic, with people saying harmful and destructive things. And often, I'm afraid, zealots on either side of the issue take over, hampering constructive dialogue.

On the other hand, as you share with individuals what is going on in your life, they will be able to ask questions, think, and hopefully respond in a Christian manner as they try to process this very difficult revelation.

I don't want you to retreat from talking about this, but I do want you to be wise in whom you talk to and how you communicate. (Jesus' statement about being "wise as a serpent and innocent as a dove" seems to be appropriate here.) My feeling is that if you deal with this one-on-one, you will be a better resource for people trying to make sense of this, and that your witness for Jesus Christ will be better served as people watch you deal with this in a personal way. One-on-one, people will see the anguish and care with which you are dealing.

You asked if anyone from your class had come to me with concerns. No one has. You asked about others in the church. And as I mentioned to you, people have called and asked questions about your situation, but they were questions of concern. Yet, even with the questions, there has not been anyone who has even suggested that you leave the church. However, as this becomes more public, I think it would be naïve to assume that there won't be a mean statement here or there. That is my rationale for asking you to step aside as a teacher. I don't want you to become a "lightning rod" for emotional fears and prejudices. I truly think you can best make sense of what is happening to you and with you on an individual basis. Lou Anne, lead with your best gifts in this matter and lead with the spirit of Christ to guide you. My sense is that He will grant you wisdom and courage, but most of all the gift of appropriateness, knowing when to speak and when to remain silent.

…You matter a great deal to God and to me.

Your brother in Christ, Bob

When I read Bob's letter that first time, I felt a cold churning inside me at having been asked to step aside as a Sunday School teacher. The churning was a mixture of hurt, disappointment, and relief that I would no longer have to spend hours and hours every week preparing a lesson.

Looking back twenty-four years later, I ask myself what I expected from my pastor. After all, I had always been a member of a church denomination known for its fundamentalism and its exclusion of people who were different. My pastor had gone far above what I should have even hoped for from him, and I finally realized how blessed I was to have had him as my pastor during this time of upheaval in my life. Today, his reasons for asking me to resign make perfect sense, and I appreciate Bob's kindness and consideration.

After reading his letter several times, I immediately forwarded it to Barbara and Janie, then took a long, fast-paced walk. As I strode along, I prayed for strength and guidance as well as thanking God for giving me some good days recently.

Barbara immediately replied, agreeing with our pastor's advice.

Lou Anne,

I think he is right about dealing with issues "without prayer and preparation." I think he's right about people being better able to deal with your situation one by one rather than publicly. You gave me that grace, not knowing how I would respond. I know you better than most, and I'm not homophobic, so knowing about your sexual orientation wasn't that big a deal for me personally, though you know I grieved to discover the depth of your pain and how long you'd been dealing with it alone. You must consider how you can best give people an opportunity to be (become) the people God created them to be (Which is what you're discovering and living out yourself).

If one occurred, how would a public discussion affect you? There's a huge difference between wanting people to know and being the subject of a public discussion. How would such a discussion affect those who love you? I include your Jim in that category as well as your children, your mother, and your friends. Would it be an opportunity for "the body of Christ" to mature, or is there a greater chance it will drive some to instant decisions they wouldn't make if they'd had time to think about it? I don't have good answers to those questions.

Bob's told you how he thinks you can "be a better resource for people trying to make sense of this." How do you think you can be the best teacher? You'll always be a teacher, you know. You couldn't help it if you tried—you were born to be an educator, trained to be an educator, gifted to help people learn. You've been a terrific Sunday School teacher, and you've resurrected that class from the dead. You have every right to keep on teaching it, and the class has the right to have you as its teacher. But you know as well as I do that commitment to following Christ means we're not allowed to insist on our rights.

There's the writing, of course, and I fully expect your account of your experience to be published—though I hope that's far enough in the future for you to have the perspective to understand fully what your experience is…

I can't carry your load, but I'm grateful that you allow me to keep you company on the journey. I've learned so much from you already…

Grace and peace to you today and all your days,

Barbara

How fortunate I was to have Barbara help me with my thinking. She's wise and articulate. When I responded to her, "Give me the freedom to change my mind hourly, and that is what I am doing—trying to work through it… Barbara, you know I would never deliberately cause problems in the church. It's just that I'm not yet absolutely convinced that I must give up my class."

That's when she reminded me how long it has taken our church to elect women deacons and how long she and her husband have worked toward that end. She finally felt the church was getting closer to reaching that milestone.

"Sometimes it's extremely irritating to those of us who are quick to have to move at the pace of the slower members of our flock, but that's the speed at which flocks move, isn't it?"

17
FACING MY FIRST REJECTION

I volunteered last year to serve as secretary for a task force established to create a local Christian Women's Job Corps. This is an organization I could really support—one that educates women who are currently unemployed and on welfare, so they can eventually secure a good-paying job. I loved my work with this organization and appreciated the hard work of Gwen Patterson, the young woman who led the group.

After sharing the "Out emails" between Jim and me, I wasn't surprised when Gwen called to ask if she could drop by for a visit. She was one of the most fundamental, legalistic Christians I felt I would ever talk with about my sexual orientation. Consequently, when we visited, I shared more of my past with her than anyone else. I wanted to witness her reaction and learn how bad it might be for me when people like her knew who I really was.

Gwen stayed for an hour and a half. I wanted her to realize I hadn't chosen this sexual preference, as many fundamentalist Christians believe. I wanted her to be aware of the frustration I'd experienced dealing with prejudice and bigotry in the media and mindsets around me. I wanted her to understand the long-lasting, adverse effects gays experience by marrying outside their preference because it's expected of them. I can't deny I tried to stun Gwen by explaining the agony of thirty-seven years of unnatural heterosexual sex from a homosexual's viewpoint. I also relayed my concern regarding an incident in one of our task force meetings.

Before the meeting began, about eight members started talking about *Angels in America*, a controversial play about the AIDS crisis, which was scheduled to be performed at nearby Kilgore College. Negative opinions about this play abounded throughout East Texas, and a form of political blackmail occurred when the Gregg County commissioners rescinded $50,000 in support of the college's yearly Texas Shakespeare Festival in retaliation for hosting the play. The play centered on homosexuals, and that evening, nearly all these task force women began venting their blatant prejudice toward homosexuals. Dumbfounded, I had sat there, not moving, not saying a word. I wanted to get up and leave the room, but I didn't. I regret I didn't have the nerve to say, "I find this talk very offensive," but I just sat there, silent. I was the secretary, and they depended on me to take notes. So, I listened to these Christian women, now voicing their support of banning the play.

While visiting with Gwen that afternoon, I told her, "What I heard that evening was obscene bigotry. I'm not certain I can fit into a group like that."

"I just don't know what to say," Gwen stated. "I hope you're not still battling suicidal thoughts."

"No, I'm not," I reassured her, "and I haven't since I asked for a divorce almost two months ago."

"I still want to be your friend, Lou Anne. Feel free to call me anytime."

"Thanks, Gwen. I appreciate that."

"Will it be all right if I pray for you?" she asked.

"That would be wonderful. Of course, you can." I said, bowing my head.

Gwen prayed a beautiful prayer. She's gifted in that capacity, as her petitions to God rolled off her lips in an almost poetic form. I only hoped she would be as willing to listen with the same fervency as she prayed.

A few days later, I received the following from Gwen:

Hello, Lou Anne,

I've really been thinking about you and praying for you. Your pain is so beyond my abilities to address that right now, all I can do is pray. You are a very dear person, and I value you and your friendship. I was thinking about our conversation on Tuesday and realized that I never answered your question about coming to the task-force meetings.

At this time, I don't see wisdom in your participation. I doubt this is a surprise. Considering the conversations between the members concerning the homosexual play in Kilgore[9], I'm afraid you'd feel uncomfortable. I can't speak for the others, but if you're not comfortable, others in the group might not be either.

Lou Anne, I don't want our friendship to end. I do need to ask you to bear with me while I pray for guidance. Can we walk as friends?

Blessings,

Gwen

---

9   *Angels in America*, a Pulitzer Prize winning play about gays in America, was
     scheduled to be performed at nearby Kilgore College despite the hostility in
     East Texas toward gays in general. Preachers were preaching against the play,
     citizens were withdrawing monetary support from Kilgore College because
     of the play, and scathing headlines and letters appeared in local newspapers
     rallying anger against the play.

It was difficult for me not to feel hurt at Gwen's reply despite her attempts at kindness. Instead of addressing the group and asking them to be considerate of the feelings of others, she merely asked that those of us (me) with "uncomfortable feelings" leave. Feeling jilted and a little ill at ease, I shared Gwen's letter with Barbara, who wrote back with an encouraging reply.

Lou Anne,

It's good that the friend from the Christian women's group is still a friend, more for her good than for yours. Ultimately, you're going to be okay, though you've just begun a part of your journey that will likely take you places you can't foresee. That's true of all of us, though, to varying degrees.

I've always thought of the word "valiant" when I thought of you, Lou Anne, and never known why. Now that I understand more about you, I see valor. (Did you know that valor has its roots in a word that means worth, by the way?)

Barbara

I replied:

It's interesting that you used the word "valor." Laura and Janie both say I have courage, but I feel just the opposite. I'm terrified of the future and the fact that I haven't faced the tip of the iceberg in what will inevitably come to test my emotions, my resolve, and my ability to make the right decisions. It's as if I am teetering on the edge of a cliff, not knowing which way I will fall. At times, I feel as if I'm taking it one day at a time, and other times, I feel I'm existing an hour at a time. I keep telling myself my life will get better, but I know it will get much, much worse before things improve. I just keep telling myself to hold it together for a little longer.

After those initial emails, Barbara and I kept up a running email correspondence all day. She encouraged me to be patient and try to become comfortable with myself. Finally, she made a statement that I'll never forget.

About valor—people think John McCain is a hero because he endured less than five years of captivity and torture. You endured almost thirty-seven years, and I believe you're still working your way out of captivity.

Although her words validated my years of suffering, I felt a twinge of guilt having my thirty-seven years with Jim compared to actual physical torture. Jim's words sometimes made me feel "little" and "inept." He'd never apologize to me for his words, but the more I turned Barbara's statement over in my mind, the more I realized I did suffer a type of torture year after year by having to pretend to be something and someone I really wasn't.

I suffered from constantly feeling a need to protect the children from Jim's anger. I suffered in accepting my role as an obedient wife, which involved holding my tongue when I disagreed with decisions he made about one of the children. And I suffered by remaining in a marriage out of fear—fear that if I were not careful, Jim would divorce me and take custody of the children. He occasionally threatened me by saying, "I'm going to declare you an unfit mother and take the children away from you." I knew if he ever found out I was gay, he could do just that.

While I never lost my children, Gwen's email legitimized my fears of loss. I was being pushed out of service at the Christian Women's Job Corps because being gay came with feelings and perspectives that the organization wasn't ready or willing to interact with. Empathy and education were supposed to be our guiding lights—the tools we used to empower and equip women in our community. However, it was clear that the group lacked both when it came to improvement.

I believe God wants us to help others and that we are uniquely equipped to help in a certain way. My way wasn't at the Christian Women's Job Corps; I began to wonder if a path of service for someone like me even existed, or if I'd have to create my own.

18
THE PAIN OF BELONGING

*A*fter my interaction with Gwen and the Christian Women's job Corps, the reasons for Barbara and my pastor advising me to move slowly was beginning to sink in.

Hate against gays was occasionally making the news, allowing everyone a front seat to the protests of Westboro Baptist Church from Topeka, Kansas. Pastored by Fred Phelps, the church was infamous for public demonstrations against homosexuality, traveling all over the U.S. holding signs that said such hateful phrases as "God Hates Fags" as well as painting that message on their bus. I personally witnessed them in action two years after my coming out. It surprised me how the hateful messaging of this motley crew could resonate with so many people.

Barbara and Pastor Bob were encouraging me to give people time to adjust to my disclosure of being gay. Members of the church found this an uncomfortable subject and preferred to simply ignore it. Conflicting with that type of group thinking was my daughter's attitude. I felt torn between generational experiences and views.

Laura was twenty-one and simply did not understand the church members' attitudes and prejudices and the potential problems my coming out could cause within the church. Her generation is much more open and tolerant. Months prior to my coming out to her she said to me one day, "Mom, I have lots of gay friends, and I'm convinced they can't help being gay."

Just a year earlier, her dad's prejudices, and those that marked our generation, were brought to her attention when she cut her long hair for the first time. She asked her dad, "How do you like it?"

Jim replied, "I didn't know I was raising a butch!"

After much thought, I decided to follow my pastor's advice and resign from teaching my Sunday School class. Janie was the only class member who knew I had asked Jim for a divorce and was privy to the knowledge of my sexual orientation. I hated to resign with no one else knowing why. It seemed inconsiderate, callous, and likely to become the source of more gossip than just being forthright. We were usually a small group of only seven to nine women who, before the lesson began, freely shared with each other what was going on in our lives. We were very close, but I had never shared of my unhappiness in my marriage, and they had no idea I had even asked Jim for a divorce, much less that I was gay. They were simply in the dark about the emotional upheaval I was experiencing.

After thinking about it for a while, I decided another member of the class, Carolyn, would be the best replacement for me. She was always very kind and loving toward everyone and she was the only member of my class who had attended seminary where she had studied theology and biblical studies. Despite the fact Carolyn was grounded in fundamentalist religion, I knew she had a good, open heart, and, as my replacement, deserved to know my reason for stepping down. I trusted her to be the same kind of safe and understanding person Laura, Barbara, and Janie had been.

Coming out was good for my soul even though I had to endure the emotional upheaval that always took place as I waited for the other person's response. Every time I found the courage to reveal my sexual identity, I felt lighter, freer, released from a type of prison. Only those who have walked in shoes like mine can truly understand the feeling. I spent many years worried that someone would somehow figure out I was gay. I was constantly afraid. It kept me tied up in knots, governing my life, and turned me into a different person—a person I didn't even recognize. My life had become a life of pretense.

I knew Carolyn liked me—we were church friends— and respected me under my guise of heterosexuality. I have found that coming out to people who already respected you to begin with, wasn't too challenging, as it simply opened their eyes to realize: sexuality doesn't determine character. We are all just people and shouldn't be treated any differently based on our sexual identities.

I informed her that our pastor thought I should no longer teach our class, and along with that letter, I included a copy of Dr. Watson's recent letter, and the coming out letters shared between Jim and I.

Carolyn replied the next morning.

Lou Anne,

You probably thought that I would be knocked out of my chair when I read your email, but I wasn't. Janie and I have discussed this issue in the past. I, like Dr. Watson, think there is too much homophobia and hurt associated with it. I certainly will be discreet with the information. If I were you, I would not make a public statement in the class and would be very careful about who I shared it with. I would hate to see you hurt further by all of this. And I hate the thought of losing you for a teacher.

You are such a wonderful leader, but you need to follow God's direction in that one. You have so much to share with others, and I know how much I gain from our classes.

I must admit that I am still very convoluted in my feelings about homosexuality. I have really wrestled with the Baptist Old Testament doctrine about Sodom and Gomorrah and the wickedness there. I also know that Jesus was the last person to condemn anyone and was most loving and understanding. I am so sorry that you have had so many feelings of depression and wishes for death. I KNOW that is not what God wants. I certainly do not think homosexuality is a sin. People can be involved in unhealthy relationships whether heterosexual or homosexual. I still struggle with the idea of same-sex relationships. I don't have any idea if you just didn't want to live a lie anymore or would like to have a life partner. That is totally between you and God. I couldn't and wouldn't pretend to give an opinion on that one.

Lou Anne, be assured that this does not affect my respect for you or our friendship in any way. I don't know many people who would have had the courage to face the situation head-on like you have. I admire you for that. I grieve at the pain you have suffered and just wish there was some way I could help make it better. Thank you for trusting me enough as a friend to share this information with me. Like I said earlier, I honor your privacy in this matter. I would be glad to talk with you any time you need to.

Carolyn

I thanked her and told her that I was learning other ways to look at the Old Testament verses she referred to, and shared these new interpretations with her.

Next, I wrote to Barbara and told her that I was leaning toward resignation. She encouraged me to use the word "sabbatical" instead.

When Jim called that week to discuss some details of our financial arrangement, I shared with him that I would soon be taking a sabbatical from teaching my class. I also mentioned that Dr. Watson had told me members of the church were starting to contact him about me.

Jim exclaimed, "Well, surely they aren't coming in support of you!"

I found his comment strange. Did he want me to be condemned by others?

I replied, "Dr. Watson says they're contacting him out of concern for me," and I asked him to hold while I read him the letter Pastor Bob sent to me, being sure to emphasize the last line: "'I think you will be pleasantly surprised by all the support you will find among church members who think very highly of you.'"

Jim had nothing to say afterward which tickled me. I felt he was both stunned and disappointed that I was not receiving condemnation from our pastor and fellow church members. He was probably expecting everyone to have the same negative views on homosexuality as he did, and be much more vocal about them, as he had often been in our home. Thankfully many weren't. Instead the injury and opposition I encountered more frequently was that of toxic theology leeching out from the words and small, sometimes subtle actions or reactions of those within my church group who cared about me. It wasn't a pain that came all at once, or maliciously, but intermittently, like the defensive stings of a thousand different bees that gave no real chance of recovery before the next one landed its sting in me.

Prior to teaching the Sunday School lesson that week, I privately handed to our class president, Patsy, a sealed envelope containing copies of the coming out letters I'd shared with others. I wasn't certain I could properly handle her reaction in that public setting, so as I handed her the envelope, I said, "Patsy, I really would appreciate you not opening this until you get home. It will be better to have the privacy of your home to read what I'm giving you."

Patsy was a "good Baptist", and I was not counting on her reaction being particularly supportive, but I felt that she, as our class president, deserved to know why I would be stepping away from teaching as well.

I spent the afternoon brooding and thinking, contemplating the direction my life was going and anxiously awaiting Patsy's response. I had about decided she was not going to call when the phone rang at 4 pm. I could hear shock in Patsy's voice. She did her best to be loving and kind, but she simply didn't know what to say to me. What she came up with was, "Lou Anne, all of us have sin in our lives." Over and over, she repeated that statement, "We all have sin in our lives."

As she tried to assure me with her assertion that we are all sinners, I wondered What makes my being homosexual a sin?

She had no knowledge of whether I'd ever acted upon my same-sex desires, but she obviously considered me a sinner simply because I was gay. I don't know how many times she made that statement, but I never threw it back at her in any way. She was in a situation where she wanted to be kind, but just didn't know the right words to use.

She said, "It's been obvious in the class that you are very tense when you teach the lessons." Until she made that statement, I had never thought about that. I should have.

"I'm always fighting tears and emotions," I admitted to Patsy.

"Lou Anne, that's pretty obvious," she said.

She mentioned a class member who was concerned that her statements a week ago on homosexuality might have upset me when she stated that sexual orientation is a choice.

Patsy then stated, "We had a neighbor once whose husband was gay. Several times he tried to commit suicide, and no one knew why.

Finally, they divorced, and he moved to Dallas. It was in Dallas that he was finally successful in his next suicide attempt."

Patsy proceeded to explain that everyone in the class had problems "of one kind or another" and took time to reveal some to me, that both did and didn't surprise me.

"But that's the problem." I replied. "We don't share our heartaches with each other so we don't support each other in the ways we genuinely need."

My conversation with Patsy that Sunday afternoon drained me. Being referred to over and over as a sinner simply because I was gay caused "my hackles to rise." I wanted to argue that simply being a homosexual did not make me a sinner, but I knew that kind of argument would be non-productive. I was simply glad that "sinner" was the worst label she used, and delighted that, overall, she seemed to show kindness and concern, though I quietly doubted that she, or any other women could understand my struggle or the support I needed. I wasn't always sure myself. Regardless, the whole interaction took a toll on me, and I left the conversation depressed and teary-eyed. To help myself feel better, I decided to eat supper at the church where the food is always wonderful and comforting.

I was not disappointed in the simple meal. However, my emotions were overcoming my stoicism and I continued to get teary-eyed off and on during the service that followed. Afterward, I visited with Barbara who was sitting at my table. Noticing my shaking hand on my glass of iced tea, she reached over and steadied it. Thank goodness for Barbara.

From the outside looking in, I know many don't understand why I was working so hard to "swim against the tide," but the sincere truth was, I wanted to remain active in my Southern Baptist Church to live as proof that being gay doesn't make someone who believes any less of a Christian. I knew of no one trying to live openly this way in a church. Being gay and declaring yourself to be a Christian simply wasn't done.

Only four years earlier my denomination had declared that "even a desire to engage in a homosexual relationship is always sinful, impure, degrading, shameful, unnatural, indecent and perverted."[10] In the 2000 Baptist Faith and Message statement, the Southern Baptist Convention equates homosexuality with adultery and pornography, declaring, "In the spirit of Christ, Christians should oppose ... all forms of sexual immorality, including adultery, homosexuality and pornography." Southern Baptists were called upon to "love the sinner and hate the sin" at the same time they were also told that marriage and sexual intimacy were to be between one man and one woman, for life, declaring that homosexuality is not a "valid alternative lifestyle."[11]

Homosexuals were not ordained as preachers. They were not allowed to hold any position of leadership in the church. Homosexuals were welcomed as active church members only by hiding their sexuality.

Back in 2000, as I was first coming out, I understood their fear and their hesitancy because I'd lived with it my whole life. This understanding and compassion made me patient and determined to do whatever was asked of me. I was convinced that by stepping down from teaching, by keeping my head low, and remaining pleasant and active in the church, God would use me to open their hearts and minds, and eventually welcome others like me in.

The following week, I began working on my last Sunday School lesson for my class. It was a lovely April day so I spent time just sitting

---

10   Southern Baptist Convention's 1996 "Resolution on a Christian Response to Homosexuality"
11   https://www.hrc.org/resources/stances-of-faiths-on-lgbt-issues-southern-baptist-convention

and reading some of the Psalms from my New International Version—and crying, keeping the tissue box beside my chair. One of the passages I recall reading was from Psalm 139: 1-6; 13-16.

> "You have searched me, Lord,
>   and you know me.
> You know when I sit and when I rise;
>   you perceive my thoughts from afar.
> You discern my going out and my lying down;
>   you are familiar with all my ways.
> Before a word is on my tongue
>   you, Lord, know it completely.
> You hem me in behind and before,
>   and you lay your hand upon me
> Such knowledge is too wonderful for me,
>   too lofty for me to attain....
> For you created my inmost being;
>   you knit me together in my mother's womb.
> I praise you because I am fearfully and wonderfully made;
>   your works are wonderful,
>   I know that full well.
> My frame was not hidden from you
>   when I was made in the secret place,
>   when I was woven together in the depths of the earth.
> Your eyes saw my unformed body;
>   all the days ordained for me were written in your book
>   before one of them came to be."

These words reassured me that God was not only aware of my existence and my occasional feelings of despair but was guiding me in the direction my life needed to take.

Another passage was from Psalm 13: 1-2; 5-6.

How long, Lord? Will you forget me forever?
How long will you hide your face from me?
How long must I wrestle with my thoughts
and day after day have sorrow in my heart?
How long will my enemy triumph over me?
But I trust in your unfailing love;
my heart rejoices in your salvation.
I will sing the Lord's praise,
for he has been good to me.

Barbara had written to me earlier, saying that my sabbatical could be a healing time for me and for others. But an icy coldness swept over me. I put my arms through a sweater and wrapped my legs in a throw blanket, then looked out my window onto a cold, dreary April day. Unrelenting pain had lodged itself in my heart.

I read somewhere that we have three choices in life: to run; to spectate; to commit. I had decided to commit, to open myself up to my church friends and acquaintances as their example of a homosexual, a being they have been taught was an abomination in the eyes of God. Even though I expected rejection, it still hurt when I wasn't fully embraced. However, I continued to believe I was being given a unique opportunity to alter long-held misunderstandings about those in the LGBTQ community.

We all have a need to belong. The American Psychological Association[12] stated in 2012 that the pain of rejection is not much different from the pain of a physical injury.

---

12   https://www.apa.org/monitor/2012/04/rejection

Human beings rely on social groups for survival. Besides my family, my social group at this time in my life was my church. It had always been a primary social group for me, especially during those 14 years I was a stay-at-home mom. Now that I was revealing my sexual orientation to members of my "social group," I was jeopardizing my standing and even my continued inclusion. And yet I strongly felt this was something I had to do and that I have been destined to do—to admit that I am gay, and to serve as an example of a gay Christian.

I received an email from Gwen Patterson of the Christian Women's Job Corps. Her four-page, single-spaced letter ended with these paragraphs:

I miss you. I love you in the Lord as a sister. I know that you are going through much pain and suffering, and probably have more to come. I hurt for you and cry for your choice. But I still do not reject you, only the choice you are making.

I am praying that "the Lord will hedge you in and grant you repentance that will lead to a knowledge of the truth and that you will come to your senses and escape from the trap of the devil, who has taken you captive to do his will (2 Timothy 2:25b-26)."

Seek counsel with those who have won the victory over the temptations of homosexuality. When you are ready, help will be available from caring brothers and sisters in Christ.

Yours in Christ Jesus,
Gwen Patterson

I kept seeing the words "escape from the trap of the devil" jump off the page at me. I understood the context of the phrase and Gwen's intention in sharing it with me but despite her goal of shaming me into repenting of what she considers a great sin, all I felt was a deep relief. I had already "escaped from the trap of the devil" which had ensnared me for over 40 years into believing I had to pretend to be straight to be loved by God and by fellow human beings. I had discovered I could be honest about my sexual identity and the result was not a feeling of shame but a feeling of freedom, of relief. I had thrown off that yoke of pretense and fear, no longer allowing the devil to have a hold on me, infusing me with fear, shame, and guilt. I told myself that I was finally free to be the person God created me to be. Free to live my life in the way He ordains.

19
MY HEDGE OF PROTECTION

*W*hen I awoke very early the following day, I immediately sat down and wrote to Barbara, sharing my concern about becoming emotional when I taught my last lesson this coming Sunday, the 9th of April, especially knowing the divorce was scheduled for the Tuesday after, at 8:15 in the morning. "Just one more step along this road I'm on." I wrote, ending with, "Know of anyone who'd give me a tranquilizer to use that morning? I'm serious."

To my great surprise, Janie called a while later, and we talked for over an hour and a half. I was so depressed yesterday because she hadn't called, but now I was floating on air. As always, she was very supportive and quite upset that I was leaving the class. She said her husband couldn't believe I had been asked to resign.

After my chat with Janie, I finally received a reply from Barbara to my earlier email, which was full of news and support. Contact your doctor and ask them to prescribe a mild sedative.

I decided to take Barbara's advice and drove to my doctor's office to be worked into his schedule. This meant a two-hour wait. As I sat there, I re-read another letter I'd just received from my brother Tom, whom I'd recently come out to.

Tom, 22 months younger than I, was my playmate as a child, and together, we learned the art of compromise. He'd play dolls with me, and then I'd play "cowboys and Indians" with him. I probably enjoyed "cowboys and Indians" as much, or more, than he did.

I always felt that Tom was more intelligent than I, but because he heard a different drumbeat, his grades weren't as good as mine. As an adult, he was over six feet tall and ruggedly handsome, with a commanding presence. After graduating from college, he began a lifetime of adventure and socially conscious service, including two years in the Peace Corps in Santa Cruz, Bolivia, followed by two years in the Teacher Corps (now known as the "Teach for America Program") in Rio Grande City, Texas. In the late 1960s, he attended the New York Institute of Photography, where his understanding of photography led to his dismissal as a student so they could hire him as an instructor. He and his wife participated in Woodstock in 1969, where he took many freelance photographs that he later sold to The New York Times, Rolling Stone magazine, and the Museum of Modern Art in New York City. At the time of his writing this letter to me, he was living in Culver City, California, amid film industry people, which certainly included gays.

Dear Sister,

Your letter made me smile. I didn't even have to be sitting down to read it because the only part of it that was a big surprise was that you were speaking up and speaking out. Congratulations.

Mom has never talked to me in any depth about you. Back when you roomed with Karen, she said a couple of things that indicated she was worried, and I know she wanted you and Karen to separate. I acted like it was no big deal, even though I secretly thought the two of you were in love. Whatever she thought, she kept it between her and Dad.

I don't have any advice about talking to Mom. Our family (and South Texas culture) was so hung up about sex that even though Mom has become more tolerant, she still has a way to go as far as accepting people without prejudice. Don't let the bottomless pits pull on you. It must be quite a shock to do what you are doing. I don't think I would ever have that kind of nerve. Your confidences are safe with me. I wish you the best.

As always,

Tom

I smiled, then tried to read the mystery novel I'd taken to the doctor's office, but I couldn't concentrate. Thoughts of Janie kept coming to my mind—the kind of thoughts I shouldn't have.

When I was finally called into the examination room and Dr. Morris entered, I quickly told him exactly what I'd been going through. By then, I was fighting the urge to break down and bawl. "I just need something to get me through this next Sunday when I'll be teaching my last Sunday School lesson," I managed to say.

Dr. Morris told me about several available medications, but decided Xanax would be best for me because it takes effect quicker than the others.

That night, I took my first Xanax, and when I awoke the next morning a little after three a.m., I took another one. It worked. I slept until 7:15! Unbelievable.

I rolled over in my mind the advice my brother, Tom, wrote in his letter that I shouldn't talk with Mother unless she heard it from someone else and made the conversation necessary. He and I both knew how she aspired for her children to adhere to society's standards. She would be humiliated to know she had a gay daughter and would attempt to shame me into hiding my sexual orientation again. Tom then encouraged me to learn to have fun, try not to do too much too fast, and be easy on myself. He also advised me to explore the feelings of affection I've bottled up for so long.

Talk to other women who AGREE with you rather than with those who disagree with you. Find a gay and lesbian support group in Tyler, Longview, or Dallas and attend their meetings for a while. Skip church and go elsewhere some weeks. Concentrate on developing one or two close personal friendships. It doesn't mean you'll have sex, but it does mean you'll be putting your time and energy into exploring yourself rather than combating or converting others.

If you were shooting rapids down a canyon river (which, incidentally, you are!), and you could see a huge standing hydraulic turbulence, wouldn't you steer around it rather than into it? And can't you apply that same wisdom socially? The very thought takes me back to hippie days when the question was: Would you rather fight or make love? Which is better for you personally? Which sets a better example for humankind?

It's not your job to lead others, and it's not their job to help you. It's your job to save yourself. The first step in that direction is to get help. Find women who have already been where you are and let them guide you. Tell them your story and then listen to theirs.

Tom then provided numerous websites and phone numbers for organizations such as PFLAG (Parents, Families and Friends of Lesbians and Gays); SPROUTS, a group of women questioning their sexuality; TWIGS, a group of gay women in society, and GLAAD (Gay and Lesbian Alliance Against Defamation); along with Dallas's suicide and crisis center and another Dallas group that promotes the validity of same-sex couples.

"Okay. I've spoken my piece." Tom wrote.

My hunch is that as soon as you find another woman or two with whom you can openly share, the suicidal thoughts and terrible sadness will evaporate, and you will have a chance at the happiness that eluded you while you were trying to live a life molded for you by others.

My love and best wishes go with you, sister.

Tom

I forwarded his words to Barbara, then cried for hours without stopping. Not only did I experience Tom's love and concern, but his wisdom overwhelmed me. He knew exactly what he was talking about. Being a commercial photographer brought him into contact with all kinds of people, and so did his living in Culver City, California. I felt certain he had some close friends who were gay and who felt comfortable in being fully known by him.

Barbara agreed with Tom's advice and encouraged me to follow it and also search for online resources. She mentioned www.truluck.com, which contained Rembert Truluck's story and a ton of Bible commentary. He was gay and a former Baptist preacher who went to Baptist seminaries and taught in a Baptist college. His resume was full of other Christian-based accolades and accomplishments. I enjoyed reading his story. Sadly, he passed away in 2008, and his website no longer exists.

After several days of sadness and depression, during which I agonized about my reply to Tom, I finally wrote back.

Tom,

Just to know that you perceived the love that Karen and I felt for each other overwhelms me. You're right. I never learned how to have fun. Karen and I had fun. But behind that fun was the ever-present awareness that society and parents prohibited our relationship from being permanent. We savored every moment we had together as if it were our last—and sure enough, that day came sooner than we anticipated.

After we separated, fun, joy, friendship, and love went out of my life, and, as you so aptly put it, I began to live a life molded for me by others. I became a shell of a person, a person I eventually came to hate. I spent my life distancing myself from ever forming a close friendship with a female for fear of what might happen to me. And I know now that was a wise decision on my part because I have fallen hopelessly, desperately in love with my friend, Janie, who is heterosexual and has no idea what I feel toward her. It's killing me, and I must get over this. I am in the depths of an emotional turmoil that I have never faced.

Thanks to your suggestion, I have contacted a local chapter of PFLAG and have been given their meeting date, time, and location. I plan to go. It's going to be tough, but I've never had an opportunity to talk with someone who has endured the kind of life I have endured. I need to do this.

I appreciate the references you sent. I've spent my whole life in denial, never even reading about homosexuality. Even now, I've read only two books on the subject. I believed if I ignored the subject, it would go away. Now I know differently.

Dear, dear brother, thank you so much!
Lou Anne

By mid-afternoon, a letter arrived from my daughter, Laura, saying she would soon graduate from Texas Tech University and encouraging me to continue the hard work I had started.

Hey Mom!

I think about you all the time and hope you're doing all right. Just remember that lots of people love and care about you (me being #1). You're doing the right thing, which isn't always easy.

I love you and can't wait till you come to Lubbock before graduation and we can pack up my belongings together!

Laura

Her letter brought a smile, along with a feeling of warm hugs, and bolstered my resolve to face whatever came head-on. I looked forward to helping her move from Lubbock to Austin at the end of May, following her graduation with a degree in Family Financial Planning, and felt equally proud of her accomplishments. We were both graduating from one season of life into another, and I felt that I would ultimately be ok with her support and Tom's wisdom, along with so many others.

After such an encouraging morning, I spent the rest of the afternoon at Mother's and arrived at church in time for the Wednesday evening meal prior to the service. I sat with Barbara, her husband, and two other couples at a table. When I got up to refill my iced tea, Carl Atkins, one of the men seated there about my age, asked me, "How are you liking retirement?"

Without thinking, I laughed at him and said, "That's the funniest question I've heard in a long time," then walked away to fill my glass.

I realized later that Barbara had tried to cover up for my rudeness by saying, "Lou Anne's going through some really tough times right now."

"She made her bed, and now she has to lie in it," was his reply.

During this exchange, the others who had eaten at our table had already left to volunteer with various children's choirs, leaving only

Barbara, Jack (her husband), and Carl. Barbara told me later that Carl's comment upset her husband so much that he outed me to Carl.

Barbara said that Carl took it quite well and seemed sympathetic, but Barbara was upset with her husband for blabbing and told Carl to keep this information confidential—that Jack shouldn't have said anything.

Carl retorted, "I have to tell my wife, of course."

Barbara must have really climbed all over her husband for talking about me, but strangely, it didn't bother me that the truth was being told. I told her not to worry about it and to assure Jack I wasn't upset with him. After all, I figured it would eventually all come out anyway. What was wrong with one more person knowing about it?

When I returned home from church, an email from my brother, Tom, was waiting for me. In it, he urged me to get a substitute to teach my Sunday School class.

You don't owe anyone any explanation. And you don't need anyone else's approval to be who you are. But to do this, you must be beyond the crying state, and you've written that you're still there. Don't fight it. Let it last if it wants to, for it's a process that releases old, blocked emotions. You'll eventually reach the point where your tears turn to smiles and laughter.

Then again, maybe the Xanax will kick the weepiness out of you immediately, and you can handle everything with equilibrium. Personally, I'd opt out of Sunday School ahead of time, let someone else take over, go for a walk in the woods on Sunday morning (if it's not stormy), and let events take their own course.

Now, I've got to quit offering advice. Once again, I congratulate you for being willing to be in touch with all of yourself. At times, I used to wonder what happened to that tough little sister I used to play with— the one who rode pretend wild horses and shot pretend cowboy villains and who often demonstrated that her biceps were bigger than mine. Now I have every confidence that she's survived and will be part of your life again.

More power to you...

Tom

Later, Janie called, and we talked for a refreshing full two hours, until well after midnight. We discussed her plans to travel to Austin the next day, her experience of falling in love almost instantly with her husband, Charles, and her yearnings for time to herself. After finally hanging up, I called Laura, who was still awake, and had apparently been trying to reach me.

"What in the world were you doing on the phone all this time?" she asked after calling and getting the busy signal for longer than she liked.

"Talking with Janie."

"You sound so much better tonight, Mother. I bet it has to do with your conversation with Janie."

"Yes, I'm sure that's the reason. I so enjoy talking with her."

As our conversation continued, I quickly learned why Laura was so desperate to reach me. As it turns out, Jim calls her often to confide his own feelings, and their conversation tonight surprised her. Laura told me, "Gwen Patterson from the Christian Women's Job Corps recently called Dad and kept him on the phone for over an hour. She talked about you, Mom, and how wrong you are in choosing to be gay. 'I'm praying for her,' Gwen told him. She also predicted you would come to your senses and return to Dad because the Bible clearly shows that what you are doing is wrong. Well, apparently, Dad finally got fed up and told her that if she believed everything that was in the Bible, then she'd know that women are never to speak up in church. That ended the conversation."

I was shocked to hear Jim seemed to snap back at Gwen on my behalf and immediately emailed Barbara to tell her everything.

Perhaps change was possible. It certainly was happening within me, so why should I be surprised that Jim or others like him might come around to accept and defend me just as I am? I had spent weeks agonizing over what others thought of me, analyzing every word, noting every intentional glance in the other direction or passive-aggressive comment, and I had almost forgotten how much love surrounded me.

Any intense worry I still felt evaporated the next morning with a final encouraging email from Carolyn, written at one a.m. She said that even though she would be in Waco on Saturday, she planned to attend Sunday School this week, as this would be my last day as their teacher, and she couldn't bear the thought of missing it. I learned after the fact that she had to make an extremely late drive home on Saturday night and was deeply touched. Her actions demonstrated her support and the importance of our friendship.

Sunday would no doubt have its challenges, but it would also have its bright spots, and I chose to look for them as the day drew closer.

20
THE LAST LESSON

*S*unday, despite taking Xanax, I awoke earlier than usual, giving myself plenty of time to shower, wash my hair, get dressed, eat, and review my last Sunday School lesson.

I knew I was in trouble when I felt myself growing on edge and teary as I read passages that spoke personally to me. I practiced reading without thinking, but it didn't work. The tears still came. I was determined, however, to deliver this last lesson. I'd worked hard on it, felt it was well-prepared, and I wanted to teach it. I kept reminding myself to *just read the lesson without trying to ad-lib*. I knew that it would be much safer to keep the tears at bay, and I went over and over it aloud until I felt capable of getting through it with ease.

I attended the eight-thirty a.m. worship service and even then, occasionally fought back tears. The Sunday School lesson was from Luke 13:10-17 and was titled "What's More Important—Rules or People?"

Although this was an assigned topic, it was a very fitting lesson for my situation.

The day's group was larger than usual as I stood at the podium where I had placed my notes. My determination to deliver this final lesson kept me going and made me read more than usual. I remained worried that my emotions would take control of my determination, but I pressed on. I opened by explaining to the class that Jesus was a great teacher because He forced people to think, which angered others, especially the ruler of the synagogue.

As I spoke, I did just fine with the exposition of the Biblical passage, and then I switched gears:

"I began this lesson talking about Jesus being a great teacher, and one of the attributes of a great teacher is the ability to enable the student to find inner direction. A great teacher helps you find your own goal. When you begin marching to a different drummer, those around you no longer determine your goals; instead, you find a new direction from God. Many of us are guilty of "radar living," so our radar is always on, picking up moods. We're other-directed, always trying to fit in and be right with the crowd.

Jesus refused to be other-directed. When he was warned that King Herod was out to get him, he replied that this sly fox would not set his agenda. He will continue to minister for the next three days and beyond, with no change of plan."

I paused here to look up and noticed how attentive everyone was. *Are they waiting for me to slip up?* I reminded myself to have the same resolve as Jesus; *no change of plan, Lou Anne.* I looked back down at my notes.

"It seems to me there are two ways that those who are other-directed can be trapped. They can try to please others or be stubbornly determined to rebel against all suggestions or directions. To be inner-directed means that our inner voice dictates our agenda, that 'still, small voice' of which the Bible speaks in I Kings 19:12.

Robert Louis Stevenson wrote, 'To know what you prefer instead of humbly saying Amen to what the world tells you that you ought to prefer is to have kept your soul alive.' That's what Jesus demonstrates for us toward the end of this chapter in Luke. We have kept our soul alive when we are inner-directed through the voice of the Holy Spirit."

Somewhere in this part of the lesson, my emotions began to surface. My voice started to break, and tears sprang to my eyes. I finally just had to stop. At that point, I explained to the class, "I really thought I could do this, but I'm not certain I can." After hesitating for a moment, I took my notes with me and sat down.

Someone in the class said, "Just give it a few minutes."

I did, but time wasn't helping me gain control.

Janie said, "I'm going to pull my chair over next to Lou Anne. Carolyn, you pull your chair up on the other side, and the rest of you move close. Let's surround Lou Anne and let her know how much we care for her."

Slowly, bodies began to move, and chairs shifted, surrounding me in patient, loving silence until I regained control. Having petite Janie nearly snuggled up on one side, and Carolyn exuding strength on the other, helped calm me as I haltingly continued:

"I'm not going to sit here in front of you and say that the Holy Spirit is directing me to make a change in my life, but I'm also not going to say that it isn't true. Time will tell. I *can* honestly say that I am taking a route in life that's in tune with what Robert Louis Stevenson wrote. In other words, I'm keeping my soul alive by knowing what I prefer in opposition to what the world tells me I ought to prefer.

I'm making some changes in my life, and these changes remind me of a story I recently read in Dr. James C. Denison's daily devotions that illustrates in a very vivid way what seems to be happening to me."

Janie and Carolyn continued to squeeze next to me, doing their best to provide support.

It was Barbara who suggested the devotionals to me earlier in the year, and when I first read the one I used in this lesson, I was so struck by its application to my situation that I printed it out and saved it. The metaphorical story I shared was about planning to "go to France" by plane and, upon landing, realizing you ended up in Germany with an unsympathetic pilot who could do nothing more than ask you to explore and try to enjoy this new destination. I expressed to the group that this was exactly how I'd felt.

"The entirety of my first 60 years of life has been spent preparing to live as a heterosexual wife and mother, abiding by the rules of society, teaching Sunday School classes, and always being an active participant and leader in my church. Despite having packed and planned for this 'trip,' I've unexpectedly found myself on another."

In my mind, "going to France" represented the continuation of who I've always been, but suddenly, I found myself in a different country: a land where I was now living openly gay, and I was sure I'd "packed" all the wrong things. Secretly, at the time, I felt wholly unprepared to live the life of an openly homosexual woman, no longer leading in the same ways I once did in my church.

"My life will be very different from the one I have been leading, and I was prepared to continue leading," I confessed.

Denison's metaphor continues with the pilot showing his unsuspecting traveler around the new destination and saying, "It's beautiful." I explain to the class of ladies, now all leaning in, captivated by the analogy. "I realize that I never knew all of this was here. Germany is wonderful. And quite often, I run into people who are busily coming and going from 'France.' They say, 'It's a wonderful place.' And I say, 'Yes, I know. I was supposed to go there. I had it planned all along. But my pilot had a different journey for me, and my pilot took me to a different place, but it's beautiful, too.'"

The tears came again, so I waited a few minutes before finishing the lesson by saying:

"You see, I'd planned to teach you ladies for several more years. I really enjoy this class and look forward to it each Sunday. I thought this was what I was supposed to do, but now I know that it isn't, and I'm being led in a totally different direction. I'm hoping that someday, I can leave Germany and come back to France, but I don't know if that will ever be possible. So, I'll be stepping down as your teacher after today. You'll have a substitute next week, and I've asked our associate pastor, Wilson Rhodes, to find you a permanent teacher soon. I'll keep reminding him of this need, but you need to keep reminding him also."

Most of the ladies were shocked, as I had only told Janie, Carolyn, and Patsy about my plans to step down. I hung my head, fighting off tears, unsure of what I'd see if I looked at everyone's faces. No one said a word as I continued.

"I read a sermon this past week delivered by a Canadian pastor that may help explain some of the changes taking place in my life. He described two ways I can talk to you. I can speak to you as a group, laying out concepts drawn from scripture, and I hope and pray that you latch onto them and apply them in your own situations. Or I could speak to you individually so that I wouldn't need to talk in generalities. Speaking one-on-one is much riskier than speaking in great sweeping statements.

It involves relationships, trust, and honesty. You can't hide in face-to-face, soul-to-soul communication."

Everyone's attention clung to me as they seemed to hang on to my every word, so I continued.

"I think Jesus knew this all too well. In today's gospel story, in Luke, where our lesson started, Jesus was in the synagogue teaching a bunch of people. Then, suddenly, a woman appears, and Jesus stops teaching to call her over to him. A group message just became personal. That's the way Jesus works best: one-on-one, face-to-face, soul-to-soul. Only then does He have our full attention. And I think the lessons I'll be sharing in the future will be one-on-one instead of group lessons. That seems to be where I am being led."

We ended the class in our usual way, by all standing in a circle, joining hands, bowing our heads, and reciting together, "May the Lord watch between me and thee while we are absent one from the other."

Afterward, each member hugged me and told me how much she loved and appreciated me, until Janie and Carolyn were the only ones left in the room with me.

Once the crowd had dispersed, Carolyn's husband walked in and joined us. All three gave me a pep talk, and Carolyn's husband said, "You shouldn't resign, Lou Anne. You really shouldn't."

"I must. You know I must," I replied.

"No," he said. "I don't think you should. I don't think you should at all."

Janie then joined him by saying, "My husband said he doesn't think she should resign either. He thinks it's just awful she's been asked to quit."

Carolyn and her husband invited me to lunch, but I had no appetite and decided it was best to head home. Carolyn understood and said she'd come by my apartment later that afternoon.

Although their affirmations at the end of class were loving and encouraging, my nerves were taut. I knew I needed to resign, and this was one of those occasions when the longer the issue is drawn out, the more difficult it becomes.

Later in the day, after returning from a walk, my heart soared when I heard Janie's voice on my answering machine.

"Hello, Precious. It's Janie. I'm just calling to say 'hello,' that 'I love you,' and that I've had two calls from Sunday School class members today. One, I think, had no clue as to why you resigned from the position of teaching, and one, I think, knew exactly. The one who knew exactly said, "We're going to Germany together." So anyway, I wanted you to know that everybody loves you and is very distressed that you've left. You wouldn't believe all the positive things class members have said about you. You need to know this. These wonderful and understanding ladies love you. I just wanted to pass that message on to you. I love you, girl. Bye."

Carolyn came over later to visit, and we had a long, frank conversation. Afterward, we went to Paco's for Mexican food, and I amazed her with how much I ate. I enjoy Mexican food almost as much as I enjoy being with Carolyn.

The following day, she left a message on my answering machine.

"I think it is evident that the word is out, and you are officially out of the closet—be that as it may. For the most part, the response has been very caring. I didn't feel that most people were shocked but truly concerned and had lots of questions. I've tried to be very positive. I haven't brought the subject up with anyone, but they all say, 'You do know what's going on, don't you?' I let them tell me. They question whether you left Jim for another person, and I assure them that's not so—that you had to find release from an unbearable situation and live a life you felt was honest. Maybe things won't be as bad as feared. I'm sure you've had calls and questions, too. My prayers are with you on Tuesday morning as you go to court to finalize your divorce. I hope all goes well. If there's anything that I can do, please let me know.

You know my thoughts continue to be with you. You're a very special friend, and I'm proud to say so. Relax, eat, take a few deep breaths, and I'll talk to you soon!"

The thing was done. My last Sunday school lesson was taught, and my fears were again overpowered with compassion.

Stepping down was difficult, but I realized it was the first step out into my own adventure, where my learning and unlearning would truly begin.

21
ADJUSTING TO A NEW NORMAL

*A*fter the success of Sunday's lesson, I got quite courageous and attended a PFLAG (Parents, Families and Friends of Lesbians and Gays) meeting the following evening after handbell practice. I've never forgotten the date of that meeting: Monday evening, April 10, 2000. Driving to the church where PFLAG met took courage, but not as much as it took for me to step out of the car and walk into the beautiful yet modest St. Francis Episcopal Church. I entered the lobby at the rear of the main sanctuary and saw no one. Heard no one.

After peeking into the dimly lit sanctuary to see if anyone was present, I walked down the hallway, looking and listening, trying to determine precisely where PFLAG was meeting. In just a few moments, I heard the muffled sound of talking and located a group of 25 to 30 people sitting in a circle in the church's fellowship hall. With apprehension and an inner voice telling me it would be less stressful to turn around and head back to my car, I realized that everyone seated looked "normal."

I'm not sure what I was expecting but having been indoctrinated with the lie that homosexuals were all destined for hellfire, I guess I expected to see people who looked and acted differently. That's not what I saw at all.

I arrived late because I had sat in my car too long. The meeting had already started, and I hurriedly looked around for an empty chair and spotted one to my left, next to a woman about my age who seemed to be alone.

Despite my anxiety, I looked forward to meeting others like me. I later learned the woman I sat next to was Brenda. She, too, had been married and had divorced her husband of 20 years, raising her two boys on her own. She was attractive with a short haircut like mine and was over 11 years younger than I.

The group was almost evenly divided between adults of all ages, mostly men sitting with men and women with women. I later learned they represented a cross-section of our city in terms of occupations, talent, and economic status. Partners sat comfortably beside each other, and a few were openly affectionate. Those who belonged together were relaxed and at ease in letting others know they were partners, as any heterosexual couple would be.

I'd only seen openly gay couples once before when I attended a Metropolitan Community Church in Lubbock about three months earlier. At that time, my breath was taken away when I walked into the church and saw same-sex couples sitting together, either holding hands or one draping an arm around the other. I'd sat toward the back of that sanctuary with tears in my eyes during the whole service. They were beautiful. I envied their happiness, their sense of ease and relaxation, their freedom to worship together as partners, and their taking communion together with their arms around each other. The whole scenario was more than I could contain. Oh, how I longed to have someone to share my life with.

Following that service in Lubbock, I stayed for a fellowship and met some of the congregation. I was wonderfully ministered to and cared for by numerous warm, loving people. Now, I was seeing the same scenario and experiencing the same type of atmosphere in this PFLAG meeting, which seemed very similar to a church service.

Much of the PFLAG discussion dealt with Christian beliefs and the treatment gays have received from their churches. The speakers confirmed that God truly does love us.

Afterward, we divided into small groups and were invited to share our personal stories. I told mine, mentioning that my divorce was to be finalized the following morning. When I said I'd been married for thirty-seven years, everyone was amazed I'd stayed that long. I was an oddity in their eyes. Most of them had been married at one time or another and had children from those marriages, but their relationships had ended much sooner.

Some told stories which were heartbreaking, especially those who lost their children simply because they were gay. I had always feared this might happen to me, and was thankful my children were now grown.

By the time the meeting ended, I had relaxed, made new friends, and was looking forward to the next meeting, confident that PFLAG was a good place for me to be.

The next day, Tuesday, April 11th, I awoke earlier than usual to the reminder that my divorce was to be finalized that day. Heading to my computer, I updated Barbara about the people in my class who knew about me and told her about attending the PFLAG meeting. On that subject, I explained that they were "A great group of people" and expressed my surprise at all the talk about religion and God, as well as my heartache that so many felt ostracized from their churches.

Our lawyer was just walking in when I arrived at the courthouse that morning, so I joined him. Jim was already there. Since we had been able to work everything out on our own, we used the same lawyer and split the cost. We signed the necessary papers and then appeared before the judge.

The procedure was cut and dried. He asked for my name, whether I had lived in Smith County for a certain amount of time, and the same question about the state of Texas: did I feel that our differences could not be worked out? Did we have any children under the age of eighteen or any expected? Had we agreed on the financial division of property, and so on? The judge asked Jim only three or four questions and allowed him to say whatever he wanted or contest anything. He chose not to speak, so the divorce was finalized in just a few minutes. Barbara had offered to come with me, but I was glad I'd turned her down. Everything went very smoothly and quickly.

After we left the courthouse, Jim said he had parked in our church's parking lot, about three blocks away, so I asked, "Would you like a ride to your car?"

He readily accepted, and I drove him there. After parking next to his car, he took my hand and said, "I wish it had never come to this."

"I wish it hadn't either," I said.

"I still love you, but I hope we can find someone else to be happy with."

"I hope so, too. I really appreciate how nice you've been. You could have made it rough on me."

"I never wanted to do that." He said, beginning to cry. He quickly exited my car. I drove away with a heavy heart, knowing his pain would be my only regret. I was free—out in the light—and would never hide again.

The next day, I awoke feeling terribly sad. An old friend who'd recently outed himself to me wrote to let me know about a gay-oriented church in our community. St. Gabriel's, located south of Tyler, had a congregation of about 100 warm, friendly members and held an Episcopalian-style service. The pastor was a gay woman, and most of the congregation was female.

He warned that I might not feel at home there since I was a Baptist, but he said I could meet some like-minded people and would probably enjoy discussing the pastor's interpretation of the issues in Leviticus.

"If you want to attend the church," he wrote, "I'll attempt to leave my church (St. Mattress *grin) and go with you. It's been several years since I've been there, so most won't know me."

I laughed out loud and replied with thanks. I needed that laugh more than anything else that day. Despite the fun invitation, I explained I planned to stick with my church and the people who knew me. I'd made the decision weeks ago to embrace my situation as an opportunity to live unashamedly as a gay Christian and let others see what that looks like.

At the time, I reasoned that members of the church would have a chance to understand better and hopefully accept homosexuality, as I served as a good example. I foresaw a mutual coming together, acceptance, and understanding of the truth, and being part of this new experience excited me.

Just as I thought the worst of my struggles were over, later in the week, one of my Sunday school class members contacted Patsy, our class president, with concerns about me. Patsy took that opportunity to share "what was troubling her," and our pastor's request that I no longer teach.

That classmate then wrote to me, explaining she and Patsy agreed to pray for me and that she was sorry I was having a difficult time. She said she didn't understand and knew others could be cruel, but the women in my class all sympathized with me, and she would always be willing to talk to me.

"Even if we hold different viewpoints, we can still be friends and agree to disagree," she wrote. "Know that I still love you as a sister in Christ, just as I always did."

Another friend from church, with whom I'd recently had a long conversation, called me at least five times that day, concerned about me and seemingly fearful that I might commit suicide. I understood why she was worried, as I had been crying almost constantly after recently sharing my story with her. (These were still the sad days when I woke feeling depressed and ready to cry at the slightest little thing, but messages like these made me feel encircled by love.) I felt fortunate to have so much support from members of my church.

About a week later, I drove to the Austin area to visit Linda, my cousin from North Carolina, who was visiting her son and his family. She's almost two years older than I am, and as children, we spent a lot of time together.

Her dad was four years older than my dad, and they looked very much alike, even up to their bald heads. Whenever we visited them on a Sunday and went to church with them, these two brothers would be invited to sing a duet in the church service. Their voices blended beautifully, and I loved to hear them sing.

As Linda and I talked one evening, the subject turned to children, their behaviors, and whether those behaviors were learned or innate.

With three children of her own and a lifetime of experience caring for the children of others, Linda stated, "I believe people are just born a certain way and that not all behavior is learned." As she pursued this line of thought, she told me her son-in-law's brother had died of AIDS.

"I'm firmly convinced this young man couldn't help the fact that he was gay," she said.

"I totally agree with you," I replied. "I'm the same way."

Without responding verbally to my confession, she raised an eyebrow with a questioning look on her face.

"Yes, I'm gay."

She and I had no opportunity to talk until the next evening when we went for a walk, but before we reentered her son's home, I asked, "Would you like to talk about my being gay? If you don't, I certainly understand."

"Yes, I would," she replied, so we remained outside as I told her my story. Although tears came to my eyes a few times, I never actually cried, which convinced me I was making emotional progress. Linda was very kind and receptive, which amazed me because she's been a Southern Baptist all her life, and her parents were very strict. Once, when we were children and playing a card game in her living room, her mother rushed in, saying, "Put those cards away! Hurry! Put those cards up! The preacher's walking up the sidewalk. I don't want him to see those cards!"

We quickly did as she asked, and I found the incident rather odd. My parents played cards often, especially Canasta, so I'd never been taught that playing card games was of the devil, but Linda was brought up in a much more conservative atmosphere.

Later, as she and I headed to our separate bedrooms, I handed her copies of Jim's letter in which he wanted to know why I wanted the divorce, my reply to him in which I came out, and my pastor's letter to me. The next morning, when she returned them to me, she simply thanked me for sharing. I was disappointed she made no comment as I yearned for her to ask questions and show interest in my life and who I was, but I suppose she was reluctant to discuss the subject. Despite her belief that people didn't choose to be homosexual, I felt her religious background held her back from discussing such a forbidden subject.

The following Wednesday evening, when I attended the church supper and prayer meeting, I sat at a table that included Carl Atkins, the fellow I'd been so catty and rude to three weeks earlier. Thank goodness he spoke to me in a friendly manner and carried on a short conversation with me. I thought perhaps he'd forgiven my rude words, for which I was glad.

Several older women approached me to compliment me on my handbell playing at the evening service. "How in the world do you play two bells in each hand?" they asked. I laughed and said something about it taking a lot of practice.

I was pleased that members had a good impression of me, as it confirmed that my attempts at changing their perceptions of homosexuals may be working. Barbara also sat at the supper table with me and, in a private moment, said, "Mary Lou Reynolds approached Georgia Hunt (two church members about our age) asking if what she'd heard about you was true. Georgia told her it was. If Mary Lou's heard about it, you can assume everyone in that class knows or soon will."

The class she referred to comprised more than fifty women about my age. Their monthly class meeting was the next night, and I was invited as an associate member (meaning that while I taught a class, I couldn't attend theirs, but as a member of their age group, I'm always invited to class socials). Hearing Barbara's news caused me to lose courage and have cold feet about attending. Upon returning home from church, I wrote to Barbara.

Barbara,

When I invited Nancy Grayson, who doesn't drive at night, to ride with me to tomorrow night's party, I didn't realize everyone would probably know about me. Do you think that she might prefer not to walk in with me? Would you mind checking and seeing, because I would certainly understand. I'm reaching the point where I feel I'm doing a friend a disservice by just the two of us being together for fear others might say something about her. In fact, I've thought many times I may be soiling your reputation by sitting beside you as much as I do. I'm starting to feel that old pull toward going back and being the loner that I used to be.

Lou Anne

Barbara replied the next day.

Lou Anne,

Just talked to Nancy. She says you're friends because she thinks you're a terrific person, and she doesn't care how many people know that. She just likes you. Both of us are enjoying a new freedom (for lack of a better word) in our friendship with you now that you aren't a committed loner anymore. We'd greatly prefer that you not crawl back in that hole. I can't imagine that being seen with you would damage my reputation in any way. (What does that generally is my shooting off my big mouth!)

Barbara

I attended the party, gave Nancy a ride, and enjoyed eating, visiting, and playing games. I was glad I went.

Though I knew I was "out" to many in this group, I had no idea how many. Consequently, I felt somewhat nervous when I walked in and immediately looked around for Barbara but didn't see her. I admit I wanted to use her as a crutch. I realized later she was in another room of this huge home. When we began gathering for fellowship and games, Barbara spotted me, came over, and gave me a hug.

Upon returning home, I wrote to her that more than one pair of eyes kept watching us when she greeted and visited with me. And that wasn't my imagination working overtime. "You are hurting your reputation by being so friendly to me," I warned. "Perhaps we shouldn't sit together when we're around others. We don't need to raise eyebrows and instigate questions that should never be raised."

When she didn't respond to this email, I eventually cornered her about it. She said she'd asked her husband if he'd noticed anything, and he said he didn't. She then asked another friend if she'd spotted anything, and the friend seemed amazed that Barbara had even asked such a question.

"After that, I decided not to poll the whole department!"

I loved the way Barbara made me laugh at myself so often and urged me not to take my day-to-day concerns so seriously. I hoped I would soon find a way to live as relaxed and carefree with myself as she was, and as I had seen those gay couples at PFLAG. Would I ever truly be one of them?

22
PROBLEMS & POSSIBILITIES

*J*anie came by my apartment that Saturday to drive me to a wedding shower. Just when I thought I'd finally begun to control my emotions, I took one look at her, and all those resolutions disappeared. My feelings swamped my logic, leaving me nauseated. I desired her beyond words, and I was thankful that she seemed to enjoy having me as a friend. Surely, I'd never do anything so foolish that she wouldn't want me around anymore, but that fear of making a fool of myself kept me alert whenever she was near.

The next day, on Sunday, April 30, 2000, as soon as I returned home from church, I turned on CNN's live broadcast of the Gay Rights Rally in Washington, D.C. This was the first one I'd ever watched, and it impressed me. The speakers were neatly dressed, well-groomed, and spoke intelligently. I'm not sure why I was afraid it might be otherwise, except that I was as misinformed about gays as everyone else was within the circles I grew up in.

When the cameras zoomed in on same-sex couples openly showing affection for each other (a hand on a shoulder, two partners back-to-back, slowly moving rhythmically together to music, some with arms loosely around each other), tears sprang to my eyes. How I envied these couples. I had lived unaware of this world—so far away from it—yet deep inside, I'd always yearned to be a part of it.

I spent the afternoon watching the broadcast and occasionally wrote down statements made by the speakers. I loved what the mother of two gay children said: "Having a gay child is the ultimate test of unconditional love."

I continued to fantasize about Janie, and it was driving me nuts. I knew it was wrong, yet the forbidden enjoyment attached to it didn't stop my thoughts.

Several days later, on May 4, Janie called. "Lou Anne," she said, "Wilson Rhodes (the church's Associate Pastor in charge of Sunday School) phoned me to ask if I would substitute as a teacher for our Sunday School class. We ended up having a very long conversation, and I told him that it amazed me how everyone could respect you as an outstanding Christian one hour, and then the next, after you were honest, no longer thought of you in the same way."

As I listened to her, I thought immediately of the scripture in John 8:32 that proclaimed, "...the truth will set you free," but I knew that the freedom it referred to was only an inward feeling. I was finally and truly free in that respect. It was a wonderful state to be in, but the irony of being open and honest about my sexual orientation meant it placed me in a different kind of bondage to the prejudices of others.

Janie repeated how she'd told Wilson I was the very best Sunday School teacher she'd ever had, that everyone in the class loved me and wanted me to remain as their teacher, and that if he considered me unworthy to teach, then everyone in the church was unfit because she considered me one of the best Christians she'd ever known. She praised me up one side and down the other and said Wilson admitted he'd heard I was a good teacher.

She also told him that I was so good that I even advised her not to sit beside me because people might think things about her that weren't true. "Wilson," she said, "I plan to continue to sit by Lou Anne. I have a very good marriage of thirty-three years, and I love my husband, Charles. You need to know that Lou Anne is not hitting on any of the class members," she informed him.

Her words shocked me. "Did you really say that to him?"

"Yes, I did. That, and more."

"Did you use the term *'hitting on?'*"

"I did! I thought he ought to know you aren't doing something like that."

That idea had never occurred to me. Could anyone ever think I was that type of person? I wasn't even confident I knew what "hitting on someone" meant, but I assumed it implied making some type of sexual overture or suggestion.

I'd never had any desire to hit on anyone! In all those years since Karen and I parted, I'd never desired a particular woman other than my present infatuation with Janie, probably because I'd denied myself any close friendships over the years.

Now that a desire for Janie consumed me, I found many other emotions lingering over the years, peeking out from their hiding places. My heart was warming up, and I was learning to care for others in new ways. But these new feelings were scary. I felt unstable, almost dizzy, in that I wasn't sure which way I needed to lean. I wanted to care for others, a key characteristic of Christian virtue. Caring could also expose my heart to painful experiences such as hurt, heartbreak, anguish, and torment. I sincerely wondered if it was worth it. Wouldn't I be better off not feeling anything at all? Undeniably, yes, I would, but as all these thoughts flooded my mind, Janie repeatedly told me things like, "Lou Anne, you're such a good person. I've never heard a bad word come out of your mouth."

Wanting to change the subject, I told her that Patsy, our class president, was ill and that I'd taken supper to her last night. "See," she said, "that's what I mean! You're such a good person!"

Again, wanting to change the subject, I said, "Speaking of our class, I can't decide whether to join you on Sundays. If you have a substitute, I'm afraid I might make her uncomfortable, and I don't want to do that."

"That's what I mean, Lou Anne! You're just too good! You should certainly continue to come to our class. You won't make anyone feel uncomfortable," she said.

I felt like Janie had me on a pedestal I didn't deserve. When she'd decided to tell me about Wilson's phone call, she'd said, "I don't want us to have any secrets from each other."

She was so right, yet I continued to hide my feelings toward her. It would be a terrible mistake to tell her how much I was in love with her, but I also supposed I should tell her the truth. However, just writing down these thoughts made me nauseous, so I had to think about something else.

Janie told me she had called our departmental director to see if she had talked to Wilson about replacing me. She hadn't.

"Does she know about me?" I asked Janie.

"Yes, Precious, she knows. And she also told me that quite a few in our department would not be accepting of you and what you are. She told me she could easily name several of them."

I immediately thought, *All the more reason to remain in that department, to be an example of a gay Christian.*

Sundays continued to be decision days. Which class should I attend: my old class or Barbara's? I was constantly being pulled from both sides, with Janie encouraging me to stay put and Barbara repeatedly telling me to stay away from my old class. She was always writing me to that effect.

Lou Anne,

Please consider not attending your class for a while, and I mean a minimum of three to six months. The people in that class who aren't comfortable with your situation can't express themselves freely so long as you're there, and they need to. Discussing it among themselves will work in your favor more strongly than your continued presence in the class and department will. Your feelings are involved in something stronger than a teacher-class relationship there, and this emotional pull creates a temptation and risk that could harm you permanently, not to mention the danger to your cause and the church body as a whole.

-Barbara

Barbara's letter halfway angered me. Her advice to stay away from my class for three to six months seemed unreasonable. That's a long time. Her letter also scared me as she pointed out how my feelings for Janie might become evident to others in the class. I certainly didn't want anyone to become aware of my "unnatural affection" (as they would see it) for a classmate. That would be the worst thing that could happen, so I gave Barbara's suggestion serious consideration. Looking back now, I'm glad I did. Even though I didn't appreciate her advice at the time, I realize now that she was thinking only of me and what would be best for me. This wonderful friend, whom I now think of as "saving my life," died a painful death due to cancer in 2006, and I so wish she were still here for me to visit.

I confided to Barbara then that I was in a hopeless situation regarding Janie. "I'm constantly torn between wanting two different things that are completely incompatible."

I had recently heard a statistic that a person in love thinks of their partner up to 85 percent of the time, and I could certainly relate to that statistic, although I felt I was making progress. After all, I'd been in love with Janie for more than eight months. It was time to shake off my addiction, and, like an alcoholic, I was taking it just one day at a time. Sometimes, even an hour at a time. But I was convinced I could do it. It was this sense of determination that I shared with Barbara.

"At times, I think I'm much improved, and then at other times, I feel I'm reaching a very dangerous crossroads."

This truth scared me and kept me in knots around Janie. Several times, I'd come close to doing something that would have been so normal for me, like offering comfort to her in the form of a gentle touch or a holding of hands, but I stopped myself, keenly aware that others might sense how I felt toward her. Each time, my brain would kick in at the last minute, and logic would take over, leaving me shaking when I realized what a close call I'd experienced. Forty years earlier, my love for Karen prompted me to edit my life, pretending she was just a friend when, at that time, she was everything to me. Now, I was in a very similar situation, having to pretend Janie was simply a friend when she was everything to me.

Past our usual bedtimes, Barbara and I continued to write back and forth about such things. She told me I was too close to my situation and that it was risky. I took that to mean that I was too emotionally invested in Janie to realize how my facial expressions, body language, and words might reveal how I truly felt about her, and she was right. I could ruin myself and my reputation if it became known I was in love with a married woman in my Sunday School class. I would no longer be seen as a "good Christian" and become useless in the cause I was determined to support.

This feeling of having a mission came to me long before I asked Jim for a divorce. I think of it as a type of backlash against fundamentalist preachers who demeaned gays by calling homosexuals an abomination and accusing gays of choosing to be gay, telling them all they needed to do was to "pray away the gay." That's simply not true. You can't pray away the gay. All you can do is pray for strength to keep pretending to be straight, which never ends well.

I attended my second PFLAG meeting and thoroughly enjoyed it. The attendees talked about their partners or their loves. I enjoyed their laughter, humor, friendliness, and openness in living out their Christian faith.

That night, all those who had attended the Millennium March in Washington, D.C., reported on their experiences, sharing many positives, such as the fact that the people who attended looked so "normal." Members of the queer community are often ostracized because the media (as all media does) creates shortcuts to simplify stories and the concept of identity by suggesting it can only look, act, and be a certain way to qualify. This is why, despite the majority of the Millennium March attendees looking like any other person you'd sit next to in church, work beside in the office, or live next door to, CNN chose to interview only the most eye-catching, loud, and proud group of queens sure to make conservative skin crawl. According to the reports we heard at the meeting, all the participants (bold and beautiful or relaxed and down-to-earth) were friendly, kind, thoughtful, and considerate toward each other, and they made a good impression on the citizenry who encountered them.

Our local participants carried signs that read, "G O P (Guilty of Prejudice)," "I Love My Gay Son Unconditionally," and "Focus on Your

Own Family." One of the members, who carried two of these signs held back to back, said that many people came up to her to ask if they could take their picture beside her. One fellow wanted his picture taken by the 'Unconditionally' sign so he could send it to his mother as a Mother's Day gift. She hadn't contacted him for seven years. Obviously, she didn't love him unconditionally, and her rejection devastated him. Still, this sign was a way to demonstrate that this kind of love for her son was possible and did exist.

The following afternoon, I visited with Barbara for two hours. When I was ready to leave, she sent me home with a loaf of homemade bread which became my supper; I smothered the thick slices with butter and fig preserves feeling full in body and in spirit.

During our visit, Barbara alluded to a conversation she'd had about me with a male friend who thought I should talk to a psychologist to determine if I really was gay. "What did you say to him?" I asked, bewildered.

I asked him, "You mean just like you did when you were a teenager and realized you liked girls?"

I loved Barbara's snide remark, which forced him to reconsider his misguided suggestion. I would have never had Barbara's kind of nerve at that time in my life, but I've now found it! I thought, *Go, Barbara, Go!* She had given the perfect reply, and I was so proud of her. What a friend!

Even though she knew I didn't need a counselor to tell me I was gay, she continued to urge me to find a counselor to help me deal with the tremendous emotional upheavals I was still experiencing; however, I knew no counselors. None of my family had ever used a counselor, so I had no idea who to contact or how to choose one who was "gay-friendly." I certainly didn't need a Christian counselor who would urge me to "pray away the gay" and "turn back to God."

Then I thought about Brenda, the woman I had met at PFLAG, who had told me *she* was a counselor. She and I had gravitated toward each other at the meetings—not only had we sat next to each other at both the meetings I had attended, but we participated in the same small group when we divided up. She was kind, and I felt safe with her nearby. When the May 8 monthly PFLAG meeting ended, we shared email addresses at her suggestion.

Although I had yet to send her an email, I was surprised when I received one from her two weeks later telling me she had just returned from a camping and canoeing trip to the Buffalo National River in Arkansas. I replied to her the following day:

I envy you your trip! Sounds wonderful. I've been wanting to ask you a little more about what you do. One of my friends from church has been almost demanding that I find a counselor. I'm really doing much better, but I still fight some heavy emotional battles. That's probably to be expected, considering the drastic turn my life has taken. But maybe we could get together someday. I'm finally able to talk without a box of tissues close at hand.

She replied almost immediately, which, for some reason, surprised me. I knew she was working regularly and had assumed I might not hear from her for a day or two. She explained:

The counseling I do these days is more of a ministry than an occupation. I'm trained in psychology (master's level) and biblical counseling and certified as a pastoral counselor. I simply sit with folks, listen, and share whatever the Spirit lays on my heart. I'd be happy to sit with you sometime if you want. Tissues aren't an issue. I've gone through cases of them myself!
Take care,
Brenda.

I was intrigued by her reply because I had never had an opportunity to share what had gone on in my life with another gay person. I eagerly wrote back, sharing with her Jim's and my letters to each other before telling her I looked forward to visiting with her.

I reminded myself that Barbara was leaving for Italy the next afternoon and would be gone for three weeks, while Janie would be leaving on a 10-day trip to the Northeast in just a couple of days. Just knowing they wouldn't be available made me feel nervous and lonely. Brenda's emails were a godsend, and I wondered if I was about to make my first gay friend.

23
COUCH CONFESSIONS

When Janie returned from visiting her sister in Austin, she sent me an email, which is unusual. She usually just calls, but she wanted me to know she was back in town and that she would soon be leaving on another trip to the Northeast.

I telephoned her, and she excitedly told me,

"I got to hear Rabbi Harold Kushner speak. Lou Anne, I know you have heard of him. He is the author of *When Bad Things Happen to Good People.* He talked about his newest book, which I had purchased, titled *"How Good Do We Have to Be?"* I want you to read this little book, Precious. It talks about how we can learn to accept ourselves, knowing we aren't perfect. The book isn't very long. In it, he gives us a new understanding of shame, guilt, and forgiveness. It's such a good book. I'll loan it to you the next time we see each other."

We visited on the phone for well over an hour before I attended my weekly Bible study. I was eager to read the little book she mentioned, as I knew I was wrapped up in feelings of guilt and shame surrounding my gayness, divorcing Jim, and feeling as though I was depriving my children of a home with both parents.

Knowing Janie would be leaving in a few days, I decided to call her again to tell her I'd like to bring some papers over for her to read about the Biblical interpretations of homosexuality, since Janie had a gay son. Also, I wanted to have an opportunity to pick up the Kushner book she mentioned. The visit was going along fine until Janie asked, "How are you doing, Lou Anne?"

"I'm still experiencing a lot of pain, Janie. Climbing back into my hole looks very inviting."

Janie asked, "What's causing your pain?"

"I can't talk about it."

"Yes, you can. Tell me."

I became quiet, afraid that one small sound or movement might reveal the truth. When I was confident the words had been held back, I simply repeated, "I can't talk to you about it."

"I know what's causing it," she stated. "I've known for a long time, and it's time we talked about it."

I stood up, grabbed my purse, and said, "I need to go. I can't stay any longer."

"You've got to stay and get this out in the open," she insisted. "You're in love with me, aren't you?"

My heart stopped. How did she know? I'd been so careful. What did I do that somehow revealed my infatuation with her?

At her revelation, I felt weak all over: deflated, like a balloon. My mind emptied as I sat back down on the sofa, placing my purse on the floor. I didn't want to think of anything. I bent over, holding my head to my knees as I wrapped my arms around my lower legs. Then I began to wail, "Don't, don't, don't, please don't."

My most private secret was being brought out into the open, and I felt as if I were drowning. I wasn't sure I even wanted to take another breath. I was so ashamed and embarrassed about my feelings for Janie. To think that she was aware of my love for her was something I was having difficulty comprehending. All the time I was trying to conceal my crush on her, she already knew. *What a foolish person I had been.*

Janie began to rub my back as I stayed hidden, my face in my lap, hugging my knees like a child. I was shutting everything out of my mind, vaguely hearing Janie say, "Oh, Lou Anne. I've known about this for a long, long time. I'm just not inclined that way. I can't be in love with you like that."

"I know. I know." I gasped between sobs, "I've always known."

"I feel honored that you feel this way about me," she said. "You're such a wonderful person—so brilliant—but look at who you've fallen in love with. You're seeing me through rose-colored glasses."

Straightening up and turning toward her, I saw Janie's face full of loving kindness, gentleness, and compassion, and I was stunned that it was directed at me. My heart made a joyful leap as I replied, "Janie, I have never seen you through rose-colored glasses." With a bit of a smile, I declared with all the sincerity I could muster, "But you see me that way. You think I'm brilliant, but I'm not at all."

"Lou Anne, what are we going to do? We've got to decide."

"I thought you'd never want to see me again once you found out how I feel about you."

"That's not true. You're my friend." She smiled, "I talk with you about things I don't discuss with anyone else. But if being with me brings you pain, we shouldn't be spending time together anymore."

At that point, I stood up and paced the room, first toward the door, then over to a front window, where I briefly leaned my head against the glass. As I walked back to the sofa where she was still sitting, I laughed and shared, "I do feel a certain amount of relief in getting this out in the open." And I did. A tremendous burden had just been lifted off my shoulders, only to be replaced with shame and embarrassment. *How could she stand to be around me?*

"I know how painful love is, Precious. I've been there." Janie then confided in me her experience along this line.

Then it was my turn to admit, "The despair isn't as great when I'm with you, Janie. I want to be your friend, but I can't believe you'd want me anywhere near you."

Janie took a deep breath. "You have to realize how long I've been aware of your feelings for me, yet we've continued to be friends all that time."

"How long have you known?"

"Since October of last year."

It was now May 31st. I sat stunned, unaware of the tears still clinging to my cheeks.

"You mean you've known I was in love with you for almost eight months?" Wondering what I had done wrong to give myself away, I asked, "How did you know? What did I do?"

"I just knew," she explained. "I sensed it. It wasn't any one thing."

I've been such a fool, I thought, as I worried about what this could mean to Janie's well-being and her reputation. The two of us enjoy sitting together in our Sunday School class; we sit together at various social functions, and those who know us are aware we are good friends. Instinctively, I warned her, "Janie, I don't want anyone to link your name to mine. I don't want you to be hurt by being friends with me. Now that I am admitting I am gay, others will assume you and I have that type of relationship."

"You're right. They already are!" Janie exclaimed, exasperated.

"What do you mean?" I asked in a panic.

"Don't kid yourself. People already think things like that, but it doesn't bother me. If someone were to come up to me and say something, I'd just quit going to church."

Her statement shocked me. I never expected her to say or think such a thing.

I knew she mustn't quit the church. Her statement hit me like a bombshell. Not only would I be the cause of a family leaving the church, but I could conceivably be the cause of discord throughout the church because she probably wouldn't go quietly. I'd only ever seen Janie this feisty—so willing to take on the world— one other time, and that was back in August when we had our first real conversation, and she admitted that her son was gay, that he was loved by God, and deserved the love of others. Now, she was boldly advocating for me in the same way, not just by saying these truths but by living them.

Concerned that she might follow through with her threat, I quickly explained, "That's the wrong thing to do, Janie. That would convince them that what they said, or thought, was true."

Calming down, she replied, "I hadn't thought about that, but you're probably right." I saw Janie wilt a little before my eyes. She probably thought that leaving the church would be a sign of defiance. If anyone should leave the church, I felt it should be me. If a choice had to be made, I was convinced the church would much prefer I go than to lose Janie and her husband.

"You have so much courage," she continued, "and I don't."

I knew she was thinking that leaving the church would be seen as a sign of weakness, a way to hide your face from those who consider you sinful, whereas staying and facing "your enemy" was courageous in her eyes. She was just caught up in the moment, thinking that my being open about my sexuality was more daring than her support of me, but both were bold moves.

"Who else knows about this?" she asked.

"Barbara. She guessed it."

"Laura knows, doesn't she?"

I was stunned that she even thought I had told my 21-year-old daughter that I was in love with a married woman. I quickly said, "Oh, no! I haven't told her. I haven't told anyone."

"Laura's bound to know."

"I certainly hope not," I said.

"Why does that bother you?"

"I just don't want my daughter to know how weak her mother is."

She gently rubbed my forearm in reassurance. Her touch sent electricity through me, and it felt divine. It was what I'd always dreamed of. Her soft, gentle, loving touch felt better than anything I had imagined. *Don't move*, I told myself, wanting to prolong that moment as long as possible.

Then she said, "Oh, I just don't know what to say." She continued, "Tell me what to do. Did I cause this?"

"No, you had nothing to do with how I feel," I reassured her.

"This happened a long time ago, didn't it?"

"Yes, nine months ago, back in August,"

A patient silence filled the room, and then I said, "I'm too old for this, Janie. I'm feeling things that teenagers feel."

"It's because you didn't have an opportunity to date normally."

"You're right." I agreed. "I'm totally inexperienced."

After another pause, Janie named friends who regularly travel together for a week or two every summer, while their husbands stay behind. "Do you think everyone assumes they are a gay couple? No." Janie continued, "No one thinks anything about it," she said. "And my good friend, Lisa, and I used to walk down the street together and into stores together holding hands so that most people won't think things about you and me."

"Oh, but they will because I'll be labeled as gay, and whoever I'm with will have that label attached to them."

"Well, it just doesn't bother me, Lou Anne. You've got to promise me you'll contact the woman from PFLAG and talk with her. Don't you want to?"

I stopped to consider her question. I'd never been one to ask for help, always thinking I should do everything myself, and had always equated seeing a counselor as a sign of weakness. That fact, plus the dread I felt in admitting to a stranger that I had fallen in love with a married woman, made me hold back from seeing anyone. Then, I recalled my visit with Dr. Kerns in Lubbock. He had been very kind, and I had nothing but positive thoughts about that visit, so I answered, "Yes, a part of me does."

"I think she's reaching out to you in kindness, and you need to be willing to talk with her. If something develops between the two of you, that would be great, but you've got to open yourself up to new relationships. You really need to find someone to be with. You've got a lot of years left, and you don't want to spend them all alone."

My heart was still so wrapped up in Janie that I couldn't imagine wanting to be with anyone else. *Surely, she realized what I thought.* Still, I promised to contact Brenda.

As Janie walked me out to my car, I could tell she was undecided about giving me the usual hug. By keeping a lot of distance between us, I let her know it wasn't at all necessary, and she almost took me up on it, but at the last minute, she said, "Oh, give me a hug, Lou Anne." And I did. Her arms around me always felt so good.

As we said goodbye, Janie said, "Call me Lou Anne. I want you to call me."

"You just don't know what a game I play with myself as to how long I can go without phoning you."

"You can phone me every day if you like. That'd be just fine. If you don't, I'll be calling you! I love you!"

"I love you, too."

I drove away, marveling at what a turn my life had taken. I was amazed and overwhelmed that my most private secret was now out in the open to Janie. *How foolish to assume she wasn't aware of my feelings for her. How dumb I was!* Though I could finally laugh a little at the thought, I still feared how many others could see the truth. I hated even thinking about it, but I worried more about my future meeting with Brenda. It would be the first time I ever spoke openly with another gay woman.

When the phone rang early the next morning, I knew it had to be Janie. No one else had called me so early. She told me she had written two long emails to me and lost them. She was thoroughly disgusted with her lack of computer skills, and I was terribly disappointed, to the point of feeling sick, not being able to read those letters. I wanted to know so badly what she had said.

After a few minutes of laughing about the emails and discussing how she had known I was in love with her, I said, "Janie, do you think love has to come from God?"

"Yes, I do. It can't come from the devil. I don't even believe lust comes from the devil. If it weren't for lust, we wouldn't have procreation."

"Janie, you're different," I said, as we laughed.

"Yes, I am, Precious."

My heart soared every time she used that pet name for me. Years later, at her memorial service in 2024, I learned that she used that pet name for many people, not just me. Even after all those years, my heart sank a little at the thought.

"I just wish I could get over this, and it wouldn't last much longer," I confessed.

"Well, sometimes it can take a long, long time."

"That doesn't give me much hope!"

"You need to meet someone you can have as a partner, to share life with. I really want that for you. Right now, you're in some kind of adolescent stage, going through things you should have experienced long ago."

Wanting to change the subject, I said, "Janie, I know you and your husband, Charles, tell each other everything, but I'd feel very uncomfortable if he knew I'd fallen in love with you."

"I haven't told him, Precious. This is just between the two of us."

Toward the end of our conversation, Janie said, "You have to promise me that if our friendship brings you too much pain, you'll tell me."

"I promise."

After we hung up, I began thinking about a Ted Loder meditation that reads, "Expose my shame where it shivers, crouched behind the curtains of propriety, until I can laugh at last through my common frailties and failures, laugh my way toward becoming whole."

My hidden shame of falling in love with Janie was fully exposed, and I found I'd lost my appetite again and didn't sleep much. Instead, I spent my time thinking, thinking, thinking of Janie's knowledge that I was in love with her. Over and over, I heard Janie's confession ringing in my brain, "I know the source of your pain, Lou Anne. I've known it for a long, long time."

This new setback had thrown me. *Was I that transparent?* I was amazed that the thoughts of suicide hadn't started entering my mind regularly, triggered by this intense feeling of exposure. *Could I continue to look her in the eye? Could I keep my thoughts about Janie at bay while feeling this vulnerable?*

My well-ordered, well-structured life was still crumbling, and what I was left with was the shell of a person I wasn't even certain I knew. It felt as though there'd been a death in my family, and it had been *me*. I was gone.

Why had I fallen in love with Janie? How many times had I asked myself that question? *Why Janie?* Then again, who else?

I had no friends, just acquaintances, and that's all Janie was—an acquaintance—a member of the Sunday School class I taught. But I saw something special in her, something different. She was kind, loving, and tenderhearted toward all people, even those like me. I fell in love with Janie because she was a good person, someone I enjoyed being around, someone who lifted my spirits, and someone with whom I could talk openly, precisely as it was with Karen.

When I allowed myself the freedom to dream, to fantasize about Janie, I felt bodily reactions—a hollowness within me followed by a type of constriction in my chest, and then this pain. I had to get over it.

Soon after lunch, I emailed Janie and reassured her that she had done nothing she shouldn't have done. I told her I didn't think I had done anything I shouldn't have, but admitted I still felt ashamed, embarrassed, and humiliated, and pondered constantly what was happening to me.

Was what I was going through truly a part of God's plan for my life, or was the devil having a field day tormenting me?

I found myself drawn more to that second thought.

I already anticipated how Janie might respond, and she was right; I needed to keep my meeting with Brenda.

Brenda's small, 2-bedroom home was less than a ten-minute drive from my little apartment. Inviting me in, she indicated I could sit on her sofa just two or three steps away. She relaxed in a stuffed chair off to the side, and we started visiting. I told her everything. Although I didn't bawl like I had in the past, I used a bunch of tissues, and as promised, she was prepared.

When I told her that I felt like I had a brick cylinder inside me that had developed a crack and allowed my emotions to begin to escape, she liked that analogy. She sat relaxed with a small journal in her hand as she listened intently to my statements. Focusing her brown eyes on me, she told me she'd always used the idea of a bucket that finally becomes so full of emotion it begins to spill over. This analogy was based on the theory that we can only contain so much emotion before it must escape.

When I completed my story, Brenda asked, "Do you want advice?"

"Yes, please."

"I wouldn't tell your mother about your sexual orientation. She may not want to know. Tell her only if she asks."

Relief flooded my mind, but I still dreaded the thought of talking with Mother someday. I sincerely hoped she would never ask.

Then Brenda prodded, "Do you realize that you and Janie have no future?"

"Yes. I've always known that."

"You know you and Janie can never have a physical relationship?"

"Yes. I've got to get over my feelings for her."

"Then, whenever you begin fantasizing about Janie, picture yourself walking along a beach with Jesus. Every time the thought of Janie pops into your mind, force yourself to picture that beach scene instead."

A beautiful, sandy beach with waves gently lapping the shore has always been a pleasant, peaceful scene for me. The thought of walking in tandem with Jesus, the epitome of love and acceptance, made the vision idyllic. I was ready to grab whatever reasonable advice was offered to end my nine-month-long misery. The suggestion made sense, and it might work for me. *Yes*, I thought, *this is something I can do.*

"You said you cry and feel sad but aren't certain why," Brenda pointed out. "It's important that you focus on what's making you cry.

Identify the cause. If you think you don't know, take a guess. Your best guess is your best answer. Grieve over that thing. You'll never be able to fill up your empty shell until you've grieved through all the issues causing the tears. And you can't do that until you identify them, which can be very difficult."

Brenda was eleven years younger than I, but her wisdom seemed to be beyond our combined years, and I was grateful that I took Janie's advice and met with her.

I thought our time together would end shortly after she shared her wisdom, but I ended up staying until almost nine that evening. We learned we both have quite a bit in common: we had both been schoolteachers, were both Southern Baptists, both divorced after many years, and both had grown children who knew we were gay and continued to love and accept us.

Before I left, I was pleasantly surprised by her suggestion that we go out for pizza together sometime. The offer pleased me, and I looked forward to another opportunity to visit with Brenda.

24
BRENDA

Almost six full days had passed since Janie told me she knew the source of my pain, and five days since I'd heard from her. I fell into despair and kept telling myself just to survive. That was my only goal for the day. I wanted so badly to die. I finally left the apartment and rented four videos. *Just stay alive. That's all. Just live.* I told myself.

Early the next day, Janie finally called. I couldn't believe it! When she heard my hesitating voice as I said hello, she asked, "Lou Anne, is anything wrong?"

"I just thought you didn't want to talk with me anymore."

"Oh, no, no! Not at all."

And off our conversation went. She sounded like her old self as she shared with me all the plumbing problems she'd been having at her house. My heart became so much lighter as we caught up, though I was sad to know that both Janie and Barbara would be off traveling with their families soon.

In the coming days, I continued to fight my depression by journaling my thoughts and activities. My primary support team, Barbara and Janie, were now traveling, leaving me "alone." Having visited Brenda only two days before, I started using her as my sounding board. I emailed her, asking her questions about herself, not only because I was curious but also because suicidal thoughts had returned, and I needed to have something else to think about.

My mind was grateful for her prompt and thoughtful replies:

Hello Lou Anne,

I, like you, have lived most of my life in the box of safety and meeting others' expectations. Only in the last three years or so have I begun to truly know and live from my adventurous spirit.

After sharing information about the beautiful excursions she had recently taken on her latest outdoor adventures, she answered my question about which church she attended.

I now worship on Sunday mornings at St. Gabriel's Community Church, a small evangelical, nondenominational, gay-friendly church here in Tyler. Since my summer in Wyoming, I have viewed church in a different way than I once did. I'll share it with you sometime.

Hope you have a good day!

Brenda

Weeks passed. I assumed Janie was back home, but she hadn't contacted me. No calls. No emails. Nothing. She could have been ill, had a family emergency, or something could have happened to her elderly parents, but still, I pictured her here in Tyler, choosing not to contact me. How was I going to stand not ever visiting with her again? Not ever seeing her again. As the days continued to pass, I wasn't in the mood to write or do anything. Life was a struggle, and I was in total misery.

Eventually, Barbara returned from her trip, so I shared with her all that had been going on, especially my conversation with Janie, in which she admitted having known the source of my pain for many months. Several days earlier, I had also informed Barbara about my contacts with Brenda and her advice, emphasizing how highly I thought of her and how much I valued her friendship.

Lou Anne,

Brenda's advice sounds terrific—grounded in faith, pragmatic (I hate pie-in-the-sky advice), and positive. Next time you see her, tell her about your sleeping problem (if you haven't) and see what she thinks. That concerns me, especially right now when I am sleep-deprived myself and know how it feels.

Your mother may already know as much as she wants to. Using a mental image of beach-walking with Jesus to substitute for thoughts of Janie is a positive suggestion, it seems to me. Have you tried to identify specific things that draw you to Janie? Obviously, the attraction is primarily physical, but I think there's more, and maybe part of it is Janie's openness about her emotions, which is something you haven't allowed yourself to experience. Perhaps when you recognize what that part of the attraction is, you'll be better able to recognize those qualities in someone else. (Remember, I'm a journalism major, not a therapist, so give any suggestion I make all the attention it deserves!) I think you'll be able to identify the cause(s) for the tears as time goes on, too.

Barbara

Barbara's letter made me chuckle as I wondered why I was drawn to Janie. I replied:

Barbara,

It was probably learning of her openness and acceptance of homosexuals. What a bombshell to have someone sit and talk with me about a subject I'd always refused to bring into consciousness, and to have that person verbally demonstrate love, kindness, and acceptance toward people I'd always been taught were abominable. Who would have thought a Christian existed who displayed a loving acceptance toward homosexuals?

A recent television special called Love Chronicles stated that we all have a certain chemistry, so when we meet an individual under intense conditions, we're drawn to them, hence my attraction to Janie.

Lou Anne

Despite Brenda's encouragement, my internal climate was so darkened by my deep sense of isolation and loneliness that I saw only a glimpse of light.

One of those glimpses was an email I received from Brenda, which told me she planned to attend the gay pride parade in Houston that weekend with some friends from the gay community in Tyler. They were all younger, with partners, and Brenda admitted that, at times, she missed the company and friendship of someone nearer her age (and not in a relationship) who could identify with her experiences. She hadn't found many single, fifty-plus-year-old lesbians freely walking around in Tyler, Texas. This made me crack a smile.

She ended her message with, "Lou Anne, as you express your appreciation for my staying in touch and offering friendship, in all honesty, I also appreciate you. May you have a peaceful night's rest! Psalm 4:8."

Perhaps Brenda was someone who could understand the loneliness I felt.

The next afternoon, after my regular doctor's checkup, I replied to Brenda, telling her that I'd lost weight during this stressful period in my life. The doctor had now put me on Prozac, but I couldn't comprehend how a medicine could help a depressed person when I knew my depression was an emotional response to my situation.

Brenda,

The only gay women I know are the few I've met at the PFLAG meetings. There's not another gay woman in Tyler that I know.

I envy young gay women. To have the courage to come out when you're young would be wonderful. I never felt that option was available. But after this awful experience with Janie and the painful emotions that keep me tied up in knots, I don't want to ever fall in love again. It's pure misery.

I think the time has come for you to tell me a little more about yourself. So far, our friendship has centered on my problems, which is rather selfish on my part. Tell me something I don't know about you, maybe how you met your husband, why you married him, or something. Were you ever in love with him?

Lou Anne

Brenda wrote back that my doctor should have explained how Prozac could help me. She said I was apparently clinically depressed because of the lengthy duration of my emotional stress, which had slowed the chemical processes in my brain. She compared the mishap to a four-cylinder engine that had begun to hit on only two or three cylinders. The Prozac should jump-start my brain, she assured me.

Then she told me a little about herself.

Lou Anne,

I started dating my ex-husband between my junior and senior years in high school. He was six years older. I was intelligent, competent, and most likely to succeed as valedictorian of a small high school. Right out of high school, I went to a large university only to discover that I was shy, insecure, lonely, and had no sense of my own identity outside the roles I maintained in small-town USA. Of course, this is all from a backward glance.

Brenda

When Brenda asked me out for a light dinner Friday evening so we could continue swapping stories, I didn't hesitate. That sounded like fun, and I looked forward to the opportunity to visit with her further and to learn more of her story, which I felt was still mostly untold.

Though I'd enjoyed the evening of conversation with Brenda, I felt no better the next day. I was terribly depressed, lying face down in that bottomless hole. All I did was lie around, cry, and do lots of nothing. This was my second day on the Prozac, and I couldn't tell that it was helping me. I looked forward to Friday when I would have a reason to get out of the house and talk with Brenda some more.

When Barbara wrote the following morning to ask how I was feeling, I confessed that I thought Janie might want to end our friendship.

She replied that Janie would tell me if that's what she wanted to do and further encouraged me with these words:

Please, if you go into a funk, let it be one that you enter on a somewhat realistic basis, and not one you slide into on imagination alone. Work on imagining something wonderful you'd have to cope with. Emotions are notoriously unreliable indicators of truth.

She asked if I'd been able to exercise and recommended it if I hadn't. She also suggested that a Dairy Queen Butterfinger Blizzard might boost my mood.

You're going to be well, and you're going to truly enjoy your life again before this year is over—and, quite possibly, before this month is over. I'm glad you're going to see Brenda, and I'm glad it'll be in a restaurant.

I responded immediately, thanking her for the encouraging words about Janie.

Barbara,

I tell myself old women aren't supposed to have feelings like I'm having. I know that just accepting the fact that I am gay is a big enough jump for anyone, but to even begin to fathom my being in love with another woman must stretch anyone's limits of understanding!

Thanks for not preaching to me about it but just guiding me through. I continue to need that.

As I signed off on Barbara's email with thanks, I took her up on the idea for a Blizzard, though my favorite will always be a Heath Bar over a Butterfinger. I assured her that I usually walked about an hour every day and normally performed various exercises for about twelve minutes each morning, but that had been going by the wayside. When I walked, I usually kept a small notebook with me that contained all the poems and biblical chapters I had memorized. As I walked, I mentally recited them. But I hadn't done that lately because I couldn't focus for long stretches of time.

Barbara quickly replied.

Having accepted that you're gay (which took about 35 seconds since it explained quite a few things), I have no difficulty accepting your being in love. I do have a problem (as I'm sure you've noticed) understanding why it makes you a touch irrational from time to time. Please feel free to call me on my own periodic fits of irrationality!

I laughed at her reply, realizing how nutty I was when it came to Janie. What a blessing to have an intelligent friend like Barbara who sees through my crazy thoughts and bravely expresses her opinion. Still, even though I knew I was being foolish, a part of me couldn't release the fear that Janie was deliberately avoiding me, and I wallowed in despondency.

Three days later, Barbara wrote that she hadn't heard from me and wanted to know if I was okay. She asked me to talk to her about something, so I shared my concerns about Janie with her.

She hasn't been in Sunday School, and she wasn't at a wedding this afternoon that I know she was invited to. Several people came up to me at the reception to ask where she was, but I hadn't heard from her for nineteen days. My emotions are like a roller coaster. Thank goodness I don't stay down for three or four days in a row. If I did, I wouldn't still be around.

Barbara, several of my class members approached me on Sunday and told me they all thought I needed to leave [your class] and return to [my original] class as a member. It's flattering to be wanted, and since I enjoy being with them so much, it's quite a temptation.

Lou Anne

Friday finally arrived after what felt like a week that would never end. It was June 23, and the East Texas heat was already beginning to creep in for the summer, so Brenda and I agreed to meet at Jason's Deli, where we could enjoy the crisp coolness of veggie wraps. I don't recall thinking of the meal as a date, but I guess that's what it was. It was refreshing to leave my apartment and meet someone for dinner, especially someone intelligent and interesting. I had so many questions to ask that, even though I usually have difficulty finding subjects to talk about, I had no trouble talking with Brenda that evening.

I continued to relish the similarities we shared between our upbringings and adult lives. Still, I kept reminding myself that I'm over 11 years older than Brenda, which seemed like a significant age difference. Because of that and the guilt I was still holding about my thoughts of Janie, I couldn't allow myself to imagine the possibility of our having a future together. I was just happy to have a friend who intimately understood my struggle and with whom I could relate. Little did I know, at the time, the important place Brenda would eventually hold in my life.

When I told Barbara about Brenda, she asked if she could meet her sometime. She said that Brenda sounded like someone actively involved in figuring out life and helping others do the same.

She also said that, based on her personal experience, she doubted I could return to my class without teaching and urged me to wait at least six months before deciding what to do.

I wouldn't wish what you're going through right now on my worst enemy, but I'm learning to know you so much better, Lou Anne. And I like that, as I'd always believed I would. You have so many strengths, and right now, you're feeling so weak. I wonder if realizing how little control any of us really has over our lives is a prerequisite to experiencing the reality of God in a new and powerful way.

Above all, Barbara knew of my many weaknesses and failures as a human being, so when she acknowledged my strengths, I felt uplifted and renewed. I absorbed her compliment like a man dying of thirst when offered water.

But her advice to stay away from my class for at least 6 months was most disappointing and halfway angered me. She was undoubtedly right about God being more real, vital, and loving when someone is at their weakest. She reminded me of II Corinthians 1:3-5 where the scriptures say: "Praise be to the God and Father of our Lord Jesus Christ, the Father of compassion and the God of all comfort, who comforts us in all our troubles so that we can comfort those in any trouble with the comfort we ourselves have received from God. For just as the sufferings of Christ flow over into our lives, so also through Christ our comfort overflows."

I wrote to Barbara the next night that I'd swallowed my pride and called Janie. Her husband, Charles, answered and explained that Janie was touring Texas with a friend visiting the state for the first time and expected her back the next night. He sounded very friendly, which relieved my mind considerably, as I'd feared he might know of my feelings toward his wife.

Barbara's answer made me smile, "I read this two or three times and considered not saying, 'Told you so!' But I'm weak. So, . . . told you so."

I awoke the next day feeling better. Usually, I can tell within a few minutes of when I get up what kind of day I'll probably have, which amazes me. No tears at all! And no effort all day to keep them away. My mind went to the Prozac and the hope that it was finally working.

By Day 11 of the Prozac, I'd had no tears for three or four days. Amazing! What a change. Brenda was right; the medication was finally beginning to "jump start my brain," as she said it would. I was starting to hear the bugles of the cavalry riding to my rescue.

After three weeks of no contact or communication, Janie finally called, and we had a pleasant, long conversation about what was happening in our lives. By the end, we both agreed that despite Janie's many destinations, I had certainly had the more interesting experiences, most of which revolved around my time and conversation with Brenda. But the event that took the cake was chauffeuring around my friend Greg, whose wife was in my Sunday school class. Greg is quadriplegic and wheelchair-bound, so a day with him is a day spent in unavoidably close proximity. I assumed he knew I was gay, but I was wrong. That's when I discovered how much more difficult it is for me to "out myself" to a male. His reactions were so different!

"I'll take you to a gay bar," he said attempting to break the ice, "so you can have a good time. I'll even pretend to be gay myself, which shouldn't be too hard since I'll be sitting in this wheelchair."

My embarrassment was impossible to escape and peaked when he said, "All you need is to have a good romp in bed. That'd get you over your depression."

Greg didn't know very much about homosexuality and thought I was just mixed up. Our conversation covered various topics, and he was surprised to learn I'd been the one to ask for the divorce, thinking, I guess, that Jim may have had some woman he wanted to be with. He was unaware, almost shocked, that Dr. Watson, our pastor, had asked me to take a sabbatical from teaching my Sunday School class after I'd confided in him. The unfairness of it floored Greg—that my sharing of confidence had led to what might be conceived as a punishment.

When Sunday arrived, I continued to head to Barbara's class. That's when I spotted Janie in my former Sunday School department directly across a wide hallway. My heart started racing. I hadn't seen her for three and a half weeks, and I immediately turned and walked into my new department to avoid her. I didn't think I could properly handle our greeting each other.

When classes were over, I spotted her again as she visited with friends in the other department. Still wanting to avoid her, I headed straight for the staircase despite my yearning to speak with her. She looked gorgeous. I had to muster all my willpower to walk down the stairs. However, when I reached my car, I decided to sit and wait for her to get to the parking lot. Shortly thereafter, I spotted her coming toward me. At that point, I opened my door and called to her when she was only a few cars away.

Excited to see me, she hurried over and greeted me with a hug. "How are you doing, Precious? It's been ages since I've seen you."

We stood beside my car and visited for about ten minutes, and Janie was as friendly as ever. "Give me a call, and let's meet for lunch some day this week," she said.

Her invitation relieved me; she still considered me a good friend. But I knew I'd never call her and set a date for us to get together. Nevertheless, her words were welcome, and I couldn't help but hope she might phone me.

In desperate need of a distraction, I asked Brenda if she'd like to go with me to a patriotic-themed concert in the park on Friday, July 7, featuring our local high school band. She gave a little laugh and said, "I was going to ask you to join me. You just beat me to the punch. Why don't you drive to my house, and we'll eat a simple meal before the concert?"

"Sounds great. Why don't I pick up a Greek salad from Bruno's? We'll split it. You know how huge those salads are."

"Great idea. See you at 5:45."

I picked up the salad as planned, and we ate in her tiny kitchen while discussing plans to get to the park. She suggested we walk and carry our lawn chairs. I'd never walked to the park from her house and wasn't certain if this was a good idea. I knew where the park was, but sitting in her kitchen, I had no idea how far we'd travel. She grinned and explained, "Really, it's only about five blocks."

Seeing her confidence, I agreed to walk because I certainly didn't look forward to hunting for a parking place on the streets once we got there. I was pleasantly surprised to discover the walk wasn't bad, even carrying our fold-up lawn chairs. I was impressed with how capable and confident Brenda was, and how she saw those same traits in me, despite my doubts.

When we reached the amphitheater, we went down to the front row and set our chairs off to the side of the permanent seating, where the view was perfect. We could see the band and enjoy watching people arrive. I was even more grateful for having walked and brought our chairs as we saw others squirming to get comfortable on the hard, permanent seats of the amphitheater. The casual dress code of the event was another plus of the evening, in addition to the amphitheater being located to the west and providing shade on a hot July evening. Eventually, the whole hillside was dotted with chairs or quilts for families to sit on.

The music was grand, and we enjoyed sharing the evening together in public. By the end of the concert, we also learned that we both played in our high school bands and enjoyed good music.

When Barbara and I corresponded that evening, I told her that Brenda agreed to have lunch with the three of us on Saturday. Both women were essential to me, and I wanted Barbara to realize that Brenda was a good and trustworthy person. When I had first told Barbara that I planned to meet with Brenda as a counselor, she had warned me that Brenda might be a lesbian who would take advantage of me. I was aware of her concern and felt confident that all her fears would be allayed once she met Brenda.

The lunch with Barbara and Brenda lasted two hours and was very pleasant. I did little more than sit back and listen because both these women grew up in Kilgore (about thirty miles east of us in Tyler) and had much in common to talk about.

Later, Barbara wrote,

Lou Anne,

I enjoyed visiting with Brenda and would have liked her if I'd just met her somewhere without your involvement at all. Remember I'd suggested the possibility of an emotional involvement with her, and you said she was way too young? Well, it crossed my mind that there's about the same difference in your ages as there is between my sister and her husband. Brenda's not that young, especially considering her maturity. You two may never have an emotional attachment, but if not, it would be because the chemistry wasn't there, not because of her age.

Barbara's words gave me a lot to consider. I wasn't sure if Brenda was even interested in a potential romance, but the possibility stirred my curiosity nonetheless.

photo provided by the author

MY LIFE, MY MINISTRY
August 2000 – December 2015

25
A LIVING TESTIMONY

At our monthly PFLAG meeting that week, the president of the Dallas chapter shared his surprise when his son came out to him as gay. He and his wife were caught completely unprepared. After the initial shock wore off, they not only accepted him as he was but have since become strong supporters and advocates of gay rights. I found this interesting, along with my desire to immediately share details of that night's meeting with Brenda, who stayed home sick.

A bond was forming between us, and I called her as soon as I returned to my apartment to ask how she was doing.

Since our lunch with Barbara, we were corresponding regularly and becoming good friends. It made sense that I felt an emotional pull toward her. She was lesbian, single, and seemed like an ideal person to fall in love with, but I struggled to feel the emotions my logic knew were there. I blamed this on the Prozac, which made me feel void of all complex emotions at the time. Still, it was refreshing, and I began to take it as a good sign that the logical part of myself yearned for a closeness with someone. This seemed a healthier start than the connections my heart seemed to form on its own in the past. I hoped these feelings of stability and certainty were a sign of an upward trend. The combination of medication, new friends, and the support of the PFLAG group helped, as one day, I found the courage to share my story with an old family friend, Corinna.

When Jim and I lived in Austin, a couple named Corinna and Ed lived next door. Their children and ours freely moved between our homes and yards, as her two sons were the same age as our three boys. Even though Corinna was two years younger than I, she had a grandson the age of Laura. I very much enjoyed having her family live next door to us.

I came out to her by sending the long, all-important letters Jim and I wrote to each other when we first discussed our divorce. Not long afterward, when I happened to be in Austin, I contacted her. She invited me to her home for a visit, where we enjoyed a good conversation, during which I felt she accepted my being gay with no reservations.

In August, Corinna wrote that she was so glad I'd told her my story because that was the way, one by one, she believed our society might come to accept homosexuality as just another way to be. She'd told a couple of her friends without mentioning my name or those connected to my story, and it made them think about the subject differently, as if I were someone close to them. "Little by little, these conversations will make a difference," she said.

At times, I felt as if I were just twiddling my thumbs regarding my efforts in encouraging the acceptance of gays, so Corinna's letter was a bright spot, which I shared with Barbara.

Barbara wrote that she was rereading a book of meditations and, for some reason, found herself in the chapter on "Testimony." This chapter discusses testimony as an important part of the healing taking place all over the world through Alcoholics Anonymous. Testimony requires a person to be truthful and willing to share their truth. It also requires the rest of us to support one another as we rise to speak the truth about what we have seen and heard.

Barbara then explained

Lou Anne,

This struck me in the context of your friend's comment about conversations. Testimony about how life is lived comes in all forms: personal, from the pulpit and platform, and written. The testimony that has been most effective in my own life has been that which is shared in the context of living that life, the testimony given to maintain a relationship, and the testimony that's required in the context of community. Which is why I (and your friend, I assume) are much more moved/changed by your kind of testimony than we are by the testimony of others, though I do understand why that very public testimony is necessary to provide encouragement and assurance of acceptance.

I thanked her for sharing these thoughts and confessed that I didn't speak to more people because I feared the subject might upset them and cause them discomfort and embarrassment.

Barbara replied that I'd know when to speak to individuals, though I might cry occasionally when I did. Her following comments intrigued me.

I'm not sure self-control is all it's cracked up to be. Maybe we need to know we're vulnerable and human, and maybe other people need to know that about us, too.

I had struggled all my life to maintain self-control and protect myself. Now, I'm learning that being vulnerable and showing emotion reflects my humanity and authentic self more than trying to repress myself.

A few weeks later, my empathy and vulnerability were tested when My 89-year-old mother's hip broke on the evening of August 11th. I stayed with her for several weeks while she was in the hospital, then the ICU, then back to the hospital, and then to physical therapy. Many days, I only left her for an hour or two to go home, shower, and put on fresh clothes. This schedule kept me exhausted and sleep-deprived. Luckily, Brenda visited my apartment on Saturday, August 26th, which gave me a much-needed break from caretaking.

It had been four and a half months since we first met at the PFLAG meeting on April 10th, and this was the first time she'd been to my apartment. She picked up supper for us and brought a video from the library to watch.

I felt odd about the evening, asking myself if this was what others would term a date. Yet we never touched each other. If a man had been visiting instead of a woman, he would have made a move of some kind. The idea of sitting close to her, just enjoying the physical nearness of another person, appealed to me, but we kept our distance.

Later, after she left, I asked myself why homosexuals were so often perceived as more promiscuous than heterosexuals. That certainly wasn't my experience, and it didn't appear to be Brenda's either. I understood that many publicly gay celebrities (like most celebrities, to be fair) seemed to have many sexual partners, but surely they didn't represent the entire gay community or experience. Perhaps the myth of hyper-promiscuity got its roots in demonizing homosexuality as sinful; that was certainly the majority of the information I'd come across online for the last eight months as I searched to better understand myself, to no genuine end. Nothing online reflected my internal or current external experience. I was beginning to think the only way to know myself and better understand homosexuality, in general, was to continue spending time with people like Brenda and me. What did the straight men online—most of them evangelicals—know about me or others like me, especially if they were too afraid actually to get near enough to know us?

Six days later, Brenda and I joined a group of about twenty people from St. Gabriel's for a Labor Day pool party held at the home of a female couple. Relaxing among this friendly group was just what I needed. Most of us stayed in the pool to find relief from the blazing sun. This was my first gay/lesbian party, and I had entered a different world.

Most of the crowd consisted of couples who enjoyed the freedom to show affection openly toward their partners. Alcohol was available, and I wasn't accustomed to parties with alcohol. I'd led a very sheltered life and stuck to my soft drinks.

Toward evening, some of the women began to lose their inhibitions—due to the alcohol, I assumed. One couple, with arms around each other, shared a hammock. Feeling a touch of envy, I kept letting my eyes stray in their direction. Other couples in the pool occasionally kissed. The backyard had a tall privacy fence, and couples who usually had to hide their fondness for each other in public places were free in this setting to openly express their affection. Yes, it was a different world, but I liked it.

These feelings of comfort and peace, however, were short-lived, as the Sunday School lesson the following day dealt with perhaps the most famous of the infamous "six biblical passages" used to condemn homosexuality. Although the broader lesson was from Romans 1:18-32, Barbara never mentioned homosexuality until her concluding statement. She explained she had no time to discuss that part of the passage at that time. She then handed out her "Lesson Leftovers," information she

239

didn't have time to discuss with the class, which she regularly shared at the end of each lesson. Her leftovers included, among other things, "Views of Some Texas Baptist Leaders on Homosexuality," which had been distributed at the Baptist General Convention of Texas last year (1999):

"*Russell H. Dilday, Jr., president, BGCT (Baptist General Convention of Texas):*

According to the Bible, God's ideal for sex in marriage is one man and one woman in a monogamous relationship for life. Any divergence from this ideal is contrary to God's will and, therefore, sinful. Homosexual practice is a perversion of God's plan and is described in the Bible as an abominable sin. Of course, there are other perversions, such as adultery and premarital sex, which the Bible also condemns as sexual sins."

Barbara later told me that she chose these less-condemning statements from among the nine listed in the report:

"*David Currie, director, Texas Baptists Committed:*

Homosexual activity is sinful, as I understand the written word of God. Practicing homosexuals should not be elected leaders, nor should persons practicing greed, hatred, anger, and prejudice (as a lifestyle) be church leaders. The church must balance Christ's call and example of treating sinners with grace and love while affirming biblical morality and the truth that things are clearly right and wrong."

"*Phil Lineberger, president, BGCT 1990-91:*

I do not believe homosexual activity is natural or biblically acceptable, but I do believe people who have these tendencies need to be treated with respect as human beings created in the image of God."

"*Phil Strickland, director, Texas Baptist Christian Life Commission:*

I believe that the Bible teaches that homosexual practice is inconsistent with Christian living. The Bible teaches the same about adultery, vengefulness, greed, self-righteousness, and an unforgiving spirit. This is to say that while homosexual practice is a sin, it is not the only sin, but one sin among many that estranges us from God. We follow Jesus as we welcome all sinners to repent, to receive the forgiveness of God, and to enter into the fellowship of God's people."

After reading what she considered to be the least hurtful statements, it was no wonder that I and many others feared not being welcomed into the faith I grew up in. Even the most tolerant leaders of the church considered me a sinner simply because I was gay.[13]

A few days after her lesson, I said to Barbara, "I dislike that phrase 'hate the sin, love the sinner.'" She replied, "I'm not crazy about it myself and can certainly understand why you wouldn't like it. I see no sin in being born with a specific sexual identity. Still, I can't find any part of the Bible that condones any sexual relationship other than a faithful heterosexual marriage. Obviously, the same is true for premarital sex and adultery. I imagine few people in any Sunday School class are free from all sexual sin, but I doubt few would be honest about that fact since they don't have to be."

She continued, "I can't imagine interrupting a friendship because of any judgement I might make about someone else's sins. This would leave me with zero friends—and no one who'd be willing to be my friend

---

13   The Southern Baptist Convention, as of 2024, still does not affirm same-sex marriages or female pastors, and it still lists homosexuality as a form of "sexual immorality." This viewpoint really hasn't changed since 1996 when The Texas Baptists denounced homosexuality in the same category as adultery, incest, and pornography.

since my sinful characteristics would be painfully obvious to anyone who'd spent much time with me."

I tried to analyze Barbara's opinion about homosexuality. I concluded that she accepted the fact that people don't choose to be homosexual, but she felt pretty strongly that sexual relationships between homosexuals were sinful. This struck me as a fascinating contradiction and pained me a little. Still, I appreciated that Barbara extended kindness and care to me. I could not deny that she was a dear friend, and I appreciated her attempts to understand me and my homosexuality. The learning process is rarely perfect and often has flaws.

Barbara and I exchanged several letters that night that reminded me how much her loving friendship overshadowed any theological differences we may have had since my coming out.

In her message, she said she remembered feeling unclear about who she was as a person in high school and college. She had also attended Baylor University and tried to imagine what it must have been like for me in much more difficult circumstances. She had no problem staying aware of the pain I had endured for so many years, never knowing if anyone cared about me for myself or just who they thought I was.

"One good thing about pain," she wrote, "it certainly makes a person compassionate—and we all need a certain amount of compassion."

I replied that I'd focused on her statement about never knowing if anyone cared about me for myself and told her she was right.

"I played a role all my life." I wrote, *"I always tried to be good and follow all the rules. I wanted to be accepted, and I especially wanted my parents to be proud of me. I knew they suspected I was homosexual, and I knew they believed homosexuality was sinful and totally unacceptable for their only daughter. I walked this tightrope all my life, pretending to be someone I wasn't to please my parents and make them proud of me.*

I never let my guard down with anyone. Even when Karen and I continued to correspond, I was always cautious and circumspect, knowing her husband also read my letters.

The loneliness hurt the most. The challenge of succeeding at whatever I attempted was always just that, a challenge. This constant striving to be "the best" became a way of life. I was trying to prove my worth more to myself than to anyone else, and I'm still caught up in that. I suppose when you do something all your life, it's difficult to change.

My willingness to share my secret amazes me. So many have told me how courageous I am, but I don't feel courageous at all—just free. Unshackled. Out of bondage."

I received an email from Frank Smitherman, the teacher with whom I once shared a classroom, and one of those male acquaintances Mother had mentally paired me with when I first asked for the divorce. Even though I had retired from teaching several years earlier, Frank continued teaching, and we stayed in contact. He knew I was gay and was the one who offered to leave "St. Mattress" on Sundays and accompany me to the gay church. Months ago, I had sent my out-of-the-closet letter to Vicki, another teacher-friend who taught next door to us in the alternative high school. Despite the passage of time, I'd never received a reply from Vicki, so I was very interested in what Frank had to say.

Dear Lou Anne.

"I've had the most amazing and refreshing conversation with Vicki. I didn't bring up the subject, but she asked me if I had received your e-mail about your being gay. I admitted I had not only received your email, but that I had known about it for quite some time.

Vicki said she still loves you as a friend and would never shun you, but she did disagree with your choice and its effect on Jim. I told her it wasn't a choice but that God had made you that way. Vicki said she just couldn't believe God made homosexuals. She also admitted she didn't *know very much about homosexuality and really couldn't make that judgement. I very politely told Vicki that she and I would have to agree to disagree on the subject and explained to her why I didn't believe it was a choice. Vicki said she was very proud of the comments your pastor made to you and acknowledged that he was a very compassionate man.*

Vicki also told me that she wanted to respond to your email to let you know that she still cared about you as a friend, but wasn't sure what to say. She and her husband, Cliff, had lengthy discussions on the subject, and she indicated she would send a message to you as soon as she collected her thoughts.

I feel you have a friend in Vicki . . . I think she's trying to keep an open mind. It was a very positive conversation. Good for you, girl!

Sincerely,

Frank

Frank's sharing about Vicki both excited me about the possibility of her acceptance and disappointed me in the sense that her acceptance wasn't immediate, something she would have to think about. She must still be thinking, 24 years later, as I've never heard from her.

I read somewhere that once an individual decides to "come out of the closet," it is a never-ending process. That's true. Occasionally, as I became more comfortable with myself and who I was, I would feel a nudge to tell a particular individual. After giving it further thought, I would usually decide that this was a step I needed to take and just do it. For the most part, the responses to my sharing my authentic self were positive, and I began developing closer friendships with more people.

The more I faced my fears of judgement and loss and gained the support of friends, the more I found myself becoming a passionate advocate for the LGBTQ community.

For example, in the same year I started coming out, I wrote to one of our local television stations that recently started carrying the "Dr. Laura" (Schlessinger) show. I told them I disagreed with their carrying her show because she had publicly called homosexuals "biological errors." I asked them how they would feel about being called a biological error. I also told them this type of obscene bigotry should be unacceptable to everyone. "True," I said, "Many intelligent people are prejudiced. It's a matter of being uninformed." I then quoted a 1989 study from the Department of Health and Human Services, which concluded that 30 percent of teenage suicides were related to "sexual identity problems" and that as many as a third of all gay teenagers attempt suicide.

Surely, this is sufficient evidence to convince any intelligent person that homosexuality is not chosen. Why choose something that brings such anguish and despair, such a feeling of hopelessness that suicide seems to be the only way to stop the pain? I implore you to use your rationale not to perpetuate this type of bigotry in East Texas. This is certainly one of the worst places for gays to live anyway. It would be wonderful to have a television station with enough backbone to say, "We won't be a part of this bigotry. We won't continue to make gays feel like outcasts or second-class citizens. We love all the people in East Texas and want to do what's best for all."

Along with these types of letters, I also corresponded with people I knew. For instance, one mother I had come out to shared with me that her daughter was gay. I encouraged my friend to love her daughter unconditionally, stating that "An unconditional love in this case cannot be 'loving the sinner but hating the sin.'"

Sending all these correspondences now made me think of my first letter of actual protest, which I sent a few years ago when I was still "in hiding".

My first letter was to the Baptist Standard, a Texas news and opinion publication for Texas Baptists, which is read religiously by most Texas Baptists. In all honesty, I remember the pervading fear I felt of making my identity known even more than the thing I was speaking out against. At the time, I didn't feel courageous, but I was bolstered by a quote I had recently come across from Eleanor Roosevelt: "You must do the thing you think you cannot do." I made myself write the letter despite the fear that someone might find out who I was and realize I was gay. However, fear kept me from signing it. That same fear also compelled me to drive to Henderson (about 45 minutes away) to post the letter in a different city, convinced it would help protect my anonymity.

I recall driving around this unfamiliar town, looking for their post office, and fearing to ask for directions. When I placed the letter in the mailbox, I made certain no one was around to see me, and then I immediately drove back to Tyler. The letter, of course, was never published because I had not signed it. I learned my lesson there.

The fear of "being known" continued to control my life, but despite this fear, I continued to write my memoir, come out to friends and family, and write protest-type letters. Interestingly, my determination to outrun and outlast my fear gradually led to my becoming a different person—a stronger and bolder person—and as fear receded, faith ironically began to take its place. Faith in advocacy, the power of people sharing their stories, and belief in myself to shamelessly pursue the mission I believed God uniquely designed me to follow.

26
AFFIRMATIONS & HEALING

*J*anie and I saw very little of each other after our May 29 "I know the source of your pain, Lou Anne" visit. Neither of us planned this separation. I missed her terribly, but the Prozac helped push the pain away. During June, July, August, and September, the happenings in our lives required us to naturally drift our separate ways.

She spent weeks of the summer traveling across Texas as a personal tour guide for a friend from up North who'd never been to the state before. Then, her aunt in Austin broke her hip, and she cared for her for several weeks. About this time, my own life had become hectic. I spent six days in Houston caring for my newborn grandson and six days in Austin helping my daughter settle into her new apartment. Then, I had visitors in my apartment for two days. Added to that were my mother's health problems, so my world was spinning ever faster, thus it seemed my mind had little time to dwell on Janie.

Looking back, I can see the long separation was a gift, as it helped me learn I could get along without Janie in my life. Although I still had some pain connected to our separation, I was no longer weepy and despondent. The things going on in my life required me to set aside my "Janie feelings," and as I did, it made room for new friendships and opportunities to grow.

Toward the end of September, Brenda invited me to her house, where nine of us gathered for food and games like Scattergories and Trivial Pursuit. Brenda is much more outgoing than I am, and at first, I felt out of place, not knowing anyone other than her at the party. However, by the end of the evening, it turned out that playing games with a group of strangers was precisely what I needed.

Although her home was small, no one seemed to mind the crowding, and there was lots of laughter and kidding around. This seemed to be the first time I had laughed in a long time. The experience made me wonder if there really could be a place I "fit" in the world outside of the roles I'd always been prescribed—a place I could be genuinely happy in.

When I finally attended Sunday School in my old class, members asked me where Janie was. I had no idea and told them so. She and I hadn't talked since July 5th, and it was almost October.

Despite the anguish our separation still brought to my heart, I reminded myself that this was the only life I could ever have regarding her. I no longer allowed myself to live in the unrealistic fantasy world I had created. I continued practicing the advice Brenda had shared with me of picturing myself walking down a sandy beach with Jesus by my side. Controlling my thoughts in this way was not easy. I struggled to force thoughts of Janie out of my head, but I managed to, and I felt like I was making headway.

After receiving two written requests from Carolyn to come back and visit our Sunday School class, I decided to do so. As our class's new teacher, Carolyn believed I hadn't returned because I felt uncomfortable in the group, and she was right, in a way, but the feeling of being ill at ease had nothing to do with everyone's knowing I was gay. My hesitation, instead, had everything to do with sitting in a room with Janie and being fearful that I'd look, act, or speak to her in some way that would let others know I was in love with her. I didn't want that to happen. I also didn't want to inflict pain on myself by being in such proximity to her. I decided to hope for the best and was ready to try it, to experiment. Besides, I continued to be upset at Barbara's "lesson leftovers" she handed out two weeks earlier.

When I attended Carolyn's class, I felt right at home. Everyone kept asking where Janie was. No one seemed to know. Then, a week later, as I again took my seat in my old Sunday School department, Carolyn walked over and sat beside me. "Do you know anything about Janie?" she asked.

"I haven't talked with her for a long time," I admitted, "but I do know that her aunt fell and broke her hip."

Then, in a surprised voice, Carolyn said, "Well, there she is now."

I didn't look. I hadn't seen her in such a long time, I wasn't sure how I'd respond. Carolyn then commented, "She's heading our way."

I finally turned around, surprised and relieved to feel no pain when I saw her. She looked as wonderful as always, and we greeted each other as she sat beside me.

When we eventually entered our classroom, I debated the wisdom of sitting beside her. Still, I decided that everyone would expect us to, and my not sitting beside her would raise unnecessary questions. So, as usual, I did what was expected of me, all the time feeling comfortable in her presence. I was excited to realize I could look at her, talk to her, and still feel no pain or anguish. Relief flooded through me, and I felt a sense of hope that the worst was over. I was healing.

I called Janie that afternoon because she had asked for details about an upcoming appearance by Rabbi Kushner, the author of a book Janie had recommended to me, titled *How Good Do We Have to Be?* We talked for a long time, which was so enjoyable. Again, I felt no pain or longing through the interaction. I was thrilled to finally feel friendship, and nothing more, toward Janie. My crush was over! Yet my desire to belong and share my life with someone was not.

One night at church, while our pastor was leading a discussion in the fellowship hall, Barbara moved her chair to sit close to her husband. That display of harmony caused my heart to ache. I felt resentment as they enjoyed each other's company and companionship. Their affection for each other was publicly acceptable, whereas Barbara's interpretation of scripture prohibited me from experiencing anything similar.

Greg, the friend I occasionally chauffeured around, sent me an email on October 9, explaining that he had contacted a counselor friend about me. Greg still had difficulty understanding my claim to be lesbian. He thought I'd jumped the gun and that I couldn't be a lesbian if I weren't having an affair with a woman. This had been a very perplexing issue for him, and I was discouraged to hear of his doubt until I read the letter his counselor friend had sent to him, which read:

Got your email. Yes, I do know something about lesbians. As with any sexual orientation issues, this one has more to do with how a person experiences intimacy with other people, and not just sexual intimacy (that's the easy part). The fact that she has not actually had genital or sexual contact with another woman would not mean that she is premature in claiming that she is a lesbian. She would know that well before she ever had a girlfriend.

Think back to being a teenager. You were pretty sure who you wanted long before you found a way to 'score' with a woman. Although you had not had any heterosexual, genital, or sexual intimacy, you were quite correct to assume you were heterosexual. In much the same way, this sixty-year-old woman can say that she is a lesbian. Sexual activity is not determinative of sexual orientation. Sexual orientation is determinative of sexual activity. You can have the orientation without ever having the activity.

Sexual orientation is so much more than a preference or a choice. It is not a matter of liking something the way we like (or dislike) cherry Cokes, for instance. It is a whole different way of experiencing the world.

In our world, it is not at all unusual for someone sixty years old to finally get around to recognizing that their true orientation is as a lesbian. Many, many, many lesbians marry and have children (sometimes finding no other options in their world at the time) and eventually recognize and find the courage to act upon their true orientation. It does not invalidate the good times and the good feelings that almost certainly were present in the marriage. It does not mean the marriage was a lie.

I think we are moving into a world that will not FORCE young people to marry. Lesbians will not be forced into heterosexual marriages. Society will not push as hard for conformity. We will celebrate diversity and welcome it even in our own families.

We will not be so quick to demonize the adult actions of people different from us. We will decriminalize consenting intimate actions between consenting adults. We will let people love whom they will.

The Church will have to quit loading the rifles of people they are setting up to persecute those whom the church regards as sinners. We will have to learn to let God be God and not get ourselves mixed up on this point and start acting like "Vengeance is mine," because the Lord said,

"Vengeance is MINE, I will repay." We can get comfortable knowing that all these years, God has run the Universe without needing me to stick MY nose in it.

If we can make some of those dreams come true, we will have worked to make our prayer come true ("Thy Kingdom come on earth..."), at least in our little corner of the earth and in our hearts.

Tell your friend that you know she did not come to her decision [to come out] easily and that it took lots of courage to say and do what she did. Tell her that you will be praying that she will find new strength each day to be the person God created her to be.

Greg, nobody can CHOOSE to become a lesbian. That is a matter of creation. (For that matter, nobody can CHOOSE to be straight; that, too, is a gift of the Creator.)

We are what we are. It is what we CHOOSE to do about it that "separates the women from the girls", in the case of this sixty-year-old lesbian.

Of course, when anybody asks me, I tell them not to wait until they're sixty to get real with themselves and their families. Get with it; time's a-wasting! Be who you ARE. Let the chips fall. Let other people figure it out; you are responsible for yourself. Don't be captive to other people's ignorance and prejudice.

Move on. And anyone who refuses to bless you, move away from that person—no one needs their condemnation.

Your sixty-year-old friend might merit a medal for valor.

What a letter! I was ecstatic upon reading it and shared it with Barbara, Brenda, and Janie, who rejoiced with me in its affirmation of my sexual orientation in such a wonderfully positive manner. I read the letter multiple times as I found it so uplifting.

Despite the struggles and moments of anguish I still felt, this letter ignited some deep reflection over the last year. I realized God had sent special people into my life to help me through the rough spots. An email friend sent me a copy of a poem by Brian A. "Drew" Chalker titled "Reason, Season and a Lifetime." It hit home when I read it, so I filed it for future reference. As I reread it, I felt it was appropriate to the past year of my life.

The first line, "People always come into your life for a reason, a season, or a lifetime..." really hit home. It reminded me of Janie and Barbara.

Janie's outspokenness in supporting her gay son is what led me to admit to myself that I am gay. Even though deep down I'd always known it to be true, I refused to admit it, especially to anyone else. Janie figured it out when she realized I had a crush on her, and instead of putting distance between the two of us, she stood by me, always encouraging, warm, and caring. Barbara, who had been merely an acquaintance, turned out to be my tower of strength, always there for me, always encouraging, always boosting my spirits, and always cheering me on despite our disagreement over certain theologies.

These thoughts continued as I moved on to words in the second paragraph: "They have come to assist you through a difficulty, or to provide you with guidance and support, to aid you physically, emotionally, or even spiritually. They may seem like a godsend to you, and they are. They are there for the reason you need them to be..."

We were only a week away from Thanksgiving, and I felt very grateful for all my friends and family members who stood by me.

The thought crossed my mind several times that day that only a year ago, I was living in misery and despair, just wanting to survive. I was so much better off now, even occasionally singing to myself as I took my walks. This year, without a doubt, I had more than usual to be thankful for.

27
MORE THAN FRIENDS

*B*renda wrote to me on October 11th: "Happy Coming Out Day! How does it feel? I think we should celebrate."

I greeted her the same way and said, "I wouldn't trade coming out for anything."

Brenda had become my go-to friend and someone I often relied on. I had no romantic feelings toward Brenda then, but I couldn't deny that our friendship deepened and could easily turn into something more. After all, we were both older, single lesbian women who seemed to have no other close lesbian friends our age and who regularly stayed in contact with each other. Anyone would agree we seemed destined to end up together. Still, having just gotten over my unwanted feelings for Janie and the anguish it caused, I was apprehensive about welcoming an emotional pull toward Brenda. Still, I couldn't deny one was beginning to grow.

At the same time, I was healing from my feelings for Janie and getting to know Brenda more; I was also attending another Beth Moore Bible study with sixteen other women. This one was about bondage and setting ourselves free. It was a hard study for me, particularly because the past week had been especially difficult. The video lesson that day focused on a specific type of bondage that's handed down from one generation to another: prejudice.

The only prejudice mentioned by the study was racial prejudice, and I sat hurt by the other unspoken prejudices that existed in our community, even in this very room; prejudices that had impacted my life decisions and those of so many others. I used a bunch of tissues but didn't think anyone noticed as I sat in the back of the room. Some in the group knew about me, but it was a small minority. I felt emotionally drained afterward and welcomed any opportunity to lift my spirits.

I wrote to Brenda the following day about a concert in Bergfeld Park at 7:30 on Saturday evening, featuring the East Texas Symphony Orchestra. They planned to play Tchaikovsky, Gershwin, Debussy, Grieg, Strauss, Berlioz, and Bizet.

"Can't beat that!" I wrote. *(Except there was no Schubert or Mozart.)* *"Anyway, are you interested in going? Many of the selections were listed in yesterday's newspaper, and they sound wonderful."*

Brenda replied that I'd "beaten her to the draw." She'd read about the concert and was thinking along the same lines, saying it sounded like a great lesson in the classics. She asked if I wanted to come over to her house and walk to the park from there, or suggested that I could come earlier, and she could fix us some dinner or split one of Bruno's half lasagnas or one of their large salads. I readily accepted, and we had a great time.

As I drove Greg around that day, I mentioned the upcoming concert and indicated my plans to attend.

"Alone?" he asked.

"No, I'll go with a friend."

"A man?"

"Now, Greg, why would I go with a man?"

"Well, what's her name?"

"Brenda."

Later that afternoon, I told him about Saving Grace, a movie I'd seen that I thought he'd enjoy. Again, he gave me his usual quiz about who I went with or if I went alone. I had to tell him again, "Brenda."

Despite my protests, he jumped to all kinds of wrong conclusions. He then asked, "Where did you meet her?"

"At a PFLAG meeting. It's a group that supports the lesbian and gay community." I explained.

Greg was a slow learner, but he kept plugging along. He tickled me with his questions. He was one of the very few individuals who showed interest in the fact that I'm gay. I talked with Barbara and Janie about my sexual orientation, but to have someone show interest and ask genuinely curious questions about my love life was surprising and caused me to smile inside. It also helped remind me that I took myself too seriously at times. It was good for me to be around Greg.

The concert in the park with Brenda was another wonderful experience, and I was thrilled when she invited me to her house the next afternoon to watch a video and eat soup and cornbread. I looked forward to it even though it wouldn't just be us. She'd also invited a male friend who didn't cook for himself, so it was a lovely, cozy evening, perfect for the fall weather arriving just in time for Thanksgiving. As I watched TV with them that night, a scene of a couple gently kissing for the first time awoke a feeling I thought had disappeared. I thought about Brenda and the possibility of kissing her, though I didn't allow myself to linger on the thought too long for fear of getting too attached.

Luckily, that angst was replaced by a wonderful Thanksgiving Day with Brenda, who invited me to attend a service with her at St. Dismas, a small, open, and affirming community. I thoroughly enjoyed the informal mass, which consisted of approximately twenty people who gathered for the service. Everyone present had had to combat some challenge that left them feeling outside "normal" society: the death of a child, alcoholism, drug addictions, and homosexuality, to name a few. We were all broken, mending people coming together to support each other, and it felt good being there. The potluck meal that followed was delicious and comforting with everyone's presence and support.

Afterward, Brenda and I went to my apartment to watch *Angela's Ashes*. As usual, we sat on the floor with our backs against the sofa. A large vicuna rug provided a soft seat, and pillows at our backs made this a comfortable viewing position.

After the movie, we saw the last part of *Who Wants to Be a Millionaire* and the beginning of some news show. As we watched the TV together, our hands occasionally touched and pulled away like we were young kids in a theater. Neither one of us wanted to be the one to make the first move to hold hands, yet we wanted the same thing. Finally, Brenda took my hand. "Do you mind?"

"No, not at all," I answered, enjoying her closeness, touch, and the warmth of simply being next to her. "The Prozac hasn't completely taken away all my feelings, you know," I added nervously.

A little later, Brenda suggested we turn off the TV and just talk, which suited me fine. I was yearning for more than simply holding her hand, and I felt certain she was holding back to avoid offending me in some way. She had always been very careful and considerate, and I was feeling a passion that had been subdued for many years. I never thought I'd feel this desire for anyone again, and I rejoiced to know I was wrong.

At my playful but sincere comment about the Prozac, she turned and faced me, then gently kissed me. My response was so positive that we were quickly in each other's arms. To this day, she teases me about my passionate response to that first kiss. And she's right. All my pent-up emotion seemed to come out with that first kiss.

Holding each other and kissing brought immediate, unbelievable happiness, accompanied by excitement to realize I was experiencing a feeling I had been yearning for many years. It was fantastic. I kept thinking, *"It's been over forty years since I've felt like this, forty years since I've held and kissed a woman."*

Being with Brenda felt wonderful. Kissing her was so natural and desirable. I'd thought the Prozac had numbed all my sexual feelings, but I discovered that night that this wasn't true. Despite our passion, we both held back. At one point, she called me "sweet," and my heart pounded. She asked, "Are you alright?" worried about me, fearful I might be overwhelmed with guilt, as she thought I was crying during a moment of stillness and silence between caresses. I assured her I was fine, just quietly thinking. All I could say was, "You feel so good to me. It's hard to describe how good you feel to me."

I had a lot of thinking to do on Brenda and our passion before I found the right words. All I knew was that the moment was blissful, and I was happy to share it with her.

Sadly, I left for Austin the following day for a much-needed break, not from the new developments with Brenda but from the everyday, around-the-clock care of my 89-year-old mother, whose broken hip from August was still requiring much-needed attention and care. Now that she could get up and around on her own, I felt a need to get away for a while. Laura was away visiting a friend in New York City and had invited me to stay in her Austin apartment, so I accepted her offer and enjoyed four days of freedom from all responsibilities.

Once I arrived at Laura's apartment, I thought about Brenda a lot and wished she were there with me. I often considered calling her, but I had no idea what I would say, except that I missed her. I've always felt more comfortable talking with someone in person than over the phone.

After spending the weekend in Austin, I picked up Laura at the airport at noon on Monday, drove her back to her apartment, and then traveled the 224 miles directly from Austin to Tyler to be at handbell practice by 5:30, arriving only five minutes late.

That evening, I emailed Brenda to come over for supper the next night. She told me later she was so delighted to know I wanted to see her again that she shouted in joy. Because I hadn't called her, she was afraid I might not want to see her again.

The following day, Janie called. I was surprised and delighted. She said it had been at least three weeks since we'd seen each other, and we chatted for an hour and a half. When she asked what was going on in my life, I told her about kissing Brenda.

"What was it like?" she asked.

"Wonderful."

"Oh, I'm so glad!"

And I knew she was. She'd been wanting me to find someone for such a long time. "Does Brenda like you?" she asked.

"I think so."

"Well, she'd have to be nuts not to be absolutely crazy about you."

"Oh, Janie!"

"No, that's right. You're such a precious person."

Five days had passed since Brenda and I last saw each other and kissed for the first time. The next morning, she responded to my supper invitation, apologizing for just then reading my email and asking, "Which night are you referring to?"

"Tonight," I replied, explaining that it would be a simple meal.

I prepared a quiche and a pistachio ambrosia salad. After the meal, we enjoyed hugging and kissing more. My feelings for Brenda were growing daily, which pleased me very much.

Brenda returned the next night, on Thursday, to use my computer, and we ended up being affectionate again. I was dumbfounded that all this was happening to me, and even happier that I felt absolutely no guilt or shame. I kept expecting those feelings to crop up, but they didn't. Despite my 61 years as a Southern Baptist, surrounded by homophobic hate and abusive use of the Bible against gays, I didn't feel sinful. I didn't feel guilty. I felt no shame. All I felt was a type of cleansing—a purity—a feeling of being where I was meant to be. More than anything, I felt a sense of relief.

Two days later, Brenda's long letter arrived by snail mail. She wrote it after she returned home the night of our quiche supper.

Dear Lou Anne,

I came home, put myself in a tub of hot water, bathed in candlelight, and (soothed by the music of Yanni) began to weep. Yanni's melodies are so passionate and soulful that they often pluck chords of emotion within me.

When I first met you, I felt some interest and attraction. I saw you not only as courageous but also as someone with whom I had some common experiences, someone who could be a friend, someone who was single and could be a partner in just doing things. And, yes, I confess to a bit of physical attraction. I've always thought you were and are cute as a bug.

As we visited and I got to see you more, I liked what I saw. You're an amazing woman—courageous, caring, desiring truth, determined to live in that truth, and having the fortitude to keep moving, growing, and being who you are and who you are becoming. I also admire your sensitivity, humor, intelligence, and playfulness.

I just wanted to be available for friendship, encouragement, and support for you, even knowing at the same time my own need for friendship, encouragement, and support. Yes, just a friend as you dealt with your full plate—leaving your marriage, coming out, your struggles and disappointments with church and friends, getting through your feelings about Janie, and then your mother's illness. And I thought I was successful in cutting off any physical or romantic attractions I might have had. (I have had a lot of practice in that, you know)

However, these last few weeks, as we've spent more time together, conversing and sharing, I've had to be honest with myself about my growing attraction—my desire to hold you, touch you gently, and kiss you passionately. I couldn't stay away from you and let the feelings die a painful natural death over time, nor could I be around you and continue to ache inside.

So, Thanksgiving evening—oh, I want you to know I was so proud and pleased to have you with me at St. Dismas—I mustered every ounce of courage I might have and said, "Let's turn the TV off and talk." I held your hand, and when you turned to me and said that the Prozac hadn't killed everything, that you were feeling something, I kissed you.

I admit I was a bit surprised but very pleased with your response— warm and tender, as if you might like me.

I don't know about you, Lou Anne, but I'm definitely in uncharted territory here. I feel happy and excited, as well as a little (a lot) of uncertainty. As I wept earlier in the bathtub, I was thinking: What do I want? This is my answer:

I want you and me to listen to Yanni's music together. I want you to hear the song "Desperado," and then you'll know my greatest fear and pain. I want to dance with you while Kenny G plays.

Yes, I want to dance with you, literally. I also want us to keep dancing—figuratively, as well. I want to keep doing the steps as whatever it is—be it friendship or relationship— develops between us into whatever it's supposed to be. I don't have a clue. I just know I'm tired of running from myself and others. I want to do it differently this time.

Well, Lou Anne, I hope some of this makes a little sense. I just want to be honest. I've said a lot about me and what I want—aren't I self-centered? I'll close with as much honesty and lack of self-centeredness as I can muster by saying I love you. I truly want for you what is best and good for you in your life.

I love you,
Brenda

I've always held my feelings very close. Many years ago, my brother called me stoic, and his observation came to mind when I read Brenda's letter. I saw my emotions staying contained on the outside while my insides seemed to be churning. I was surprised and flattered by her openness and honesty. My heart pounded harder than usual as I reread and digested her words and realized the special friendship/relationship she was offering me. I also panicked when I realized I felt totally inadequate to answer her letter. There was simply too much happening inside me to put into words. Knowing I'd see her again that night, I sidestepped, replying in kind by saying, "I don't intend to do much commenting over the Internet about the wonderful letter I just received. I'm counting the hours until I see you."

I had a date with Brenda at her house to eat spaghetti and help her decorate her Christmas tree, and I couldn't wait to be there with her.

Dressing carefully, adding a little color to my cheeks, running a brush through my short hair, and refreshing my lipstick were all it took to get ready for the evening. The whole time I was primping, my thoughts drifted, imagining the feeling of Brenda in my arms, laying my head on her shoulder, and kissing her. It was amazing I was able to get myself presentable at all. Just holding or kissing Brenda released feelings throughout my whole being that seemed new despite having experienced them when I was a teenager. When the time arrived to leave, I practically jogged out the door to my car.

Sure enough—just as I had dreamed it—as soon as she opened the door to my knock that evening, she reached out and took me in her arms, and we held each other and kissed. This became "standard procedure" every time we visited each other. Her embraces always set my heart to hammering.

Supper was delicious, and it was fun being with her. I was learning to appreciate her more and more. She was intelligent, kind, generous, respected by others, cute, and, most importantly, honorable and truthful. All I could think was *that she was one in a million*, and I felt very fortunate that she seemed to care for me in kind.

Decorating her Christmas tree didn't take long, so we had hours to enjoy holding, kissing, and talking afterward. After decades of aching to feel anything good, I found it unbelievable that life was suddenly so enjoyable. With Brenda beside me, I was now looking forward to the next day, the next week, the following year. It was unbelievable.

The following day, Saturday, December 2nd, I took Brenda with me to visit my mother so they could meet. We only stayed a few minutes, as I was fearful Mother might realize the relationship between Brenda and me. I wish I hadn't been so afraid of my mother's opinion of me, but I was. Brenda understood, and we were both glad the visit was genuinely "short and sweet."

As Brenda and I visited that night, we began a practice of asking each other, "What are you thinking right now?" The honest answers we gave to that question helped us get to know each other more deeply. Those conversations, combined with a courtship that was heating up, led us to discuss our future together. We were both longing for complete intimacy and decided that Brenda would spend the night with me in a week, on Friday, December 8th.

28
OLD FEELINGS, NEW JOYS

*W*hen I awoke on Sunday morning, December 3rd, I wished Brenda were with me, not Janie. Since October 8th, when I realized my intense feelings toward Janie had vanished, I had been feeling nothing but relief. What a gift to be free of those agonizing, unwelcome feelings. I was free to simply be friends with Janie and free to love Brenda without fear or hesitation.

During both the morning and evening services, I longed for her to be by my side that Sunday. I wanted to feel her snuggled up next to me like the other cozy couples worshiping together throughout the pews. I knew it would have been difficult not to hold her hand if she were there, and I didn't think my church was ready to see that. Even late Sunday night, I thought of her, wishing she were with me.

Wanting to feel the whole expanse of my feelings for Brenda, I decided it was time I got off the Prozac. I took my first antidepressant during the early part of 2000 when my overwhelming longings for Janie had driven me into a deep depression. However, it was now December, and eight months had passed since I began taking the drug. That pain of wanting Janie was gone, and I no longer needed the help Prozac offered me.

Brenda was now in my life, and I felt a genuine closeness to her, yet the Prozac was continuing to dull my emotions. On December 4th, I called my doctor to tell him I was ready to get off it, and he gave me a simple schedule to follow, which I started immediately.

By the time Brenda spent the night with me three days later, on Friday, December 8th, I was beginning to feel like my old self before Prozac came into my life, which made the night even more wondrous.

Feeling a woman's body next to mine for the first time in over forty years was heavenly as if I were where I was supposed to be. I felt calm, happy, and contented, with no guilt or shame. As we rested in each other's embrace, a mental image of Jesus smiling down upon us with the most glorious, approving smile popped into my head.

The feeling of His blessing and delight in our happiness was more meaningful to me than any marriage ceremony. During my thirty-seven years of marriage to Jim, I never pictured Jesus approving of our emotional connection or physical relationship. Now, I felt his approval throughout my whole being. I knew that Brenda and I had married each other in God's eyes. My happiness was so overwhelming, I constantly reminded myself it was real—that holding Brenda in my arms was no dream. I savored every minute with an awareness of a physical closeness I'd longed for for many years.

The next night, we attended an all-lesbian party, which was a first for me (not counting the pool party during the summer). Invitations went out to 117 women, and at least eighty people attended, which was amazing to me, considering a year ago, I didn't know a single lesbian. We ate lots of fantastic food. Each time I wandered through the kitchen, pans of various appetizers (such as little quiches or pigs in a blanket) were removed from the oven or slid into the oven to bake. Many of the foods served were new to me as I'd never purchased prepared appetizers, and I found them delicious.

The house was crowded, and there were few places to sit. Consequently, we tended to wander from one room to another, meeting and greeting. The lights were on in the backyard, enabling guests to wander outside. Besides the all-girls band, whose music kept the atmosphere lively, there was a Santa Claus happily pulling one girl after another into his lap. Yes, a few fellows were at the party, probably fewer than ten.

At one point, a large group headed to the front carport, where we stood in a circle and played some silly, bachelorette-type game with a dildo. I had never heard of or seen a dildo and had certainly never touched one. I can still picture the girls laughing hysterically and passing that limp, floppy plastic around like a hot potato. Despite my initial embarrassment, I laughed along with the others. I felt relieved when that game ended, and my stomach muscles could relax from all the laughing. By the time all the crazy games ended, I was convinced I had led a very sheltered life and grew excited to think that a life with Brenda held the promise of many more adventures to come.

I mailed about eighty Christmas letters that year, which announced—in addition to news of my divorce, my church activities, the birth of a new grandson, and my mother's broken hip—that I was much happier than I'd been in a long, long time. Tears sprang to my eyes as I concluded the letter with:

"By the grace of God, our suffering can be transformed into something that brings life and light to this world." I believe that is what is happening in my life, and I praise the Lord for his tender care and guidance.

May knowing that you are in the hands of an all-powerful, all-loving God bring you peace.

Lou Anne

While I didn't go into the specifics about what was unfolding between Brenda and me, I felt compelled to proclaim my happiness, to let my family and close friends know how good my life has become. I certainly didn't want to be specific as it would only bring pain to Jim and others in my family. But when you're happy, you want to shout and share your happiness with others, and these words became my muted shout in my Christmas letter.

That holiday season was made even colder by the icy weather. It was beautiful outside with all the ice, but tree limbs were breaking, power was out in many parts of town, traffic signals were malfunctioning, and the water pressure was dropping. This turned out to be a terrible ice storm in East Texas. Some homes ended up without electricity for a month or more.

I was quite surprised to receive a letter from a Dallas man Jim and I had known in the early sixties. He'd been a friend of Jim's before our marriage, and we occasionally visited his family.

He'd received my Christmas card and replied that he appreciated it and had thought of me frequently this year. His letter went on to explain that he had a note from Jim via email that shared the information about the divorce. He explained, *"Bless his heart; he's still hurting from it, but I fully understand and appreciate your feelings, too. I probably understand your vantage point more than I do his. As I explained to Jim, I've known that I'm gay for many years now."*

I sat in appreciative surprise as I continued reading,

"I had to reconcile that fact with my wife and son quite a while ago. I enjoyed your quote about transforming our suffering into something that

brings life and light into the world. Very true, indeed. My wife remarked repeatedly about how the Holy Spirit marches through our lives wearing combat boots. Also, it is a very apt expression. I still have a few cleat marks to show for that presence."

He ended his letter wishing me the best in life and expressing his desire to keep in touch with the reassurance that our friendship would remain "solidly intact."

I immediately responded, telling him I appreciated his note and understanding. "It's as if we are all members of the same club, put on earth to support each other." I wrote, "I've been amazed at how many of my friends are affected by either being gay or having a gay child. If everyone came out of the closet at once, the nation would be flabbergasted."

I then told him my story about why I married and what my life had been like. I concluded by thanking him for his honesty and telling him I was glad he had a partner. I then explained that my recent involvement with a woman had brought me peace and contentment I hadn't felt for a long time.

He answered immediately and shared his story with me, saying that his wife had had a tough time at first but later became his staunchest advocate.

"She'd remark, 'Honey, you didn't ask to be gay any more than I asked to have MS.' Very tolerant, very understanding. I was blessed to have that sweet thing in my life those thirty years—even if I WAS hiding the truth from her and me both," he wrote.

He also admitted that when he came out to Jim not long ago, he'd hit him too close to home because he'd never received a reply to his letter.

When I shared the letter I'd written to my Dallas friend with Barbara, she found it interesting that I'd recently become involved with a woman, although she had suspected it. She said she supposed I meant Brenda and hoped to get to know her better.

She also warned me to take it slow and easy in any new relationship and to be very sure before I committed to someone else.

When I answered Barbara later that day, I admitted I'd decided to let the cat out of the bag because I figured she knew anyway. I reminded her that Brenda and I had met on April 10 and didn't even hold hands until Thanksgiving.

Then I said that Brenda and I had every intention of growing old together and that, since I wasn't far from the "old" category, we laughingly talked about the future when she might use a walker to push my wheelchair.

Amidst holiday preparations and celebrations, Janie and I ate together at McAllister's and visited for about an hour and a half one day for lunch. Afterward, I wrote to Brenda about the meeting to tell her how delighted I was that my painful feelings toward Janie had disappeared.

I shared the good news not only with Brenda but also with Barbara, who quickly replied.

Now there's a Christmas gift! How are you doing without Prozac? How are preparations coming for your mother's ninetieth birthday party? In other words, are you doing okay? Is life becoming more joyful for you more of the time? Can you sit down and read a book?

Your nosy but caring friend,
Barbara

I replied that this Christmas would be much different than last year's.

It's as if I have to constantly pinch myself to be assured my feelings of happiness and contentment are real. I've just completed my two-week withdrawal period for the Prozac and took my last pill yesterday morning. This week, and possibly the next, will tell the tale.

In the spirit of all the letter writing I was doing that season, I decided to write a coming-out letter to Marta, a friend from the sixties who now lived in Oregon. I hoped that sharing my joy would only bring joy to others. Her reply pleased me and brought back memories. She said she wasn't shocked, but hadn't realized how unhappy I had been.

Lou Anne,

In the 1966-68 scheme of things, I saw only a dedicated, wonderful, beautiful wife and mother, somewhat reserved but always giving unstintingly of herself. You were the pie-crust wizard who showed me that working in the least amount of water equaled flakier crust; you shared recipes I still have; and you and Jim were always available for forays to the Night Hawk or such for food and fun. You were the one with a burning desire to write. You were the one who stretched herself to meet a most interesting variety of jobs over the years. Your Christmas letters always brought news of some additional mastery...always humble, always capable and skilled.

I admired you enormously then, and I admire and respect you enormously now. Your letter gives me a broader perspective, and I understand that only your courageous stand could relieve the pervasive pain of forty years of endurance. I applaud you and am thankful for the support of your children. Forty years in the wilderness. May you surely know the presence of the Lord as He holds you in the palm of His hand.

It seems the older I get, the flimsier and more useless our facades are, and the only true dialogue is soul to soul. I sense that is what you have shared with me here, and I am deeply touched.

Love,

Marta

Our letters reminded me that my parents never spoke openly about my homosexuality. However, one afternoon, after I had been married for almost twenty years and had already had my fourth child, Dad privately told me, "I want to apologize for what I once thought about you." His statement came entirely out of the blue. Though we had *never* openly broached the subject, I knew what he referred to. My mother had brought up the subject only once, when I was seventeen and a freshman at Baylor. My being homosexual was like the proverbial elephant in the living room.

At the time of Dad's statement, I could have simply accepted his apology and thereby let him believe he'd made a terrible mistake when he convinced Mother I was a homosexual, or I could confess that he owed me no apology because he'd been correct the whole time.

At that moment, I concluded that confessing the truth would deeply hurt him more than having judged me unfairly. I, therefore, replied, "That's all right, Dad. No problem." And that's all that was ever said between us on this subject.

Dad passed away in 1996 at age eighty-six, and I lost my chance to ever tell him I'm a lesbian. Perhaps that was best for both of us. If he had adhered to the Southern Baptist belief that homosexuality was an affront to God, then he would have condemned me and insisted I repent. On the other hand, if he acknowledged his love and support for me despite my sexual orientation, he would have probably urged me to leave Jim. That would have been tough because the children were young, and I would no longer be able to be a stay-at-home mother to them. I would have had to work a full-time job plus care for my children, with the youngest not yet in school.

When people ask me, 'If you had your life to live over again, what would you do differently?' And that's simply a question that has no answer. If I had never married Jim, I wouldn't have the four wonderful children I have, along with my six grandchildren. My children and grandchildren have enriched my life beyond measure. Sometimes, difficult paths lead to the most incredible treasures; indeed, my life now was richer than it had ever been.

Because we were taught that homosexuals are bad people, Brenda and I braced ourselves to be overwhelmed with guilt or feelings that we must be "bad." When this feeling never materialized, another heavy burden was lifted from our shoulders.

Brenda and I continued to feel contentment based on the assurance that, in God's sight, we were as married as any heterosexual couple. We knew this to be true because when we were together, we were enveloped in a sense of peace and serenity, always aware that God had brought us together and that Christ's presence was with us.

As we lay in each other's arms in the many nights that followed that first one, Brenda would sing to me. She has a beautiful voice, and I felt proud whenever she joined me at church and eventually became a member of First Baptist.

One of my church friends asked me, sometime in 2001, "Who's that cute girl who sits with you in church?" At first, her question baffled me, but then I realized she'd been viewing Brenda and me from the choir loft. I proudly shared Brenda's name with her and explained that she was my dear friend.

My relationship with Brenda blossomed for almost three years while I lived in my tiny apartment, and she remained in her small home. She worked regular hours, and although I had retired as a teacher, I became pretty active in running the office of a newly formed non-profit group that was developing a faith-based health clinic for the under-served and working poor in our community. My work at Bethesda Health Clinic became challenging and time-consuming, so Brenda and I became weekend lovers and companions.

We occasionally discussed purchasing a home together and even shared these thoughts with Sidney, a realtor friend who took the time to show us some houses. None interested us, but he was forming an idea of what kind of house we wanted. One weekend at the end of August 2003, Sidney called us to say, "You've got to come see this house. I think it's just what you're looking for, and the price has just been lowered."

We tried to put him off for a day or two, but he insisted a house at that price was bound to disappear, so we told him, "We're on our way," before quickly hanging up.

We knew almost immediately that the house was just right for us. The inside appealed to both of us because it was all white, allowing the home to reflect all the bright, natural light through the windows. We both loved all the built-in bookcases and storage areas, and when we looked out the sliding glass door that opened to the backyard, we practically gasped at the sight of a large wooden deck and the lush, green, well-manicured lawn beyond it. That yard cinched it. This brick, ranch-style, 3-bedroom, 2-bath home priced just under $100,000 spoke loudly to our pocketbooks and even louder to our hearts. Other families were also looking at the house while we were there, and Sidney kept urging us to get our bid in before they did. In less than an hour, we were signing papers to purchase our new home.

The house was an outward symbol of our committed relationship, and convincing the mortgage company to place our names on the deed became challenging. It wasn't that they didn't want to be accommodating, but they'd never had such a request. In 2003, we must have been the only gay couple for whom they'd ever provided a home mortgage. They didn't seem to know how to do it, but, in the end, like the love Brenda and I shared, they found a way, and it was done.

In the years to come, we kept reminding them that when they sent us an interest statement at the end of each year, our names needed to be on the statement, both in full. They once listed "Lou Anne McWilliams" instead of Lou Anne Smoot and Brenda McWilliams. We would just laugh, give them a call, patiently explain what we needed, and they'd do their best to comply. To make our home purchase even more special, our moving-in date was October 11, 2003, which also happened to be National Coming Out Day. It has been 21 years since we first moved in, and we continue to feel quite fortunate to have found this house and each other.

29
CONFRONTATIONS IN CONGREGATION

The three years between Brenda and my first official night together as a couple and purchasing our first home were filled with equal moments of delight, beautiful memories, and challenges. Together, we made a stunning mosaic of all life offered and threw at us.

In March 2001, Brenda and I attended the Southern Regional PFLAG (Parents, Families and Friends of Lesbians and Gays) Conference in Dallas, which allowed us to be seen in public as a couple. When we registered at the hotel and asked for a room with one bed, I felt self-conscious and concerned about others' possible negative opinions. But no more hiding, no more pretending, no more doing what was expected by getting a room with two beds and using only one. Once we'd crossed that threshold, I found it much easier to ask for one bed the next time and the next.

We often held hands as we walked across campus to attend the conference. We never held hands publicly in Tyler and enjoyed this freedom to just be ourselves. It felt so good and so right.

During the conference's many meetings, I discovered that my emotions were constantly bubbling near the surface. I kept hearing statements I'd never heard before—some I'd never really thought about—that applied directly to me. For example, in discussing gender, a speaker pointed out that a person's gender identification has nothing to do with sexual orientation. In other words, in my case, it's all right to be feminine (which I consider myself to be) yet to have a sexual orientation, making me desire a woman for a partner. Another way to put it: A woman doesn't have to look or act "butch" to be a lesbian.

Other comments that hit home included these three: (1) "The more painful the outing, the more potential for happiness." (2) "When you first hear something affirming about homosexuality, you decide to come out." (3) "Negative comments about homosexuality from family cause an individual to stay in the closet." All these statements were factual for me.

In November 2001, my mother passed away at the age of ninety. Although she and I never had another conversation about my being gay other than the one when I was 17 years old and attending Baylor, I believe she had been doing some deep thinking about the issue. She realized I'd been very unhappy in my marriage, and by the time of her death, Brenda had become a regular part of my life. My boldness was growing even before her death, and my mother was an intelligent woman. Her death permitted me to be more visible as a lesbian.

When Brenda finally joined me as a member of First Baptist in 2001, amidst these significant life events, we boldly served together as an example of a gay Christian couple in a committed, covenant relationship. We made a point of sitting together in the front rows of the sanctuary, near the center aisle so that others could see us. We were out and simply refused to hide, regardless of the setting.

Everyone was friendly to us and never mentioned the fact that we were gay. No one wanted to talk about the subject, but gradually, the members became accustomed to seeing the two of us together. When only one of us showed up for an event, someone invariably asked where the other was.

While attending First Baptist together, Brenda and I were members of different Sunday School classes and departments, primarily because of our age difference. I'm 11 ½ years older than Brenda, and she gravitated toward the Singles department, whose members were closer to her age, while I stuck with my old Sunday School class. Another unspoken reason we decided to go our separate ways during the Sunday School hour was a sincere desire to divide and conquer. By being in different departments, we were able to serve as an example of a "gay Christian" to many more people in hopes of breaking barriers where we knew they were held most strongly. In most fundamentalist churches, there is no such thing as a "gay Christian." That's considered an oxymoron. We wanted to encourage members to question that oxymoron.

Because we were in different departments, we attended the social events of both groups. That introduced us as a "couple" to large groups in both departments. The only time this became awkward was at my department's Christmas party, where a game was played pitting husbands and wives against each other. They didn't know what to do with the two of us, so we were designated as judges.

To help members know one another better, our church organized Shake and Bake groups. These groups consisted of four to five families of varying ages. Baptist Sunday School classes are organized by age, so in a large church like ours, we have few opportunities to get to know members not in our age bracket. "Shake" was the plan to mix up the membership so people of different ages could engage in church life and community together. "Bake" was the plan to get these members to eat together once a month, either in a member's home or a restaurant.

Brenda and I participated in a group in 2002 and thoroughly enjoyed it. There were three or four other couples in our group. Several of the couples were much older and have now passed away. Another couple, who were slightly older than I and good friends with Barbara, sent word through Barbara that they had no problems with my being gay or my divorcing Jim. They initially thought I had asked for the divorce so I could pursue my desire to write. Barbara quickly set them straight when she explained that while I was still married, I had written two books while caring for young children.

The youngest couple in our Shake and Bake group became lifelong friends. They brought their two very young boys to the gatherings—the only ones with children. When we met, those boys were approximately 2 years and 3 months old. It's been over 20 years, and we still see them regularly as they own Brickstreet Pharmacy, where those little boys are now men who help their parents in the pharmacy, and we are regular patrons. Every time I pick up a prescription or go in for my flu shot, and one or both parents happen to be there, I get a big hug and a "catch-up" conversation as to what is going on in our lives. They are delightful people, and I am thankful to the Shake and Bake group for our special friendship.

Because we enjoyed our first Shake and Bake group so much, we signed up two years later to participate in a new group being formed. Before being assigned to a group, I listened to a phone message left on my answering machine by Wilson Rhodes, the associate pastor. He explained that the rules had changed with the Shake and Bake groups and that non-married couples would be assigned to separate groups.

This new rule felt explicitly designed to separate Brenda and me and prohibit our participation as a couple. I wrote to him expressing my sadness and disappointment with his decision and asking him if an engaged heterosexual couple wanting to participate in a Shake and Bake group would be allowed to do so, or if they would be separated because they were technically not yet married.

In that letter, I cautioned him that mainstream churches regularly drive away people who are different with rules designed to exclude rather than include.

"Isn't it sad that churches make certain Christians feel unwelcome and/or uncomfortable?" I wrote.

He never replied to my letter.

One of my favorite church memories from Brenda's and my "mission" at First Baptist involves a visiting Bible professor from a nearby Baptist college. He had served as an interim pastor at our church in years past, and I thought he was terrific because he thought outside the box. Few Baptists, in my experience, tended to do that. He was funny, energetic, engaging, and very knowledgeable. When I heard he would lead a series of Bible studies at our church during the summer of 2005, I told Brenda I wanted to go.

We arrived early enough to sit at the front table, close to the stage where he would be standing and speaking. The study was interesting, and I enjoyed it, looking up Bible passages and taking notes. Then he read aloud Matthew 9:10-11. "While Jesus was having dinner at Matthew's house, many tax collectors and sinners ate with him and his disciples. When the Pharisees saw this, they asked his disciples, 'Why does your teacher eat with tax collectors and sinners?'"

To expound on this passage and develop its relevance to our Bible Study group, he stated, "In today's world, Jesus's eating with sinners would be like his eating with..." He began to grope for a suitable comparison, trying to wrap his thoughts around an example of a modern-day sinner. Eventually, he confidently declared, "It would be like Jesus today eating in the home of lesbians."

I could feel my face glowing red and wished the floor would open and swallow me. The people sitting behind us were aware that Brenda and I were a couple. I heard nothing else he said. I concentrated solely on breathing and keeping my cool. When the study ended and we walked out of the room, Brenda said, "He kinda got to you, didn't he?"

"Yes, he did. And I'm going to write him a letter, but I want to think about it for a few days."

And that's what I did—I just thought about it. Finally, I sent him an email, telling him how much I'd always admired him, enjoyed hearing him speak, and looked forward to his Bible studies. Then I stated that I was sure he had no idea he had a lesbian couple sitting right in front of him at the Bible study on Wednesday.

I ended my letter with an invitation: "So you'll know what it's like to eat in the home of lesbians, we would like to invite you and your wife to eat with us Friday evening."

He responded immediately and was most apologetic. His faux pas had embarrassed him to no end. After thanking us for our dinner invitation, he regretfully declined, explaining that his wife was ill. We had heard she was on chemo, so of course, we understood, but he promised to come by our house for a visit after the following Bible study.

True to his word, he followed us to our home after the next session and visited with us for about an hour. He listened respectfully to our stories. By the time he left, I was convinced it had simply never occurred to this good, kind, highly educated Bible scholar that a Christian could be gay, or a gay person could be Christian. Hopefully, we opened his eyes.

Not long after Brenda joined the church, she quickly became active in the singles department, agreeing to teach a Sunday School class, becoming the leader of the singles council, and even volunteering to answer the phones during the televised Sunday morning worship service. As a trained pastoral counselor, she was the ideal person to listen to and pray with those who called the church to talk about their problems. Sadly, Brenda's commitments to First Baptist were about to change.

In November of 2005, the state of Texas was set to vote on a constitutional amendment called Proposition 2, which stated that marriage is solely between a man and a woman. Brenda produced a flyer to distribute to our neighbors, asking them to vote against this proposition. A picture of the two of us appeared at the top of her well-written letter urging people to reject this attempt to turn our state constitution into a discriminatory document. We distributed copies of the flier throughout our neighborhood, hanging it on doorknobs. Although we found it difficult to declare our relationship in both written and picture form for all to see, we more or less gritted our teeth and did it because we felt it was the right thing to do.

When the vote on Proposition 2 was tallied, it passed overwhelmingly in Texas. In our very conservative Smith County, it passed by a little over 90%. It was hard not to feel our minority status in this area.

Very soon after our first political effort as a couple, the minister of ministries and missions at our church, Evelyn Carpenter, contacted Brenda, setting up a meeting for the next Wednesday evening church supper. Because Evelyn gave Brenda no purpose for the meeting, she assumed it must have something to do with the singles department because Evelyn served as the overall singles director.

Much to Brenda's shock and surprise, Evelyn told her that night that First Baptist had decided she could no longer hold any leadership position in the church. As Evelyn shared this crushing information, she held a copy of the mustard-colored flier we had distributed. Someone had taken the flyer to the church, complaining, we supposed, about our membership in the church and the inappropriateness of a gay person being a Sunday School teacher. Evelyn made it clear to Brenda that she was simply the bearer of the news. She was chosen for this unpleasant task because the other church leaders knew she and Brenda were long-time friends, and they hoped the decision would perhaps appear less harsh coming from her.

That conversation ended Brenda's service to the church. She no longer taught her Sunday School class, led the singles council, and was never again asked to volunteer as a phone counselor during the televised morning worship service.

This decision by our church was cruel, and it angered me. I, too, had been discouraged from holding a leadership position when I first came out, but the church's approach seemed much kinder than the one Brenda had received; perhaps the goal was always the same: not to protect us, but to protect them. Seeing this dismissal from the outside sent a hot pain through my heart.

I imagine most people would have walked away from a church that treated them in such a hurtful and contemptible manner, but we never even considered it. We continued volunteering in ways that had nothing to do with leadership positions. When either of our Sunday School classes needed a substitute teacher, Brenda and I were the ones our respective classes called upon for that job. We continued to try to serve as a Christian example of a lesbian couple, but the insults and "small" moves to exclude us sadly kept coming.

One Sunday in September 2007, an announcement was made from the pulpit that the church would be sponsoring a Family Campout on November 9-10 at our local state park. Brenda and I enjoyed camping, so as soon as the announcement was made, we nudged each other and whispered, "Let's go!"

When morning worship ended, we headed to the church lobby and picked up an application form. In the next day or two, we completed the form, enclosed our check, and mailed it to the church more than a month before the event. Then, we marked our calendar and started counting down the days until this special day arrived.

A month later, two days before the campout, I received a phone call from Wilson Rhodes asking if he could visit.

"Sure," I replied. He'd never been to our home, so I knew something was up.

When I greeted him at the door and invited him in, he stated, "I guess you know why I'm here."

"Well, Wilson, it either has to do with your hearing that I taught our Sunday School class last Sunday, or it has to do with the Family Campout."

"We'll talk about the teaching another time. I'm here about the Family Campout. We think it best you do not go." He handed me the envelope I had mailed to the church, containing our application and check.

"Has someone complained?"

"No. I don't think anyone knows you planned to attend."

"Then why do you think it's best that we don't participate?"

"We just think it's best."

"But why?"

"We just think it's best."

That's all he would say. We talked for a while longer, and I took the opportunity to share part of my story with him, but tears started to well up. I handed him a little booklet to read by Walter Wink titled "Homosexuality and the Bible." He seemed anxious to leave and not at all interested in my story, so I gave up talking with him.

Later that evening, Brenda attended the Wednesday evening service and asked Wilson the very important question: "Why did you make this decision?"

He explained that he'd had to struggle with it. This struck a nerve with Brenda, who retorted, "*You've* had to struggle?"

Later, she felt terrible about her reaction and emailed him, apologizing for not acknowledging that he genuinely had wrestled with the decision.

Brenda heard nothing from him in reply. Everyone seemed eager to tell us "no" to things and less eager to discuss why. Several weeks later, as we sat in the sanctuary waiting for the morning service to begin, he came by, thanked her for her letter, and promised to send her a reply. He never did.

I kept the envelope containing our campout application and check as a reminder of how we were treated - with punishment instead of acceptance or love. I'm not sure anyone else was even aware this occurred, but I knew Wilson had a very difficult time with my being gay, as he was one who, in 2000, when I was first coming out, couldn't look me in the eye.

Years later, I mentioned the camping incident to another church member. She was appalled that we weren't allowed to participate, but she made me feel better when she told me about her and her husband's previous experience at one of the family campouts.

"Lou Anne," she said, "it wasn't much fun. We older members babysat the kids to give the younger parents time for themselves. You really didn't miss much."

In deciding to stay at the church, we knew we would be facing a wall of prejudice and discrimination. We understood the prejudice, why church members believed as they did, and why they were convinced the Bible was clear on this subject, because we'd been indoctrinated with the same misinformation as they had been. We didn't hold them to blame but simply wanted to gently encourage a different way to look at homosexuality and homosexuals by being an example outside the box of who they usually thought homosexuals to be.

After Bob Watson, our pastor, left our church in 2009, our interim pastor, whom I'll call Rick Coates—the former dean of Truett Seminary at Baylor University—stepped in. As a former dean, he had withdrawn a scholarship from a young seminary student in 2003 because he was gay. Dr. Coates' action infuriated me, and I wrote to him expressing my displeasure with his decision.

His response made it clear he considered all homosexuals unrepentant sinners. "If I'd taken the scholarship away from a prostitute, drug dealer, thief, wife beater, pedophile, pimp, drug addict, or drunk," he replied, "would you have written?"

This previous correspondence meant I knew his opinions of gays before he preached his first sermon in our church. And sure enough, he preached openly against homosexuality and same-sex marriage. Each time he did, I stood up from my front row seat during his sermon and walked out of the church, exiting up the center aisle. The first time I did this, as soon as I reached the outside doors, I turned around to see who might have supported my action and followed me out. No one ever did. Each afternoon, I waited for the phone to ring and for a church member to call to apologize for my having to hear such prejudice—no one ever called. No one publicly stood up for me, or for Brenda.

After walking out two or three times, I stopped attending the worship service when Dr. Coates was preaching. I also stopped all monetary contributions to the church. And I stopped being silent. I sent letters to the church's finance chairman, the deacon chairman, and Dr. Coates, explaining that I could not in good conscience financially support his messages encouraging and inciting prejudice against homosexuals.

When our church called our new pastor, Kevin Wilkes, in 2011, I returned to our worship services and liked what I saw and heard. Two to three weeks after Kevin arrived, I met him for the first time on a Wednesday evening. I had participated in the Wednesday evening supper and fellowship and was leaving the church carrying a take-out meal. Our new pastor walked toward the church as I headed toward the street.

In greeting him, I introduced myself: "Dr. Wilkes, I'm Lou Anne Smoot, and I'm delighted to have you as our new pastor. You are like a breath of fresh air." Then I explained why I wasn't staying for the service: "I'm leaving the church early to take this dinner home to my partner, who has a broken ankle."

As soon as I said "partner," I could tell his mind started whirling. He, with a hopeful sound to his voice, asked, "Business partner?"

"No," I replied. "Domestic partner. We're second-class members of this church."

"Oh, surely not!"

"Yes, we are."

Not wanting to continue this conversation on the sidewalk in front of the church building, I excused myself and walked to my car.

A little over a year later, in May 2012, I sat down with Kevin in his study and shared my story. He listened very attentively and never argued or debated. After talking, he asked me, "Do you remember when we first met?"

"Yes, I certainly do!"

"Well, what did you mean when you said you were 'second-class members' of this church?"

"Kevin, we aren't allowed to hold any leadership positions here."

Not wanting to make him uncomfortable (which I now regret), I continued speaking, "I know it's because this church is affiliated with the Southern Baptist Convention, and that's their rule. I wish this church were not a member of the SBC, but I know that can never happen. We have too many members whose children and grandchildren serve as missionaries for the Southern Baptist Convention, so we'll always be a part of it."

Kevin clearly believed homosexuality was sinful, but by the end of our visit, I felt he might be wavering a little. He felt strongly that homosexuality demanded celibacy, even after I pointed out that the Apostle Paul had stated that celibacy was a gift and that it seemed pretty unrealistic to expect every homosexual to be given the gift of celibacy.

Kevin and I remained friends and agreed to disagree on the issue of homosexuality. I occasionally emailed him information, and he answered. I felt we had a good relationship even though we were poles apart.

Despite our pastor's apparent disagreement with our identity, Brenda and I continued to push against the norm. In late September 2012, we arrived at our church to have our photo made for the new church directory. If you're unfamiliar with church directories, the pictures are organized by family groups. By 2012, Brenda and I had been a family unit for almost twelve years and decided it was time for our church directory to display a photo of us together. We made sequential appointments for that afternoon's photography session. Arriving on time, we signed in and placed our names in one photo slot. The elderly lady in charge did not comment as we did this.

The photographer did as we asked—he took our picture together. Then, he suggested we have separate pictures made. We complied. Afterward, we chose one of our couple photos for the church directory. We ordered copies of the photo and individual shots to share with family members. We felt proud of ourselves for finding the courage to appear together in our church directory. This would undoubtedly be a first for us and for our church.

Five months later, I received an email from our pastor saying that he had missed us the past Sunday at church and asked us to suggest a date when we could all meet that week, if possible, to discuss the pictorial directory.

I quickly replied.

It's nice to be missed. We were in Little Rock and were visiting a small African American congregation this past Sunday. We happen to know (and admire) their pastor, Rev. Wendell Griffin, who is also a federal judge. He and I served on a PFLAG panel discussing Religion and the LGBT Community along with a Presbyterian minister, a Methodist minister, a Unitarian minister, and a Jewish rabbi. I was the only layperson and the only Baptist. I was given the opportunity to talk about my book, "A Christian Coming Out," which is due to be published in April. It was an exciting weekend.

Do you want to talk with us about the photo we chose to place in the church directory? We have a full week of obligations, but we can probably handle whatever question you have by email if that's alright with you.

He responded the next day, remarking on how busy we were and informing us that they needed individual photos for the church directory as soon as possible. He apologized and thanked me.

I told him this issue wasn't worth fighting over but emphasized that we'd wanted to try it since we'd been together as a stable couple for twelve years. I promised to have our photos to him by the next night.

He wrote back, expressing his gratitude for my response and concluding his letter with,

"I bathed my email in prayer, as I know emails can be wonderful and horrible ways of communicating. I appreciate your understanding, especially given your twelve years together.

Peace"

While my pastor and I corresponded about our church directory photo, I also corresponded with Kay Holladay, our regional PFLAG director. She wrote that they were in the final stages of planning a June 2013 regional PFLAG conference and invited me to speak at it.

Her invitation thrilled me, and I quickly accepted. Then, I told her about our recent experience with the church directory. "My book should be available by then, and I can talk about it as well as the recent church experiences."

She replied that she was tickled I was going to speak, as she felt I would be "a dynamite closure to the conference. You and Brenda are my heroes, and I look to emulate your grace. I hope your pastor learns some lessons from the two of you—and I hope he sees the essence of what Jesus taught us in you and Brenda."

In the last week of May 2013, Brenda and I drove to Asheville, North Carolina, where on June 3rd, we picked up 500 copies of my book, *A Christian Coming Out*. I then spoke to nine PFLAG groups, including the regional conference in Norman, Oklahoma, before returning home in June. The trip was a huge success, but neither Brenda nor I could wait to be back home. It was hard to believe I was the same person who just a decade before lived fearful and alone, even within herself. Coming "out"—being proud of the person God designed me to be—hadn't just saved my life, it was giving me wings.

$\mathit{30}$
THIS IS GOODBYE

On July 6th, my daughter, Laura, hosted a surprise party for me to celebrate the publication of my book, and I was completely caught off guard. The date of the party happened to be the same as my eldest grandson's thirteenth birthday, and I thought the party was for him. I even baked him a birthday cake!

As I got ready for the party, I didn't particularly dress up, as I assumed only close family members would be present. Brenda looked at what I was wearing and suggested I might want to wear a more attractive outfit. She seldom made such a suggestion, but I took her at her word and allowed her to choose from several different options. She chose the dressiest of the lot. Though I found this strange, it still didn't occur to me that I was about to attend anything other than my grandson's birthday party.

Earlier in the week, my daughter had called. "Mom," she'd said. "A neighbor of mine is having a party and has asked to borrow your two card tables and eight fold-up chairs. Could you bring them over to my house?"

I gladly took them to her yet still didn't put any of this together. When we arrived at her home that evening, I assumed all the cars parked on the street were for the "neighbor's party" and thought nothing of it.

When I walked into my daughter's kitchen carrying the birthday cake, and people who had been waiting elsewhere in the house started appearing, I was baffled. Someone pointed out a large banner with my name on it, congratulating me on the publication of my book, and I finally realized the party was for me and not for my grandson, although he and his parents had driven four hours from Houston for the event.

I was amazed at the variety of friends who attended. My daughter's beautiful home was overflowing with happy people, congratulating me. I saw friends from the League of Women Voters, and my gay friends walked in, representing both East Texas PFLAG and Project TAG (Tyler Area Gays).

Janie, who had moved to Austin a few years earlier, came with her sister, who also lived in Austin. Many purchased copies of my book that evening for themselves and to share with friends.

Later, I learned that everyone in my Sunday School class had been invited to the celebration, but only Carolyn and her husband came.

I so wanted my church family to read my book— to know me and understand me. I felt sure that if they just knew about my book, they'd want to read it. If they'd written a book about their life experiences, I'd like to read their story. I foolishly assumed they'd feel the same about me. A week later, I sent emails to numerous members of my church telling them about my book and explaining how they could order it through my website.

I'd known these members for many years, some for almost twenty-five years, but no one responded to my email. Not one.

My Sunday School teacher purchased a copy at the party, which was the only response I'd had from church members by the middle of July. That hurt, yet I felt if they wouldn't buy my book, I'd simply give them a copy.

On July 14th, after the evening service, I walked to our well-stocked church library located off the main lobby. The variety of offerings there were impressive and included more than just books on religion and theology. One alcove contained children's books, another section contained fiction, and then there were youth books and reference books. Many members patronized this library.

Feeling anxious and nervous, I carried a cloth bag containing two different books as I approached the librarian, who was sitting behind a desk at the library entrance. I knew this tall, thin, young woman as I had participated in a book group with her and others. She had a large, lovely home and occasionally hosted our group. Knowing her made me even more nervous. My heart was pounding, and I felt embarrassed as I explained that I had a book I wanted to donate to the library.

I reached into my bag and pulled out my book, *A Christian Coming Out*, and told her this was my personal story, and that I was giving a complimentary copy to the library. She wasn't overjoyed with the gift but accepted it.

A month and a half after donating my book to the library, on August 30th, I received an email from my pastor remarking that we hadn't seen each other recently except from afar and hoping that I had a good summer. Then he explained the situation with my book.

Our librarian let me know that you brought your book by to be available in our library. She has read it in its entirety, and I am reading through it now, as I did not do so when you gave me your manuscript.

While I appreciate the incredible amount of pain you have gone through in your pilgrimage with homosexuality, I do not believe your book to be what we should have in our library on the subject. You and I have already had our discussion about our biblical views of practicing homosexuality and have agreed to disagree on what the Word of God says. I cannot, in good conscience, place a book in the library advocating the practice of homosexuality, even monogamous, as blessed by God, especially as we have people of all ages and levels of Christian maturity utilizing our library.

I do believe aspects of your book could help a mature believer better understand what homosexuals, you, and Brenda in particular, have gone through, and how you have reached your conclusion. However, it is not a conclusion that I agree with, nor do I feel it represents our church's convictions.

I am reading another book entitled "Washed and Waiting: Reflections on Faithfulness and Homosexuality," *by Wesley Hill, a homosexual and theologian, and am considering making this book available in our library. It is raw, like yours, but ultimately the author concludes that while God can certainly bless him as a homosexual, he must glorify God by practicing celibacy. He believes that the Bible teaches that, to be right with God, homosexuals are to remain celibate.*

I do not know whether you have checked to see if your book is available, but I wanted you to know why it is not. I have your book and would like to keep it. I will gladly pay for it. I hope you understand my ongoing conviction regarding this and why I have made this decision.

Sincerely,

Pastor Kevin

My pastor's letter hurt and greatly disappointed me. My church wasn't interested in my story. I responded that very afternoon, saying that I appreciated him taking the time to write and explain to me about my book. I also informed him that when I'd stopped by the library this past Sunday to place a label in the book, I was told it was in his office, which I was very sorry to hear. I then went on to write:

By publishing my story, I have laid bare my life, my thoughts, and my struggles with homosexuality. I believe God has been leading me all along to write this book so that those who continue to believe that homosexuality is something a person chooses can see how ridiculous that belief is. No one chooses to be gay. It's a struggle, many times without the support of parents, siblings, society, or even church friends. In fact, the church friends usually condemn the loudest. That fact has always broken my heart and continues to do so.

Whenever Brenda and I visit a church that is open and affirming, I feel the tears coming all during the service because this is what I yearn for from my own church—for its members to simply accept me as the person I am.

One of the many letters I have received praising my book stated, "It was in some ways reassuring, in some ways shocking, and in the end heartwarming." When I saw the word "shocking," I immediately wondered which part she was referring to. But as I read on, it was I who was shocked as I read, "The shocking part was that even a portion of your church was accepting. I worked during that time with several people who went to church there. I can't imagine any of them accepting it at that time."

Jesus told us in John 4:35b: "... open your eyes and look at the fields! They are ripe for harvest." And I tell you that Baptist churches (and others) have done irreparable damage to those homosexuals who are "ripe unto harvest" because a large majority of them literally hate the church. They know they didn't choose to be gay. They know how much they've fought it, and my book documents the many, many years I struggled against it by remaining active in the church and faithfully married to my husband.

Instead of the church reaching out to gays, supporting them, and loving them, gays have been mistreated, hated, and in many cases, exiled— actually forced to leave the church.

Having said all this, let me admit that I know you are in an untenable position in this regard. Even though we disagree on this subject, if your thinking were to somehow change, you couldn't afford to lead our church in a more realistic understanding of homosexuality without losing your job. Yet, I believe my job is to remain faithful to my calling to share my story and God's greater story of His all-inclusive love.

As to believing homosexuals should remain celibate, the seventh chapter of First Corinthians talks a good bit about marriage, with Paul advocating that no one should marry. But he admits in verse seven that not everyone has the same gift of being able to go through life without marrying.

I thank you for listening to us and for taking us seriously. I realize the difficulty of this issue, but I also realize the difficulty in the 1800s of the church to fight against the issue of slavery, especially in the South, and how churches failed miserably at that time to stand up for what was right, too. The churches also failed miserably on the issue of segregation. I think I've used this metaphor before—that churches should be the headlight, not the taillight. We (the churches) are again failing miserably when it comes to the subject of homosexuality.

Lou Anne

I'm almost embarrassed to admit that for many months after my book was published, and after the unfortunate letter from Pastor Kevin, I carried one or more copies of my book to church, believing some church members would want to buy a copy. How foolish.

Only a few church members bought one. One member of my Sunday School class asked for three copies to share with her family, which made me feel wonderful, especially since she was one of the few people with whom I'd shared my manuscript. I then twisted the arm of one of Jim's good friends by sending him an email suggesting he might want to see if he could find himself in the book, since I'd changed his name.

He agreed to meet me in the Stein Mart parking lot one day in July, where I sold him a book. Sometime later, when I was volunteering at our church's kiosk on Sunday morning, his wife walked up to me when no one else was around. She said, "I just want you to know I read your book, and I had no idea what you were going through." Tears sprang to her eyes as she said, "I just want you to know I'm on your side!"

For a church member to say that to me, the only one, meant a lot to me. A few others privately expressed support to Brenda, but none that we knew of openly stood up for us.

A total of seven people from my church bought one or more copies, including those I've already mentioned. Continuing to yearn for opportunities to share my story, I sent letters in June 2014 to three women who led various book groups, offering to lead a discussion of my book for their group. I never heard from any of them, even though I regularly saw them at church.

I probably should have given up, but I didn't. In my 2014 Christmas letter, which was mailed to a mix of about 80 individuals and families, I wrote the following description of our year's advocacy activities:

"Brenda and I loaded up our little R-Pod camper for an unprecedented (for us) six-week combination book tour, speaking engagements, and vacation during September and October. Brenda did a fantastic job of arranging my speaking schedule so that I was able to share my story with ten different groups in places like Lubbock, Silver City, NM, and the Arizona towns of Yuma, Tucson, Prescott, Flagstaff, and Sedona."

Out of the twenty-two people from my church who received my Christmas letter, only four had already purchased a copy of my book, and to my knowledge, my Christmas letter generated no additional sales or interest. My church family simply was not interested in my story.

I was becoming disenchanted with the possibilities of ever being asked to share my story with members of my church family, which I had been a part of for almost twenty-six years. Everyone was nice to us, friendly, and kind, but no one seemed invested.

When we took our six-week trip in 2014, one of the choir members called to make sure we were all right. She said she was accustomed to seeing us sitting toward the front of the sanctuary and missed having us there.

On various occasions over the years, Brenda and I invited members of my Sunday School class to our home for an evening meal. The attendance was always wonderful. Our long table was filled with happy women eating and socializing together.

When Brenda's dad passed away in October of 2012, our Sunday School classes offered to prepare the meal for Brenda's extended family. We accepted their offer, and they provided a huge amount of delicious food for about fifteen people. They not only prepared this homemade meal but also came to our home and served us, then cleaned up the kitchen afterward. We had known many of these women for at least thirteen years.

I had always been quite open with my class about my sexual orientation. One Sunday in the Fall of 2014, when we were simply sharing what was going on in our lives, I mentioned how much I would welcome the opportunity to share my story within my church, perhaps even in my own Sunday School department (which had around fifty to sixty people). I could tell from the body language of those few in our room that this would never be possible. One member spoke up and said, "But we're nice to you, aren't we?"

I was shocked at her question but couldn't immediately put my finger on the reason her statement had made me feel so uneasy. Later, when I shared the event with Brenda, she quickly explained, "It's as if that's all you deserve. That's why that statement bothers you so much."

Christians are supposed to be nice to everyone, especially members of their own church and, indeed, their own Sunday School class. I was a former teacher of this class. Of course, they'd be nice to me. Why would they think that being nice to me was something for which they should be proud when they were clearly rejecting me on such a personal level?

This incident, along with all the others connected to the ministry in my book, prompted my questioning of why I continued to be a member of First Baptist. Then on Sunday, January 25, 2015, the pastor mentioned in his sermon that the Bible is very clear that marriage is to be only between a man and a woman—that same-sex marriage is sinful. He was preaching this type of political sermon as the Supreme Court was soon to make a decision involving marriage equality.

As I listened to his words that morning, I made a firm decision. I was through attending First Baptist Church. At the time I made that decision, I had been a faithful, supportive member of this church for more than twenty-six years and had continued attending for the past fifteen as an openly gay Christian.

In those fifteen years that followed my coming out at church, I never heard ugly words, I received no overt, intentionally cruel condemnation from the majority of members, but Brenda and I were shuffled into the "second-class" membership of the church in the old Southern tradition of "killing them with kindness."

The pushing out was so subtle at the start that, looking back, I can see how I was made complicit in it; believing my pastor and friends when they said that not leading and teaching would protect me somehow. There were real dangers in the world for LGBTQ individuals—that can't be denied—but as the church, weren't we called to be "not of it?"

Shouldn't I be the safest to proudly be who God made me to be amongst my fellow believers?

I'd been asking this question and many others for 76 years. That Sunday, my soul simply said, "Enough." I didn't make any grand exits or speeches or write any letters. I just quit attending.

The stings of dogma and the many small ways I was treated as less than within the church and denied participation and contribution that matched my God-given gifts—gifts I had been told my whole life He wanted me to use for His glory and to help others—had finally taken their toll. I was leaving, not because of a lack of love for God or others, but because I was tired of fighting the good fight against those who once claimed to be "my people"—my family.

Some members of my Sunday School class noticed my absence. Three members took time to call or write, telling me how much they missed me. The member who had purchased three copies of my book (for her children) wrote a long letter saying all kinds of nice things to me, which read:

"I consider you one of the most intelligent…most level-headed women I know. And there are very few of those around anymore. You have influenced me with your hard work, genuine spirit, and truthfulness. I personally can't turn my back on you because of your being gay. I see a person that I love and admire…The lifestyle you choose is your preference. We should be respectful of that. And I hope I have been. Your presence on Sunday mornings adds so much to our little group."

I appreciated her letter very much, but my heart sank at her use of the word "lifestyle" and her belief that my being gay was my choice. I had hoped that anyone who read my book and would thus be aware of my lifelong struggles with my sexual orientation would know that I never chose to be gay. My only choice was to be open and honest about my sexual identity as opposed to reliving the horrible instinct to hide who I truly was.

31
LIFE OUTSIDE THE FOLD

*B*renda continued going to First Baptist for about 3 more months, then decided to also leave. The pastor, the church, and the Southern Baptist Convention had taken a public stance on the sinfulness of same-sex relationships. She didn't leave silently like I did. She did what I should have done. She wrote letters to the Minister who directed the Singles Department, to the pastor, and to her Sunday School class (and took time to read the letter aloud to her class). She explained her need for a sense of personal integrity and authenticity as well as her desire to align herself with a congregation whose beliefs and public stance regarding same-sex relationships were like her own.

One of her last paragraphs contained this information:

"Also, for the sake of the fellowship here at First Baptist, I believe it is better that I leave. . . . I have remained mostly silent on my life and my beliefs regarding sexual orientation. The one time I did speak out in a somewhat public forum that was separate from the church, I was promptly

removed from Sunday School teaching and leadership responsibilities. I cannot continue to edit my life and remain silent . . ."

After leaving, we never again received any notifications of any kind from the church—no announcements of upcoming events, no requests for money for a building fund, nothing. I can imagine the church heaved a sigh of relief when we left.

After some time, Brenda and I began visiting First Presbyterian, where we were warmly welcomed. After about a month, we were placed on their mailing list, and the first newsletter we received was addressed to both of us. It was a simple thing, but it said so much. First Baptist, for 15 years, always sent us two copies of everything—one to each of us at the same address.

In November the FPC sponsored a Sunday Jazz Brunch which featured good friends of ours, a gay couple named Brian and Oliver. Brian conducted the small orchestra, and Oliver blessed us with his glorious singing voice. When Oliver finished singing, Brian proudly shared that he and Oliver had been together for 28 years. This information elicited polite applause, and I felt proud to be helping them celebrate their years together.

A few days later, Brian called, heartbroken. The pastor had called him in and admonished him for his "inappropriate" words. I felt disbelief. We were seriously considering joining this church as I believed it was an accepting and affirming church. I wrote a letter to the pastor expressing my dismay at his actions, and told him we would not be returning to his church.

At that point in our lives, Brenda and I decided we no longer needed organized religion. We stayed home on Sundays and enjoyed doing whatever we wanted to do. Most Sunday mornings, we watched a political talk show on TV. We discovered Sunday mornings are a wonderful time to do the weekly grocery shopping.

Do we miss church? Not really. We miss the music, especially the old gospel songs we were brought up on.

I realized my church friends were mostly acquaintances, so leaving the church did not cut me off from any "bosom buddies." Those few who I did consider friends occasionally dropped by for a visit and vice versa. Thank goodness God is omniscient and can be found outside the walls of the church.

My circle of friends had already widened, having made friends in our LGBTQ community through PFLAG as well as through Tyler Area Gays (TAG) which was founded in 2008 primarily as a social outlet for gays. Before the establishment of these organizations, members of the LGBTQ community in Tyler were hidden. Fearful. They didn't know each other or know where or how to find each other. Tyler had no gay bar, the traditional place for gays to meet and socialize, so TAG, specifically, was designed to provide new and safer meeting outlets for gays.

The young man who founded TAG, Troy Carlyle, was a close friend, and I served on the first Board of Directors for the organization. We sponsored various opportunities for gays to meet and work together: dinner groups, a weekly discussion group called "Tea at Troys on Thursdays," board game groups, a highway cleanup project, a flag football team, as well as annual events including a dinner-dance, a Holiday party, picnic, and World AIDS Day on December 1. Since the board games group was my idea, Brenda and I hosted the first gatherings in our home until we outgrew our space.

Troy and I secured a two-mile section of highway for an Adopt-A-Highway program so that two signs were displayed on a major highway close to town that showed "Tyler Area Gays." The signs hadn't been up long before bullet holes pierced one of them. Then, a while later, the other sign simply disappeared. Through much cajoling, we finally encouraged the highway department to replace that sign. We cleaned both sides of our four miles of highway for years.

Our circle of friends continued to widen as we participated in the League of Women Voters and the American Association of University Women. We began to regularly invite lesbian couples to our home for dinner and to play Rummikub, and in turn, we were invited to their homes. The friendships we formed with gays were far stronger friendships than I ever had with my church friends. And more numerous.

Brenda and I traveled extensively in our little R-Pod, a small camper that we both loved. We especially enjoyed visiting national parks and are now amazed at how many we have explored.

Brenda and I remained quite active in East Texas PFLAG—the organization where we met in 2000. In 2015 we received permission from our public library to set up a PFLAG display during the month of June, which is considered Pride Month. The display consisted of PFLAG booklets and a few colorful beads and pins. However, our city manager's office had it removed.

Brenda and I decided not to take this "slap in the face" lying down. We got busy sending a multitude of emails and making phone calls encouraging people to contact the city manager's office in support of PFLAG. This resulted in our being interviewed by both radio and TV. In less than 24 hours, the city manager's office relented, and the display was again set up in the downstairs case.

We continued setting up Pride Month displays at the library for the next 6 years with no big problems.

Then in June 2022 we experienced a repeat of 2015. Our display was removed. We again argued with this same city manager's office using their own Exhibits & Displays policy which stated the display case was to be used to make the public aware of leisure activities, health issues, and cultural awareness. His response was to rewrite their policy stating that the downstairs display case could be used only by the library and the city of Tyler. We now set up our PFLAG pride display in the 2nd floor display case, where few people ever see it.

We have been asked many times why we remained in Tyler. "Why not move to a more liberal area?" Two things kept us in Tyler: first, four of my six grandchildren live here and the youngest two are only ten minutes away. Second, we knew our advocacy would be more useful in this very conservative town which was rapidly growing into a city of over 110,000.

Part of our advocacy is flying a colorful 22" x 22" rainbow flag close to our front door to let everyone know our home is a safe place for gay people. We've flown that flag for years and have never received any type of negative reaction from anyone.

Over the years, I've given a multitude of speeches as a guest speaker at colleges, churches, and PFLAG groups across the country, participated in many marches and protests and parades; and published several books. More importantly, Brenda and I have always lived with love as our guiding light to help others however we can.

The life I was living outside the church was a life that was full and free, and abundant in outreach. It's still hard to believe I was once a quiet, fearful, and closeted Lesbian when I look at all the ways I've intentionally spoken out and attempted to show others that gay people are people like anyone else.

32
A NEW BEGINNING

*M*y youngest grandchildren call me "Grandmother" and call Brenda "Granny." One day, when my youngest granddaughter was about four, we were in Brenda's and my bedroom. She looked at our bed, pointed to the left side, and asked, "Grandmother, is this the side you sleep on?"

"No, Claire. I sleep on the other side. That's where Granny sleeps."

"Oh," she said. My answer apparently satisfied her. On another occasion, when she was about five, she announced a desire to play "wedding." I replied, "Sounds like fun. Who's getting married?"

"You and Granny!"

Not only was Claire thinking about Brenda and me getting married as early as 2012, but many of our friends had the same thought soon after the passage of the Marriage Equality Act on June 26, 2015. Numerous times, friends asked us, "When do you two plan to be married?" "Have you set the date?"

Brenda and I discussed that possibility and decided we were happy just the way things were. After all, we had been together for almost 15 years and had always felt we were married in God's eyes. Who needed society to approve of our relationship?

However, the more we were asked about getting married, the more we began to question our decision not to. Was our Christian example to the gay community being diminished by our refusal to marry? Shouldn't we take advantage of the new marriage law that so many had successfully fought for?

We finally decided to marry when one day Brenda commented, "You know, it would be nice to introduce you as 'my wife.'" I fully agreed. The first step was to obtain a marriage license. I was prepared for a challenging and unpleasant experience as we entered the Smith County Courthouse Annex. I was wrong. The clerk was pleasant, kind, and respectful, and we walked out with a beautifully decorated marriage license now framed and displayed in our hallway.

We shared our decision to marry with Laura and eight-year-old Claire, who asked, "Does this mean you're going to have a baby?"

"No, we won't be having a baby," we laughed, without explaining that not only are we the same gender, but one of us is seventy-six and the other sixty-five.

"Claire, would you like to be our ring bearer?" I asked.

"I thought that was for boys!"

Laura then interjected, "Claire, you are the only person they are asking to be a part of their wedding ceremony. Do you want to do it or not?"

"Yes, yes! I want to do it!"

Our 15th Anniversary as a committed couple was coming up on December 8, 2015, which happened to be the date for our East Texas

PFLAG's Holiday Party. That event seemed an appropriate wedding venue because Brenda and I met at a PFLAG meeting.

We therefore arranged to have our PFLAG Holiday Party in the lobby of the Unitarian Universalist Fellowship building. The setting was stunning, and we planned our wedding ceremony to take place in their lovely, glass-enclosed sanctuary set back in the woods.

We asked Father Tom Jackson, an Episcopalian priest and a good friend, to conduct the ceremony. Brenda and I chose to wear matching red and white holiday outfits and selected matching rings. The minute we saw the rings in a jewelry store, we both agreed they were what we had been looking for.

Brenda and I made all the other arrangements for the wedding, telling only a few close friends of our plans.

Soon after everyone gathered, we invited the attendees to take a seat in the sanctuary for a short surprise ceremony before the party.

The music started (thanks to a tape Brenda had prepared), and then Father Jackson, in his beautiful and colorful robes, walked down the aisle, holding a Bible, followed by the precious and composed Claire, with our rings held close to her waist in a little white box. Afterward, Brenda and I, side by side, hand in hand, entered with huge grins on our faces.

Jaws dropped, and hands were raised to people's mouths as we entered. Everyone was more than delighted that they had shown up that night for the party. Others were present who normally wouldn't attend a PFLAG gathering but came knowing ahead of time we would be having a wedding. I dare say there wasn't a dry eye in the crowd. A public, legal, gay wedding was a new experience for everyone. Same-sex marriage was legalized just months earlier, and we felt honored and blessed to be among some of the first in our nation's history to be wed. We never imagined living out the dreams our parents had for us in a way that was true to who we were; but there we were, amongst family and friends, getting married like any other couple in love.

Brenda and I each prepared our vows and, as Brenda recited hers, she surprised me by bursting into song and singing a cappella: "You Light Up My Life." The chorus of this song repeats the words "And you light up my life, you give me hope to carry on, you light up my days and fill my nights with song."

I was amazed at her courage in singing this song to me and was very touched by the words.

After the wedding, everyone moved from the sanctuary into the large lobby, where tables and chairs were set up for the party. On one table was a homemade Italian Cream Cake my daughter, Laura, had baked, beautifully decorated, and was now serving. Another table was loaded with desserts and appetizers that others brought for the PFLAG Holiday Party. It was a joyous occasion for all with lots of food and drink.

As I write this, I'm proud to say that Brenda and I have been together for 24 years, and even more proud to say she has been my wife for the last 9 of those.

I recall attending a PFLAG meeting in the early 2000s, when I was fresh out of the "closet," in which one of the women asked the group, "If there were a pill you could take that would make you straight instead of gay, would you take it?"

Several attendees immediately replied they certainly would. I was in that camp too. I'll never forget, though, what one member confidently declared, "No, I wouldn't take the pill. I like myself the way I am."

At that time, her words shocked me. She actually liked being gay? I stared at her, trying to fathom what she meant and simply couldn't figure it out. Surely, she wasn't serious. Who would want to be gay if you could be straight?

It is never an easy thing to live an authentic life in the face of conformity, or to choose life when death seems like a reprieve from suffering. I have looked both adversaries in the eye. But change, though long coming, is possible. My entire lived experience is a testament to that.

Now that I have become better acquainted with myself, I understand that woman's feelings. If someone were to ask me that same question today, I'd say, "No, I wouldn't take the pill. I like myself the way I am."

ACKNOWLEDGEMENTS

This book would not exist without the rhetoric of Marilyn Hillyer, known in the book as Barbara. She blessed me with support and advice and stuck by my side during my early days of coming out, those days when I struggled to climb out of my deep pit of despair. She left this earth in 2006, and I continue to miss her so very much.

The one I call Janie, Alice Parrish, remained my good friend and avid supporter until her passing in 2024. I so miss her smiling face, boundless energy, and unfailing encouragement.

I thank God every day for Brenda McWilliams, my wife, my friend, supporter, advisor, and treasured companion. We were married on December 8, 2015, on the fifteenth anniversary of our covenant commitment to each other. I call her "my special gift from God."

Thank you to all my special friends in our discussion group, Troy's Tea on Thursdays, for your steadfast encouragement and title suggestions.

The goal in writing my previous book was to offer my story to the public as evidence contrary to the often-held foolish assumptions that being gay is somehow "chosen" and that one can "pray away the gay." When my previous publishing company dropped me in 2021, I was heartsick and so very disappointed. The only goal enveloping my heart at that time was to produce another book somehow. I was 82 at the time and asked myself if I had the energy, determination, and time left on this earth to rewrite my book, find a publisher, and launch the new book into the public eye.

I met Amanda Nail at a dinner party two or three years later and gave her and others at the party copies of my book. Then I met her many months later at a coffee shop to talk about a storytelling venture. That's when she thrilled my heart by declaring my book to be wonderful. She is an English and Creative Writing professor, so her words carried more impact than others. I'd never heard anyone be so enthusiastic about my book. Her bubbling excitement reestablished my desire to revise and republish my book. Every time I talked with her, she lifted my spirits and made me feel that anything was possible.

She later mentioned she planned to create her own publishing company. I hesitantly approached her with the possibility of helping me rewrite my book. Her enthusiastic response was amazing. In the following months, each time my determination flagged, her positive encouragement kept me going. She has been amazing. Thank you so much, Amanda, and all of your staff at ANO Publishing.

RESOURCES
Books, Organizations, and Websites I found helpful.

BOOKS / ARTICLES

Allen, Jimmy. *Burden of a Secret, A True Story of One Family's Tragedy and the Enduring Faith That Helped Them Survive.* Nashville, Tennessee: 1995.

Back, Gloria Guss. *Are You Still My Mother? Are You Still My Family?* Warner Books, Inc. 1985

Bawer, Bruce. *A Place at the Table, The Gay Individual in American Society.* Simon & Schuster, 1994.

Barton, Bernadette. *Pray the Gay Away, The Extraordinary Lives of Bible Belt Gays.* New York University Press, 2012.

Baldock, Kathy. *Walking the Bridgeless Canyon, Repairing the Breach Between the Church and the LGBTQ Community.* Reno, NV: Canyonwalker Press, 2014.

Blum, Louise A. *You're Not from Around Here, Are You? A Lesbian in Small-Town America.* The University of Wisconsin Press, 2001.

Boesser, Sara L. *Silent Lives: How High a Price? For Personal Reflections and Group discussions about Sexual Orientation.* Maryland: Hamilton Books, 2004.

Carlyle, Troy. *The Remainder of My Life, an autobiography written in real time.* Lulu Press, 2007 and 2008.

Cobb, Joe and Leigh Anne Taylor. *Our Family Outing, A memoir of coming out and coming through.* Total Publishing and Media, 2011.

Cottrell, Susan. *"Mom, I'm Gay," Loving Your LGBTQ Child Without Sacrificing Your Faith,"* 2014.

Fairchild, Betty & Hayward, Nancy. *Now That You Know, What Every Parent Should Know About Homosexuality.* Harcourt Brace Jovanovich, 1989.

Farrar, Diana Finfrock. *The Door of the Heart.* Bloomington, Indiana: AuthorHouse, 2014.

Gomes, Peter J. *The Good Book, Reading the Bible with Mind and Heart.* New York, New York: Avon Books, 1996.

Ivester, Jo. *Once a Girl, Always a Boy, A family memoir of a transgender journey.* She Writes Press, 2020.

Johnson, Shari. *Above All Things, The Journey of an Evangelical Christian Mother and Her Gay Daughter.* Cleveland, Ohio: Changing Lives Press, 2012.

Martin, Colby. *UNClobber, Rethinking Our Misuse of the Bible on Homosexuality.* Louisville: Westminster John Knox Press, 2016.

Mason, Lynelle Sweat. *Tarnished Haloes, Open Hearts*. Macon, GA: Nurturing Faith, Inc., 2012.

Nelson, Thomas Arthur. *The Gay Samaritan*. Coppell, TX: 2022.

Rogers, Jack. *Jesus, the Bible, and Homosexuality, Explode the Myths, Heal the Church*. Louisville, Kentucky: Westminster John Knox Press, 2009.

Signorile, Michelangelo. *Outing Yourself, How to Come Out as Lesbian or Gay to Your Family, Friends, and Coworkers*. New York: Fireside Press, 1995.

Spong, John Shelby. *The Sins of Scripture, Exposing the Bible's Texts of Hate to Reveal the God of Love*. HarperSanFrancisco, A Division of Harper Collins Publishers, 2005.

Wallner, Mary Lou. *The Slow Miracle of Transformation*. Teach Ministries, 2003.

White, Mel. *Religion Gone Bad, The Hidden Dangers of the Christian Right*. New York: Jeremy P. Tarcher/Penguin, 2006.

White, Mel. *Stranger At The Gate*. Simon & Schuster, 2015.

ORGANIZATIONS

East Texas PFLAG. P.O. Box 130703, Tyler, TX 75713-0703. 903-372-9524. Facebook: https://www.facebook.com/PFLAGTyler/ E-mail: pflageasttexas@yahoo.com

Equality Texas. P.O. Box 2340, Austin, TX 78768-2340. https://equalitytexas.org/

Freedhearts.org. Facebook: FreedHearts Ministries. FreedHearts@gmail.com

Human Rights Campaign. 1640 Rhode Island Ave. N.W., Washington, DC 20036-3278. 1-800-777-4723. www.hrc.org.

PFLAG.org (once known as Parents, Families and Friends of Lesbians and Gays.) 1625 K Street NW, Suite 700, Washington, D.C. 20006. 1-202 467-8180. E-mail: info@pflag.org.

Soulforce. P.O. Box 2499, Abilene, TX 79604. 1-800-810-9143. E-mail: hello@soulforce.org.

The Alphabet Army. Empowers, educates and supports LGBTQIA+ youth in Tyler, TX.

The Glass House. An LGBTQ Resource Center serving East Texas youth and located in Tyler, TX.

Tyler Area Gays. https://www.tylerareagays.com P.O. Box 6331, Tyler, TX, 75711. E-mail: info@tylerareagays.com

VIDEOS

Fish Can't Fly, Conversations About God and Struggling to be Gay (83 min.). TJoe Murray Videos, 2005. Documentary film directed and produced by Tom Murray. www.FishCantFly.com

For the Bible Tells Me So (98 min.) by Daniel Karslake, 2007.

Gillery's Little Secret, Between love and friendship the answer is revealed. (25 min.) www.liquidfilmworks.com, 2005.

Lou Anne Smoot's Coming Out Story (almost 24 minutes) by CSpan2. #445082-1 in search engine. 2018.

Out in the Silence, Love, hate, and a quest for change in small town America. (56 min.) A documentary film by Joe Wilson & Dean Hamer. Produced by Qwaves, 2009.

Straight From the Heart: A Journey to Understanding and Love. (24 min.). Woman Vision Productions, 1994. Stories of parents' journeys to a new understanding of their gay and lesbian children. Available at https://www.womanvision.org/straight-from-the-heart.html.

There's A Wideness in God's Mercy (30 minutes). Dr. Lewis Smedes on Romans 1. Introduction by Mel White. You Tube.

photo provided by the author

AUTHOR BIO

Lou Anne Smoot is a writer, speaker, and LGBTQ advocate, with a Master's degree in Business Administration from The University of Texas at Austin. She has continued her postgraduate studies at Texas Tech and Texas State University. She travels all over the continental United States, sharing her story and experiences with others as a guest speaker. As an outspoken advocate for gay rights, she and her wife, Brenda, were recipients of the Project TAG Legacy Award in 2015 and Lou Anne was named "Advocate of the Year" by Project TAG in 2010. Her story has been broadcast on CSPAN2 (#445082-1) as well as on Texas Standard radio on June 25, 2018. The previous edition of her memoir was selected as one of the top 44 non-fiction lesbian books of all time by Around the World magazine. She has authored four other books in her time and continues her work as an advocate in East Texas, where she lives happily with her wife, Brenda.

www.ingramcontent.com/pod-product-compliance
Lightning Source LLC
Chambersburg PA
CBHW060125130626
46556CB00006B/2233